# Contents

*Using this book* ........ *iv*

## *Section 1* The National Curriculum and Study Skills

The four language skills ........ 2
Achieving levels 1–8 in each skill ........ 2

## *Section 2* Grammar

Introduction ........ 11
A-Z of French Grammar ........ 12

## *Section 3* Practice exercises with solutions

Listening ........ 35
Reading ........ 52
Speaking ........ 62
Writing ........ 73

## *Section 4* Vocabulary

Introduction ........ 95
Checklist of language tasks ........ 97
Vocabulary topics ........ 101

## *Section 5* Mini-Dictionary

French-English ........ 142
English-French ........ 173

# USING THIS BOOK

This book will help you in your homework and other activities throughout your Key Stage 3 studies in French. In particular it will help you develop your abilities in the four key skills, namely:

- Listening
- Reading
- Speaking
- Writing

The book is divided into five sections:

***Section 1:*** **The National Curriculum and Study Skills**

***Section 2:*** **Grammar**

***Section 3:*** **Practice exercises with solutions**

***Section 4:*** **Vocabulary**

***Section 5:*** **Mini-dictionary**
**– English–French**
**– French–English**

At the start of each section there is an easy-to-use chart showing you at a glance what you can find in that section, and where you can find it.

Sections 2, 4 and 5 are also arranged ***alphabetically*** to help you find what you want to know more easily.

HOMEWORK HANDBOOKS

# FRENCH

Alasdair McKeane

LONGMAN

HOMEWORK HANDBOOKS

*Series editors:*

Geoff Black and Stuart Wall

*Other titles in the series:*

**ENGLISH**

**GERMAN**

**MATHEMATICS**

**SCIENCE**



**Addison Wesley Longman**
Edinburgh Gate, Harlow
Essex CM20 2JE
England



First published 1996

ISBN 0852 29331–6

**British Cataloguing in Publication Data**
A catalogue record for this title is available from the British Library

Set in Stone by 36

Produced by Longman Singapore Publishers Pte

Printed in Great Britain by Short Run Press, Exeter

# Section one

## The National Curriculum and Study Skills

The National Curriculum in Modern Foreign Languages is the same for all modern languages. It lays down for teachers how each language in this case French, is to be taught.

In this section we give you an idea of what is required of you in each of the four language skills of listening, reading, speaking and writing. We also look at a number of useful study techniques which will help you reach the highest possible level in your study of French.

The box below will help you see at a glance what you can find in this section.

### The National Curriculum


- The four language skills ........ 2
- Achieving Levels 1–8 in each skill
  - – Listening ........ 2
  - – Reading ........ 3
  - – Speaking ........ 4
  - – Writing ........ 4


### Study Skills


- Good and poor students ........ 5
- Getting organised ........ 6
- Listening ........ 6
- Reading ........ 6
- Speaking ........ 7
- Writing ........ 7
- Using a dictionary ........ 7
- Learning vocabulary ........ 9
- Revising for tests and exams ........ 10

## The four language skills

The **four language skills** are called Attainment Targets (ATs).

**AT1 Listening**
**AT2 Reading**
**AT3 Speaking**
**AT4 Writing**

At the end of Key Stage 3, all four attainment targets have equal weight in the assessment of how well each pupil has done. So if you are quite good at speaking French, this can balance out being not quite so good at writing it. This can be difficult for parents to understand, mainly because when they learned a foreign language, writing was all-important. For most people, though, understanding and speaking a foreign language is more useful than writing it. That is why there is now increased emphasis on reading, listening and speaking.

The **learning activities** which teachers have to use include such obvious things as listening and responding, asking and answering questions, and so on. You should also expect to redraft your writing, learn things by heart, use dictionaries and reference materials, take part in imaginative and creative activities, and use your knowledge to experiment with language.

It is likely that most of your lessons will have very little English spoken in them. This is because it is important to use French for such real purposes as calling the register, saying which page to read, etc.

The **descriptions of performance** in each of the skills are quite technical, and are intended for teachers' use in assessing how well you have done. However, the different levels do reflect real progress. The government performance targets for most Year 9 pupils at the end of Key Stage 3 are that they should be between Levels 4 and 6. Clearly some pupils may be performing at Levels 7, 8 or at 'exceptional performance' at that age, while a few will be performing at levels 1 – 3.

If Level 8 seems difficult – it is meant to be. It was originally intended to be equivalent to GCSE Grade B, which is a good result for a 16-year-old. So there is no shame in not having reached that level by age 14 at the end of Year 9. Whatever level you do actually reach, remember that you can always improve with practice.

## Achieving levels 1–8 in each skill

### AT1: Listening

**LEVEL 1**

| | |
|---|---|
| Pupils show understanding of | simple classroom commands<br>short statements<br>questions |
| Pupils understand speech | spoken clearly face to face<br>from a clear tape recording |
| Pupils may need support | from repetition<br>from gesture |

**LEVEL 2**

| | |
|---|---|
| Pupils show understanding of | simple classroom commands and instructions for setting tasks<br>familiar statements<br>familiar questions |
| Pupils understand speech | in standard French |
| Pupils may need support | from repetition |

**LEVEL 3**

| | |
|---|---|
| Pupils show understanding of | short passages<br>messages<br>dialogues |
| Pupils | identify main points<br>identify likes, dislikes and feelings |
| Pupils may need support | from some repetition of short sections |

**LEVEL 4**

| | |
|---|---|
| Pupils show understanding of | longer passages made up of simple sentences |
| Pupils understand speech | at near-normal speed with little interference |
| Pupils may need support | from repetition of some items |

**LEVEL 5**

| | |
|---|---|
| Pupils show understanding of | longer passages made up of familiar material<br>past, present and future events |
| Pupils understand speech | at near-normal speed in everyday circumstances with little interference |
| Pupils note | main points<br>specific details |
| Pupils may need support | from some repetition |

**LEVEL 6**

| | |
|---|---|
| Pupils show understanding of | short narratives<br>familiar language in unfamiliar contexts |
| Pupils understand speech | at normal speed in everyday circumstances with some hesitancy and interference |
| Pupils note | main points<br>specific details<br>points of view |
| Pupils may need support | from occasional repetition |

## AT1: Listening continued

**LEVEL 7**

| | |
|---|---|
| Pupils show understanding of | some complex materials<br>some unfamiliar language<br>brief news items<br>other TV and radio items |
| Pupils understand speech | at normal speed |
| Pupils need little support | |

**LEVEL 8**

| | |
|---|---|
| Pupils show understanding of | a wide range of spoken materials<br>unfamiliar material |
| Pupils | draw inferences<br>report attitudes and emotions<br>need little repetition |

**Exceptional performance**

| | |
|---|---|
| Pupils show understanding of | a wide range of materials, factual and imaginative<br>material with a variety of points of view |
| Pupils | listen independently<br>organize their own listening |

## AT2: Reading

**LEVEL 1**

| | |
|---|---|
| Pupils show understanding of | single words<br>simple classroom commands |
| Pupils may need support | from visuals |

**LEVEL 2**

| | |
|---|---|
| Pupils show understanding of | short phrases |
| Pupils can | match sound to print<br>read aloud familiar words and phrases<br>use books and glossaries to look new words up |

**LEVEL 3**

| | |
|---|---|
| Pupils show understanding of | printed or word-processed short dialogues and texts |
| Pupils | identify main points<br>identify likes, dislikes and feelings |
| Pupils | use bilingual dictionary or glossary |
| Pupils | choose simple texts to read independently |

**LEVEL 4**

| | |
|---|---|
| Pupils show understanding of | printed or clearly handwritten short stories and other texts |
| Pupils | identify details and main points |
| Pupils sometimes | use context to deduce meaning |

**LEVEL 5**

| | |
|---|---|
| Pupils show understanding of | longer passages made up of familiar material<br>past, present and future events |
| Pupils note | main points, specific details and opinions |
| Pupils | read aloud with some confidence |
| Pupils | use reference materials with more confidence |

**LEVEL 6**

| | |
|---|---|
| Pupils show understanding of | a variety of texts<br>familiar language in unfamiliar contexts |
| Pupils | select their reading independently |
| Pupils | use context and grammatical understanding to infer meaning |

**LEVEL 7**

| | |
|---|---|
| Pupils show understanding of | some complex materials<br>some unfamiliar language |
| Pupils | use language from their reading in their speaking and writing |
| Pupils | are confident with reference materials |

**LEVEL 8**

| | |
|---|---|
| Pupils show understanding of | a wide range of written materials<br>unfamiliar material |
| Pupils | draw inferences<br>report attitudes and emotions |
| Pupils | read for personal interest and for information |

**Exceptional performance**

| | |
|---|---|
| Pupils | understand a wide range of imaginative and factual texts<br>can cope with formal and official material<br>can summarize and explain orally and in writing |

## AT2: Speaking

**LEVEL 1**

| | |
|---|---|
| Pupils respond | to single words and short phrases |
| Pupils' pronunciation | is approximate |
| Pupils may need support | from visual clues<br>from the teacher's model |

**LEVEL 2**

| | |
|---|---|
| Pupils respond | in short and simple ways |
| Pupils | name and describe objects, places and people |
| Pupils' pronunciation | is approximate but does not obscure meaning |

**LEVEL 3**

| | |
|---|---|
| Pupils take part in | brief role-plays with visual or written clues |
| Pupils | briefly express likes, dislikes and feelings |
| Pupils usually | use memorized phrases |
| Pupils sometimes | vary memorized phrases |

**LEVEL 4**

| | |
|---|---|
| Pupils take part in | simple structured conversations |
| Pupils | adapt phrases by substituting single words |
| Pupils' pronunciation is usually | accurate with reasonable intonation |

**LEVEL 5**

| | |
|---|---|
| Pupils take part in | short conversations |
| Pupils | briefly express likes, dislikes and feelings |
| Pupils refer to | past, present and future events |
| Pupils | are easily understood despite some errors |

**LEVEL 6**

| | |
|---|---|
| Pupils initiate | short conversations including past, present and future events |
| Pupils | improvise and paraphrase |
| Pupils | routinely use French for giving and receiving information |
| Pupils | are easily understood despite some hesitancy |

**LEVEL 7**

| | |
|---|---|
| Pupils inititate | discussion on matters of topical interest |
| Pupils | give and justify opinions |
| Pupils | deal with some unprepared situations by adapting language |
| Pupils' pronunciation | is good, as is their intonation |

**LEVEL 8**

| | |
|---|---|
| Pupils deal | increasingly confidently with the unpredictable |
| Pupils | discuss facts, ideas and experiences |
| Pupils' language and pronunciation | is generally accurate |

**Exceptional performance**

| | |
|---|---|
| Pupils discuss | a wide range of topics, factual and imaginative |
| Pupils speak fluently | with few errors |
| Pupils | vary intonation |

## AT4: Writing

**LEVEL 1**

| | |
|---|---|
| Pupils copy | single words |

**LEVEL 2**

| | |
|---|---|
| Pupils write and copy | short familiar phrases and simple ways |
| Pupils | write classroom signs and instructions |
| Pupils' spelling is approximate | when writing from memory |

**LEVEL 3**

| | |
|---|---|
| Pupils write | a couple of sentences on familiar topics |
| Pupils | briefly express likes, dislikes and feelings |
| Pupils sometimes | need help when writing |
| Pupils write | short phrases from memory |
| Pupils' spelling | is readily understandable when writing from memory |

**LEVEL 4**

| | |
|---|---|
| Pupils write | short paragraphs using memorized language |
| Pupils | adapt phrases by substituting single words |
| Pupils use | dictionaries and glossaries |

## AT4: Writing continued

| LEVEL 5 | | LEVEL 6 | |
|---|---|---|---|
| Pupils write | briefly, expressing likes, dislikes and feelings | Pupils write | descriptive paragraphs about past, present and future events |
| Pupils refer to | past, present and future events | Pupils use informal language | in diaries and personal letters |
| Pupils | are generally understood despite some errors | Pupils use formal language | in letters booking accommodation |
| Pupils | apply grammar in new contexts | Pupils | are easily understood despite some errors |
| Pupils | use dictionaries and glossaries to look up unknown words | | |

| LEVEL 7 | |
|---|---|
| Pupils | write on real or imaginary subjects |
| | use paragraphs |
| | improve, edit and re-draft work, using reference sources as a guide |
| Pupils make | only occasional errors |

| LEVEL 8 | |
|---|---|
| Pupils discuss | facts, ideas and experiences and points of view |
| Pupils produce | longer, developed pieces of writing |
| Pupils' language | is generally accurate |
| Pupils use | reference materials to extend their linguistic range |
| **Exceptional performance** | |
| Pupils write coherently | on a wide range of topics, factual and imaginative |
| Pupils choose the form of their writing | to suit the task |
| Pupils write fluently | with few errors |

# Study skills

This section is intended to point out how to be an efficient learner of French.

Study skills to help you to make the best possible use of your valuable time in school. These will also be of general use in preparing for other subjects.

I have also given hints and tips to improve your performance in the four language skills tested in Key Stage 3 French: Listening, Speaking, Reading and Writing.

There is some help on how to use a dictionary, advice on how to go about learning vocabulary.

Finally, there are some hints about how to revise effectively.

Because performance in French is a skill, it is improved by practice. And any good musician or sporting star will confirm that the best forms of practice contain variety.

Some students find school work difficult. Sometimes this is because the work they are being asked to do really is too difficult for them. However, in our experience this is relatively rare. What is much more likely is that the student has not organized his or her attitude or priorities well in order to get the best out of the learning experience. This is a real shame, as learning a foreign language to a good standard is much easier to do at school than in later life. One reason for this is that in school the teaching has to match a nationally agreed learning programme which is known to work.

## Good and poor students

So the foundations of success in French are laid early in your course – not so much by your teacher, as by how you personally approach your work. Let us compare a good student and a poor student, seen from the teacher's point of view.

| Good student | Poor student |
|---|---|
| Is a regular attender. | Is often absent. |
| Catches up with work after absence – usually without prompting. | Makes no effort to catch up. Needs to be "chased". |
| Always writes notes in lessons. | Lets teacher's explanations wash over him/her. Has lost notebook and/or pen. |
| Tries his/her best during pairwork. | Chats in English during pairwork. |
| Sits with a good view of board and teacher. | Sits at the back or in corners. |
| Asks when stuck. | Gives up if stuck. Claims he/she doesn't understand. |
| Does homework on time. | Does homework late, or not at all. |
| Works at a regular time. | Works when he/she feels like it. |
| Presents work – rough or neat – tidily, with dates, page numbers, titles, etc. | Work is messy. |
| Writes legibly, with clear accents. | Hard to read. Accents could be ink splodges. |
| Has obviously done a rough draft of homework. | Hands in first draft with altered letters, crossings-out, etc. A pain to mark. |

*Continued on page 6*

*continued from page 5*

| Good student | Poor student |
|---|---|
| Re-reads corrected homework, notes errors and resolves to act on comments and corrections. | Never looks at anything teacher writes except the mark at the bottom of work. |
| When no homework is set, finds something extra to do in French. | When no homework is set, does nothing except cheer. |
| Is basically interested in most aspects of the subject. | Only took French because there was no other option. |
| Quite enjoys French. Improving. | Hates French. Getting worse at it. |

The key to a successful approach is motivation. You know your reasons for taking French. Whatever they are, look for ways to succeed.

## Getting Organized

Observation suggests that successful students are organized. Many students fail to reach their full potential because they approach the mechanics of studying the wrong way.

Here are some practical ways you can get yourself organized. Parents, too, may find this useful.

1. Have set routines for work. If you have a fixed time or times in the day or week when you do homework, then you don't have to spend time deciding when to do it. Your school, after all, has a set timetable for lessons for that very reason. Set times save you time.
2. Have set times when you do not work. This ensures that you get enough leisure time. 'All work and no play makes Jack a dull boy', says the proverb. Again, you save time on decision-making.
3. Do assignments as they are set. This is particularly important in French, where one piece of work often builds on the previous one, and where you need detailed, early feedback from your teacher to support your learning. By doing work immediately, you also save the time you might spend worrying about how and when to do the work. Do it **NOW**!
4. Have a suitable place for study. The ideal location is free from distractions. Aim for a table or desk free from clutter, with good lighting, and pens, pencils, paper and reference books within reach (so you don't have to keep getting up).
5. Do a reasonable amount of study per week. This might, perhaps, be in the range of 30–40 hours weekly, including the 25–27 hours or so spent in lessons in school. Many adults work about that number of hours. You may, of course, work longer if you can do so effectively.
6. Approach topics on the 'before, during and after' principle.
   **Before** a new topic – read ahead in your textbook to prepare yourself
   **During** the lesson – take notes or take part, as appropriate.
   **After** the lesson – go over the notes and the textbook material as soon as possible.

Being organized doesn't take any more time than being disorganized. In fact, it saves time. And most importantly, it makes you a more efficient learner who will certainly do better than your disorganized fellow-students.

## Listening

This often seems difficult. Many students feel that 'they speak too fast' or 'I don't understand a word' when they hear French in class. This is especially so when they are listening to a cassette recording.

However, there are hints for making it more enjoyable.

1. Don't be put off easily. You cannot expect to understand every word at first. Concentrate on picking out words you **do** understand. Many teachers will want you to practise gist comprehension, or to listen out for the familiar amongst the unfamiliar. This is, after all, what you did when learning English as a baby. You are probably still learning new words in English (perhaps during Science or Technology lessons) and may not understand them the first time you hear them. The same is true of French.
2. Make sure you have read the tasks you are asked to do **before** the cassette is played. It is doubly difficult to read and listen at the same time. This may mean being super-attentive in class. On the same theme, it is important to have paper and pen/pencil handy so that you can react quickly when your teacher does a listening exercise.
3. Develop the ability to make quick notes from what you hear. This may be something you need to be able to do in other subjects, too. You need to know whether your listening notes need to be beautifully neat or not. In most cases, speed is more important than presentation. After the cassette has been played you will have time to work on improving presentation.
4. Work through the listening exercises and the cassette which go with this book. They have been designed to follow a typical programme for Key Stage 3 French. If you find them difficult at first, you could follow the transcript of what is being said in the answers section as the cassette plays.
5. Ask if you can use the audio material which goes with your course at lunch times, etc. You might ask to follow the transcripts which are in the teacher's book. This is especially recommended on wet, cold days! You could even make your own copies!
6. In most parts of Britain, French radio stations can be picked up reasonably well in the vicinity of Radio 4 on Long Wave/AM. These are music stations, but they also carry hourly news. A small daily dose will not be harmful, and may even do you good!
   Wavelengths: Europe 1 1647 metres
   France Inter 1829 metres
7. BBC and Channel 4 have schools programmes in French which are aimed at young learners. Current titles include: Le petit monde de Pierre; Quinze minutes; Café des Rêves.
8. If there are French-speaking visitors in your locality, (for example, a school exchange) you will probably find that the young French people are pleased to talk to you in French. Ask them about such things as schools and their family and their journey as a starting point. The teachers accompanying such parties, too, are worth approaching.
9. If your school is fortunate enough to have a French Assistant(e), be sure to take his/her sessions seriously.

## Reading

The obvious starting point is your French textbook. It will have a large amount of material in it, specifically chosen to meet the range of topics needed at Key Stage 3. You will certainly benefit from spending time working through texts you have previously done in class, or those which your teacher has decided to miss out. Use the vocabulary at the back to help you. Make a note of words you don't know without looking up - that is the first step to learning them.

Your school or local library may well have a variety of easy books in French. Some are available with English translations of the same stories. Look out for:

- Asterix
- Tintin
- The Mr Men

*European Schoolbooks Ltd.* stock these and a very wide range of other material not easily available elsewhere *(European Schoolbooks Ltd.*, The Runnings, Cheltenham, GL51 9PQ, Tel: 01242 245252).

Your teacher may have back numbers of magazines designed for learners of French, or you could subscribe to them direct. Popular suitable titles include, in order of difficulty:

- Allons
- Bonjour
- Ça va

obtainable from: Mary Glasgow Magazines, Building 1, Kineton Road Industrial Estate, Southam, CV33 ODG, Tel: 01926 815560, Fax: 01926 815563.

Many schools have 'reading schemes' which have graded material suitable for beginners. If they are used as part of your regular lessons, do be sure to make the most of the time.

A little French reading daily will pay dividends. And the more you do, the easier you will find it.

## Speaking

We say that someone who knows another language 'speaks' it. And speaking a foreign language is certainly the most useful skill in real life.

Some students feel very shy about speaking in French, especially in front of their classmates. However, you are all in the same boat. And your teacher will also have had the experience of learning to pronounce a foreign language. So it is really important right from the start to make sure that you get all the practice you can in speaking.

If the class repeats a word, phrase, or sentence, make sure that you do it as well as you can. You may not get it right first time. But if you don't take the opportunity to practise when there is plenty of 'cover' you are missing a chance you can't get any other way.

If you are asked questions by the teacher, or asked to repeat individually, do the best you can. With time your accent and intonation will improve. While others are being asked, keep quiet to give them the best chance hearing the teacher's model.

During pairwork, make *anglais interdit* a rule with your partner. You can chat in English at virtually any time. But you can practise conversations in French only in your French lesson. So don't waste the opportunuity. When you have done a role-play task once, do it again and again until you are really good at it and can do it with virtually no prompts.

Take opportunities to learn short conversations by heart. There are many phrases in the vocabulary topics of this book. They have been selected for their usefulness. Be sure you know as many as possible.

Finally, make sure that you practise reading aloud as well as silently. If you can do it well – and you will improve with practice – you will help your ability to understand French, too.

## Writing

At Key Stage 3, writing French is worth 25 per cent of the marks. However, you will probably spend more than a quarter of your French-learning time writing, because it is a useful tool for fixing new material.

At the simplest level you will be asked to copy words, perhaps into a notebook. This is not actually as easy as it sounds, as the spelling rules for French are not the same as English ones. So develop the habit of copying correctly and checking that you have done so.

In the authors' experience, it is noticeable that students who write a date and title for each piece of work, number it clearly and rule off neatly afterwards are better at French than those students who do none of these things. Be sure your work is tidy.

It is important, too, that you have:

- verb endings agreeing with the gender and number of the subject
- adjectives agreeing with the gender and number of the word they describe
- accents where they are needed
- accents pointing the right way

Check each of these points for each piece of work.

Avoid the use of ditto marks. Even if an exercise is repetitive, the act of repeating a word or spelling it is a learning tool.

Remember, too, that writing set for homework will usually have something to do with the lesson during which it was set. Indeed, there may well be similar material in your textbook from which you can get clues.

When work is handed back, the best students will want to write a fair version of any sentence which contains an error. This doesn't actually take long, and makes sure that you have really looked hard at your mistake. If you are lucky, your teacher will have shown you how to correct the work.

## Using a dictionary

Knowing how to use a dictionary is a really useful language-learning skill. Dictionaries are not expensive, and you may well find one useful. In GCSE, dictionaries will be available to you during some parts of the exam from 1998 onwards. At this stage in your French-learning career you will probably not need to spend more than £10 on a dictionary; many good ones are available for much less. In the English–French, French–English section of this book you should find all the words you might reasonably be expected to know at Key Stage 3. However, it is worth knowing how to look words up and what to look for among the many abbreviations dictionaries contain.

Useful commonly used abbreviations include:

| | |
|---|---|
| adj | adjective |
| adv | adverb |
| approx | approximately |
| aux | auxiliary |
| coll | colloquial |
| comp | comparative |
| conj | conjunction |
| esp | especially |
| f | feminine |
| gram | grammar |
| imp | imperfect |
| impers | impersonal |
| inf | infinitive |
| inv | invariable |

| | |
|---|---|
| irr/irreg | irregular |
| m | masculine |
| n | noun |
| o.s. | oneself |
| pl | plural |
| pp | past participle |
| poss | possessive |
| prep | preposition |
| pres | present |
| pron | pronoun |
| reg | regular |
| sing | singular |
| sl | slang |
| s.o. | someone |
| sth | something |
| refl | reflexive |
| v aux | auxiliary verb |
| vi | intransitive verb |
| vr | reflexive verb |
| vt | transitive verb |

When you look up a **French** word, you may find a number of possible English translations, listed with the most common first. You will then need to apply common sense to work out which meaning is most likely in the context.

You may find that a word is not listed. This may mean that it is a past participle. Check the irregular verb table.

When you look up an **English** word to find the French equivalent, first:

Make sure you know if you want a noun, adjective, verb, etc.

Then:

After finding the French word, look that up in the French–English section. You should get the word you started with, or one which means the same in the same context.

The example French–English dictionary below has been reproduced from *Your French Dictionary* obtainable only from Malvern Language Guides, PO Box 76, Malvern WR14 2YP. Tel (01684) 577433. £3.50, cheque with order.

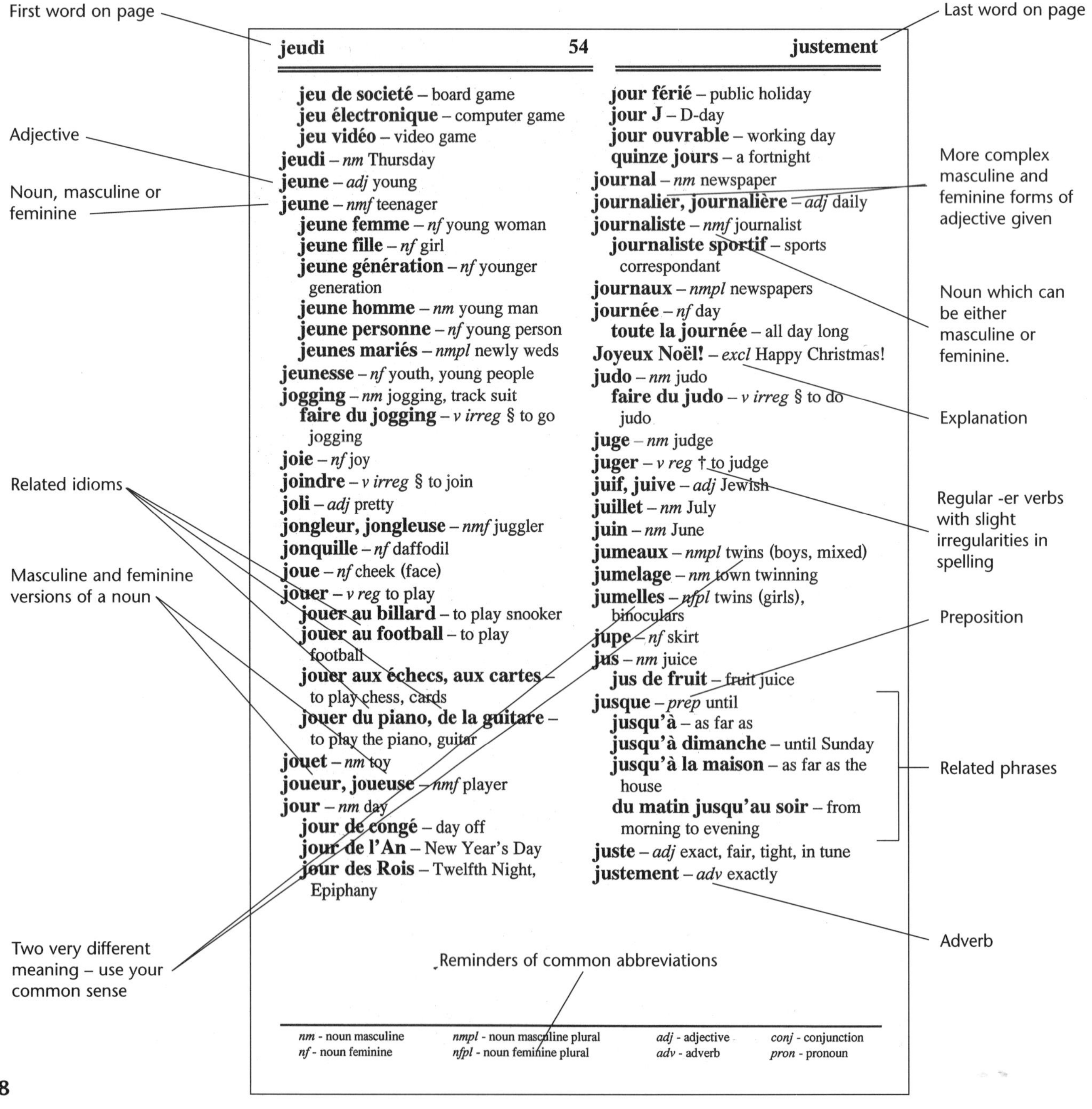


**jeudi** 54 **justement**

**jeu de societé** – board game
**jeu électronique** – computer game
**jeu vidéo** – video game
**jeudi** – *nm* Thursday
**jeune** – *adj* young
**jeune** – *nmf* teenager
**jeune femme** – *nf* young woman
**jeune fille** – *nf* girl
**jeune génération** – *nf* younger generation
**jeune homme** – *nm* young man
**jeune personne** – *nf* young person
**jeunes mariés** – *nmpl* newly weds
**jeunesse** – *nf* youth, young people
**jogging** – *nm* jogging, track suit
**faire du jogging** – *v irreg* § to go jogging
**joie** – *nf* joy
**joindre** – *v irreg* § to join
**joli** – *adj* pretty
**jongleur, jongleuse** – *nmf* juggler
**jonquille** – *nf* daffodil
**joue** – *nf* cheek (face)
**jouer** – *v reg* to play
**jouer au billard** – to play snooker
**jouer au football** – to play football
**jouer aux échecs, aux cartes** – to play chess, cards
**jouer du piano, de la guitare** – to play the piano, guitar
**jouet** – *nm* toy
**joueur, joueuse** – *nmf* player
**jour** – *nm* day
**jour de congé** – day off
**jour de l'An** – New Year's Day
**jour des Rois** – Twelfth Night, Epiphany
**jour férié** – public holiday
**jour J** – D-day
**jour ouvrable** – working day
**quinze jours** – a fortnight
**journal** – *nm* newspaper
**journalier, journalière** – *adj* daily
**journaliste** – *nmf* journalist
**journaliste sportif** – sports correspondant
**journaux** – *nmpl* newspapers
**journée** – *nf* day
**toute la journée** – all day long
**Joyeux Noël!** – *excl* Happy Christmas!
**judo** – *nm* judo
**faire du judo** – *v irreg* § to do judo
**juge** – *nm* judge
**juger** – *v reg* † to judge
**juif, juive** – *adj* Jewish
**juillet** – *nm* July
**juin** – *nm* June
**jumeaux** – *nmpl* twins (boys, mixed)
**jumelage** – *nm* town twinning
**jumelles** – *nfpl* twins (girls), binoculars
**jupe** – *nf* skirt
**jus** – *nm* juice
**jus de fruit** – fruit juice
**jusque** – *prep* until
**jusqu'à** – as far as
**jusqu'à dimanche** – until Sunday
**jusqu'à la maison** – as far as the house
**du matin jusqu'au soir** – from morning to evening
**juste** – *adj* exact, fair, tight, in tune
**justement** – *adv* exactly

*nm* - noun masculine · *nmpl* - noun masculine plural · *adj* - adjective · *conj* - conjunction
*nf* - noun feminine · *nfpl* - noun feminine plural · *adv* - adverb · *pron* - pronoun

## Learning Vocabulary

This is one of the chores of learning a foreign language. It is best to have a regular time of day (or perhaps two occasions in the day) when you sit down and spend 10–15 minutes learning vocabulary. And the sooner you start, the better – so start today!

This really requires somewhere private, or at least somewhere you won't be disturbed. So your room, somewhere quiet in school at break or lunch-time, or even on public transport, would be suitable. What is **not** suitable is trying to do it while talking to or listening to someone else, or watching your favourite TV programme. Don't kid yourself you are working when you're not.

As well as having a good place to do it, it's as well to be methodical. Work through the vocabulary topics, changing them daily. Don't try to learn too many words at once. Try to relate them to a situation, rather than just working through an alphabetical list. It's more interesting to learn, say, everything to do with changing money than just 40 words which happen to begin with the same letter.

Begin your sessions with a written test on what you did last time. This could be half French–English and half English–French. Don't cheat, but check your test afterwards with the textbook. If you did well, reward yourself with a treat of some kind. Keep a record of how you have done so you can check your progress.

Rather than simply learning vocabulary in your head from a list, it is better to be **doing** something. The best method is to write out each word or phrase two or three times. (It doesn't matter if you can't read it afterwards. Go for speed!) Make sure of accents. Include the gender for nouns. If you haven't anywhere to write, you can still test yourself using a piece of card or paper cut or folded as shown.

First, cover the English column on your list and see if you can say what the French words mean. Then turn the blind over and see if you can say what the French should

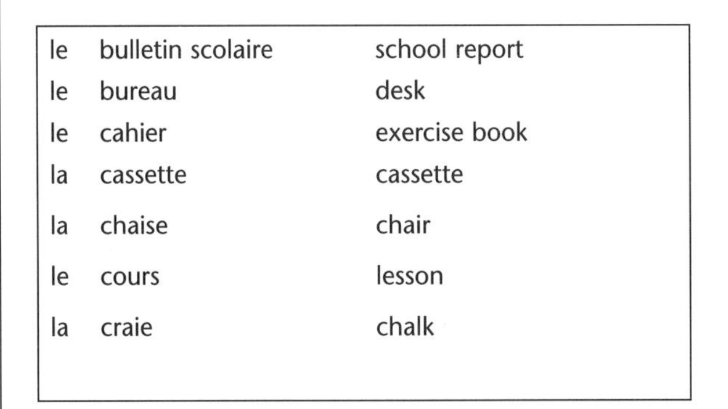


**1** Select a vocabulary topic to learn.

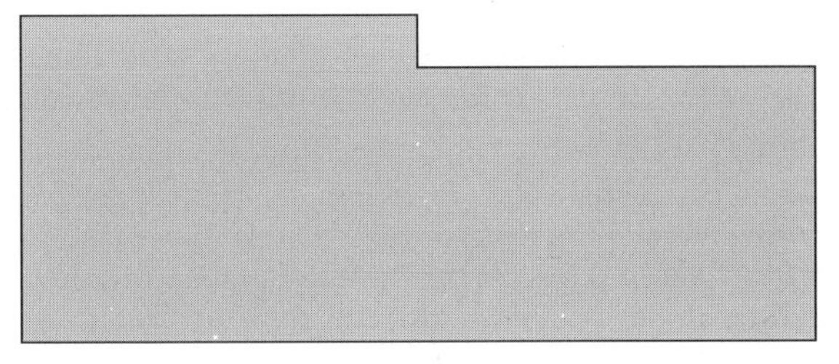

**2** Cut out the shape **blind** as shown above out of card or paper.

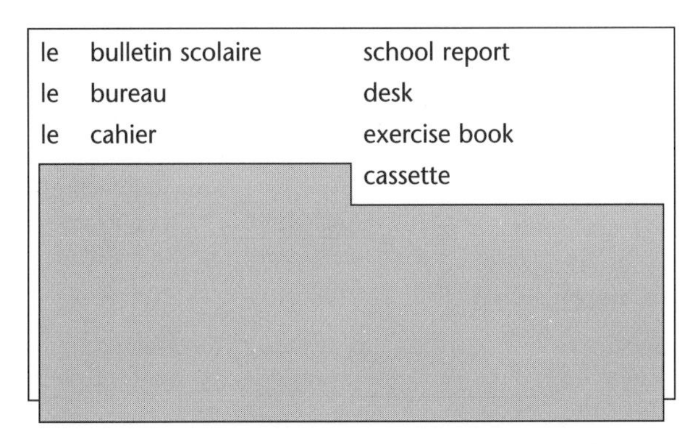


**3** Place blind over the list so that the next English word is shown. Try to remember what the word should be in French.

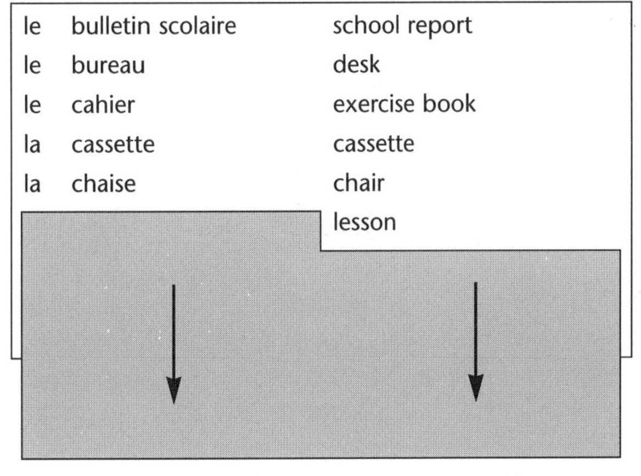


**4** Move the blind down the list. This will reveal the correct French word; check if you were right. Now try the next English word.

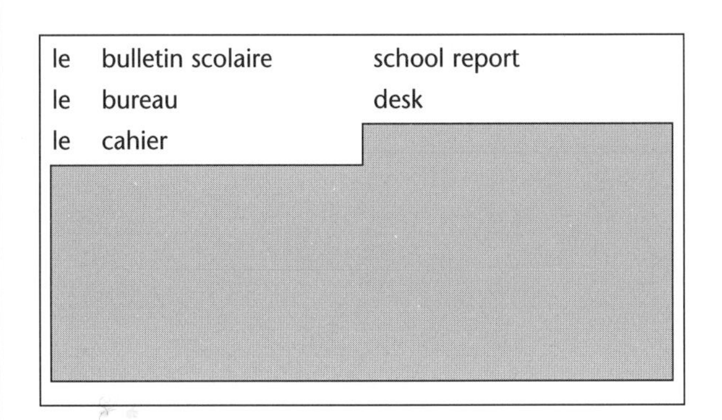


**5** When you have finished testing yourself on remembering the French words, you can turn the blind over so that the English words are covered up and see if you know what the English translations are.

be (including gender, as before). You can also use the blind to give yourself a written test. You immediately find out if you were right as you move it down to the next word. **No peeping!**

Students often like to learn vocabulary with a friend. This is fine as a way of learning what the English version of French words is, and for checking gender and past participles. However, unless someone is writing, then spelling accuracy is not likely to be improved.

## Revising for tests and exams

As I have suggested, being organized produces better results. This applies, of course, to revision as well as normal study. Here are some tips about efficient revision:

The most difficult thing about revision is overcoming boredom. By definition, you have seen things you are revising before, so you need to find ways of making up for the lack of novelty.

Many students revise ineffectively because they merely read through notes and chapters in the textbook and let the information wash over them. This is almost always a waste of time, certainly after the first half-hour or so. The key is to **do** something. Activity is an aid to concentration. In a skill-based subject like French, you will improve your performance by practice.

Try some or all of the following techniques:

1. Write notes. When reading, say, grammar rules again, make yourself skeleton notes which are sufficiently detailed to jog your memory. Some students do this on small pieces of card (index cards or chopped-up pieces of cereal packet) which they carry about with them and consult in odd moments. The same goes for vocabulary. Writing a word down with its gender and meaning will help to fix it in your memory. Another hint is to write down a phrase which contains the word and its gender. When reading texts, make a note of every word you had to look up. As time goes on, you will have to look up fewer and fewer.
2. Work with a friend. This can relieve the boredom. Pick a friend who is about the same standard as you are. Working with someone a lot better can be good for their ego, but not for yours. Similarly, working with someone a lot weaker doesn't teach you anything new. Testing each other is a good idea. But don't forget to include written testing, which is the ultimate proof of whether you know things. Because of the danger of being sidetracked, don't rely on this method of revision alone.
3. Set yourself tests. While learning, make a note of things you found hard, and test yourself later – at the end of your session, then the following day, then the following week. You have to be honest with yourself about how you got on! Keep a chart of your marks as a rough guide to progress.
4. List the topics which you need to revise. Then tick off the ones you have done
   Do not tick off ones you have missed out! The more you have dealt with, the better you will feel.
5. Set realistic targets. Don't try to do too much in one session – you'll end up frustrated and become more and more depressed. Far better to learn, say, ten words and succeed than to try to learn 56 and fail miserably.
6. Reward yourself. If you have done a reasonable stint of revision, or done well in a test, give yourself a treat- a sweet, or a coffee break, or the chance to watch a favourite soap opera. Having something to look forward to is a great incentive.
7. Don't go too long without a break. 45–50 minutes is probably the longest session most people can concentrate for without a break, – even if it's only to stretch your legs for five minutes.
8. Give yourself variety. Vary what you look at - revise different skills in French. Also, vary the subjects you do in any one session – Three spells of 45–50 minutes on three different subjects will be more productive than a three-hour 'slog' on one area.
9. Don't be fooled by other students. During the examination season, some fellow-students will be loudly proclaiming either that they 'never do any revision' or that they are 'up till 2 a.m. every evening working'. Ignore them. They are being hysterical, and may well not be telling the truth anyway. What matters to you is not how much or how little revision your friends do, but how much **you** do.
10. Most important of all, don't kid yourself that you are working when you aren't. You can't revise at all while watching TV, chatting to friends, washing your hair or eating a meal. So don't even attempt it. Instead, use these activities to reward yourself after a revision session.

Directed revision pays off. Revise early, and revise often!

## Conclusion

Learning a foreign language is an activity which can give a great deal of pleasure. You now know the most efficient way to go about it. *Amuse-toi bien!*

# Section two

## Grammar

**Grammar is often seen as boring or irrelevant. It isn't, as it allows you to generate and understand sentences which you have not come across before, and helps your reading and listening comprehension. Find out how it works, and you have the key to much more French than you could ever hope to learn by heart.**

**Not all students are taught using formal grammar in their English or French lessons nowadays. There is nothing to be frightened of in the use of grammatical terms. After all, a mechanic wouldn't attempt to describe what a spanner is every time he wanted to have one passed to him. He just uses the technical term, which is 'spanner'. These grammatical terms are the technical 'jargon' of language-learning, which give you access to the patterns of French and other languages to enable you to learn them more quickly.**

**We have defined the grammatical terms simply at the start of each entry in this section. The entries are arranged alphabetically. The box below will help you to see, at a glance, the entries presented and the pages on which you can find them.**


- Adjectives 12
- Adverbs 13
- Articles 13
- Commands – *see Verbs* 30
- Comparisons 15
- Conditional – *see Verbs* 32
- Conjunctions 16
- Days, months, dates and times 16
- Definite article – *see Articles* 13
- Gender – *see Nouns* 17
- Future tense – *see verbs* 28
- Imperfect tense – *see Verbs* 27
- Indefinite article – *see Article* 14
- Infinitives – *see Verbs* 31
- Irregular verbs – *see Verbs* 22
- Negatives – *see Verbs* 32
- Nouns 17
- Numbers 18
- Partive article – *see Articles* 14
- Past tense – *see Verbs: Perfect and Imperfect* 25, 27
- Perfect tense – *see Verbs* 25
- Plurals – *see Nouns* 17
- Prepositions 19
- Present tense – *see Verbs* 22
- Pronouns – *see Verbs* 20
- Question forms – *see Verbs* 30
- Reflexive verbs – *see Verbs* 29
- Regular verbs – *see Verbs* 22
- Tenses – *see Verbs* 22
- Verbs 22

# Adjectives

An **adjective** is a word which describes a noun or pronoun. It gives information about such things as colour, type, character, etc.

## Agreement of adjectives

Adjectives change their spelling to agree with the noun they describe. They often have a different spelling for masculine and feminine, and generally for the plural. The changes may or may not be heard in speech, but they are always made in writing.

## Patterns of adjective agreement

French adjectives have different patterns for showing agreement.

1. Many adjectives follow this pattern:

| masculine singular | feminine singular | masculine plural | feminine plural | Meaning |
|---|---|---|---|---|
| noir | noir**e** | noir**s** | noir**es** | *black* |

Others which follow this pattern include:

| masculine singular | feminine singular | masculine plural | feminine plural | Meaning |
|---|---|---|---|---|
| anglais | anglais**e** | anglais | anglais**es** | *English* |
| grand | grand**e** | grand**s** | grand**es** | *large, tall* |
| fort | fort**e** | fort**s** | fort**es** | *strong* |
| français | français**e** | français | français**es** | *French* |
| intelligent | intelligent**e** | intelligent**s** | intelligent**es** | *intelligent* |
| intéressant | intéressant**e** | intéressant**s** | intéressant**es** | *interesting* |
| petit | petit**e** | petit**s** | petit**es** | *small* |
| vert | vert**e** | vert**s** | vert**es** | *green* |

There are many more. Keep a list of them as you come across them.

2. Adjectives which already end in *-e* (without an accent!) have no different feminine form. They are actually following the same logic as in 1.

| masculine singular | feminine singular | masculine plural | feminine plural | Meaning |
|---|---|---|---|---|
| jeune | jeune | jeune**s** | jeune**s** | *young* |

Others which follow this pattern include:

| masculine singular | feminine singular | masculine plural | feminine plural | Meaning |
|---|---|---|---|---|
| bête | bête | bête**s** | bête**s** | *stupid* |
| célèbre | célèbre | célèbre**s** | célèbre**s** | *famous* |
| jaune | jaune | jaune**s** | jaune**s** | *yellow* |
| mince | mince | mince**s** | mince**s** | *thin* |
| orange | orange | orange**s** | orange**s** | *orange* |
| propre | propre | propre**s** | propre**s** | *clean, own* |
| rouge | rouge | rouge**s** | rouge**s** | *red* |
| stupide | stupide | stupide**s** | stupide**s** | *stupid* |

There are many more. Keep a list of them as you come across them.

3. Many other adjectives have slight spelling changes. Use the alphabetical list below to help you get it right!

| masculine singular | feminine singular | masculine plural | feminine plural | Meaning |
|---|---|---|---|---|
| actif | acti**ve** | actif**s** | acti**ves** | *active* |
| âgé | âgé**e** | âgé**s** | âgé**es** | *old, aged* |
| ancien | ancien**ne** | ancien**s** | ancien**nes** | *ex-* |
| blanc | blan**che** | blanc**s** | blan**ches** | *white* |
| bleu | bleu**e** | bleu**s** | bleu**es** | *blue* |
| bon | bon**ne** | bon**s** | bon**nes** | *good* |
| cassé | cassé**e** | cassé**s** | cassé**es** | *broken* |
| cher | ch**ère** | cher**s** | ch**ères** | *dear* |
| délicieux | délicieu**se** | délicieux | délicieu**ses** | *delicious* |
| dernier | derni**ère** | dernier**s** | derni**ères** | *last* |
| doux | dou**ce** | doux | dou**ces** | *soft, gentle* |
| entier | enti**ère** | entier**s** | enti**ères** | *whole* |
| fatigué | fatigué**e** | fatigué**s** | fatigué**es** | *tired* |
| favori | favori**te** | favori**s** | favori**tes** | *favourite* |
| fou | **folle** | fou**s** | **folles** | *mad* |
| gentil | gentil**le** | gentil**s** | gentil**les** | *kind, nice* |
| gras | gras**se** | gras | gras**ses** | *fat* |
| gros | gros**se** | gros | gros**ses** | *large* |
| heureux | heureu**se** | heureux | heureu**ses** | *happy* |
| jaloux | jalou**se** | jaloux | jalou**ses** | *jealous* |
| joli | joli**e** | joli**s** | joli**es** | *pretty* |
| joyeux | joyeu**se** | joyeux | joyeu**ses** | *joyful* |
| long | long**ue** | long**s** | long**ues** | *long* |
| malheureux | malheureu**se** | malheureux | malheureu**ses** | *unhappy* |
| merveilleux | merveilleu**se** | merveilleux | merveilleu**ses** | *marvellous* |
| neuf | neu**ve** | neuf**s** | neu**ves** | *new* |
| perdu | perdu**e** | perdu**s** | perdu**es** | *lost* |
| premier | premi**ère** | premier**s** | premi**ères** | *first* |
| public | publi**que** | public**s** | publi**ques** | *public* |
| régulier | réguli**ère** | régulier**s** | réguli**ères** | *regular* |
| roux | rou**sse** | roux | rou**sses** | *red-haired* |
| sec | s**èche** | sec**s** | s**èches** | *dry* |
| sportif | sporti**ve** | sportif**s** | sporti**ves** | *sporty* |
| trouvé | trouvé**e** | trouvé**s** | trouvé**es** | *found* |
| vif | vi**ve** | vif**s** | vi**ves** | *lively* |

4. Three adjectives have extra masculine forms which are used when the adjective is followed by a vowel or a silent *h*.

| masculine singular | feminine singular | masculine plural | feminine plural | Meaning |
|---|---|---|---|---|
| beau or be**l** | be**lle** | bea**ux** | be**lles** | *beautiful, handsome* |
| nouveau or nouve**l** | nouve**lle** | nouve**aux** | nouve**lles** | *new* |
| vieux or vie**il** | vie**ille** | vie**ux** | vie**illes** | *old* |

5. **Demi** does not agree when it is joined to another word.

**Example:**

une **demi**-heure

But: Il est une heure et **demie**.

## Position of adjectives

Adjectives in French, unlike in English, usually follow the noun to which they refer.

**Example:**

J'ai un pullover noir et un pantalon jaune
*I've got a black pullover and a yellow pair of trousers*

A few common adjectives, however, come before the noun. These are:

| | |
|---|---|
| beau | *handsome, beautiful* |
| bon | *good* |
| court | *short* |
| excellent | *excellent* |
| gentil | *kind* |

| | |
|---|---|
| grand | *large, tall* |
| gros | *big* |
| haut | *high* |
| jeune | *young* |
| joli | *pretty* |
| large | *wide* |
| long | *long* |
| mauvais | *bad* |
| petit | *small* |
| vieux | *old* |
| vilain | *naughty, ugly* |

**Example:**

C'est un beau garçon
*He's a handsome boy.*

# ADVERBS

An adverb is a word which describes a verb (which 'adds information to a verb') giving information about **how** something is done. Adverbs can also be used to add to adjectives or other adverbs.

In French, adverbs are formed by changing adjectives.

## Formation of adverbs from adjectives

1. In most cases, *-ment* is added to the feminine singular form of the adjective.

**Example:**

| masculine | feminine | adverb | meaning |
|---|---|---|---|
| doux | douce | doucement | *gently* |
| heureux | heureuse | heureusement | *fortunately* |
| entier | entière | entièrement | *entirely* |

2. If the masculine singular form ends in a vowel (usually *-e* or *-i*) *-ment* is added straight on to that.

**Example:**

| masculine | adverb | meaning |
|---|---|---|
| vrai | vraiment | *really* |
| horrible | horriblement | *horribly* |

3. If the adjective ends in *-ant* or *-ent* in the masculine singular form, the adverb follows this pattern:

**Example:**

| masculine | adverb | meaning |
|---|---|---|
| constant | constamment | *constantly* |
| évident | évidemment | *obviously* |

4. There are quite a lot of irregular adverbs. As these are the most common ones, it is worth learning the list.

| | |
|---|---|
| beaucoup | *a lot* |
| bien | *well* |
| énormément | *enormously* |
| fort | *strongly* |
| gentiment | *kindly* |
| lentement | *slowly* |
| loin | *a long way away* |
| longtemps | *for a long time* |
| mal | *badly* |
| peu | *a little* |
| précisément | *precisely* |
| souvent | *often* |
| tard | *late* |
| tôt | *early* |
| trop | *too much* |
| vite | *quickly* |

## Position of adverbs

The adverb generally goes after the verb (unlike in English – beware!).

**Example:**

Il va souvent au collège
*He often goes to school*

In the perfect tense it usually comes after the auxiliary verb.

**Example:**

Il n'a pas bien dormi
*He didn't sleep well*

# ARTICLES

There are three types of article you will need to be able to use: the **definite article**, the **indefinite article**, and the **partitive article** (*some* or *any*). It is also possible to leave the article out in some special circumstances.

## The definite article

This is the equivalent of the English *the.*

**Le** is used with masculine nouns which start with a consonant:

**Examples:**

| | |
|---|---|
| **le** garçon | *the boy* |
| **le** crayon | *the pencil* |
| **le** chat | *the cat* |

**La** is used with feminine nouns which start with a consonant:

**Examples:**

| | |
|---|---|
| **la** fille | *the girl* |
| **la** chaise | *the chair* |
| **la** souris | *the mouse* |

**L'** is used with both masculine and feminine nouns which start with a vowel or a silent *h*:

**Examples:**

| | |
|---|---|
| **l'**homme (m) | *the man* |
| **l'**enfant (m) | *the child* |
| **l'**heure (f) | *the hour* |
| **l'**épicerie (f) | *the grocery store* |

**Les** is always used with nouns in the plural whether masculine or feminine:

**Examples:**

| | |
|---|---|
| **les** garçons | *the boys* |
| **les** crayons | *the pencils* |
| **les** chats | *the cats* |
| **les** filles | *the girls* |
| **les** chaises | *the chairs* |
| **les** souris | *the mice* |
| **les** hommes (m) | *the men* |
| **les** enfants (m) | *the children* |
| **les** heures (f) | *the hours* |
| **les** épiceries (f) | *the grocery stores* |

The definite article is needed:

1. with nouns which refer to a particular object or person:

**Example:**

**Le** garçon est dans **le** garage
*The boy is in the garage*

2. with nouns (both abstract and concrete) used in a general sense:

**Examples:**

**Le** français m'intéresse mais je préfère **la** géographie
*I find French interesting, but I prefer geography*
J'aime **les** chiens, mais mon fils préfère **les** cobayes
*I like dogs, but my son prefers guinea pigs*

3. with countries and languages:

**Example:**

**L'**Ecosse est plus jolie que **l'**Angleterre
*Scotland is prettier than England*
J'apprends **le** français depuis deux ans
*I have been learning French for two years*

4. when speaking about parts of the body:

**Example:**

Je me lave **les** mains
*I wash my hands*
Elle a **les** yeux bleus et **les** cheveux blonds
*She has blue eyes and blond hair*

When **le** and **les** are used with **à** to mean *to/at the*, there have to be spelling changes for **à + le** and **à + les**:

**Examples:**

Je vais **au** cinéma (= **à + le**) *I go to the cinema*
Je vais **aux** magasins (= **à + les**) *I go to the shops*

No spelling changes are needed for **à+la** or **à+l'**:

**Examples:**

Elle va **à la** poste *She goes to the post office*
Il va **à l'**église *He goes to church*
Je suis **à la** maison *I am at home*

When **le** and **les** are used with **de** there have to be spelling changes for **de+le** and **de+les**:

**Examples:**

en face **du** collège (= **de + le**) *opposite the school*
près **des** collines (= **de + les**) *near the hills*

No spelling changes are needed for **de+la** and **de+l'**

**Examples:**

en face **de la** boulangerie *opposite the baker's*
à côté **de l'**église *next to the church*

## The Indefinite article

In the singular, **un/une** translates the English *a, an, any*

In the plural, **des** translates the English *some, any*

**Un** is used with masculine nouns, **une** with feminine nouns and **des** with all plural nouns.

**Examples:**

J'ai **un** cobaye qui s'appelle Pudding
*I have a guinea pig called Pudding*
Elle a **une** maison en ville
*She has a house in the town*
Nous avons acheté **des** pommes de terre, **des** oranges et **des** bananes
*We bought potatoes, oranges and bananas*

(In French, the article is repeated in front of each noun in a list)

If the verb in the sentence is negative, **un/une/des** must all be replaced by **de/d'**:

**Examples:**

| | | |
|---|---|---|
| J'ai **un** frère<br>*I have a brother* | changes to | Je n'ai pas **de** frère<br>*I haven't got a brother* |
| J'ai **une** sœur<br>I have a sister | changes to | Je n'ai pas **de** sœur<br>*I haven't got a sister* |
| J'ai **des** animaux<br>*I have some animals* | changes to | Je n'ai pas **d'**animaux<br>*I haven't got any animals* |

## Some or any: the partitive article

There are several forms of this article:
**du** is used for masculine nouns:

**Example:**

J'ai **du** fromage
*I have (got) some cheese*

**de la** is used for feminine nouns:

**Example:**

Elle mange **de la** crème
*She is eating (some) cream*

**de l'** is used for both masculine and feminine singular nouns which begin with a vowel:

**Examples:**

As-tu **de l'**argent?
*Have you got any money?*
Jean cherche **de l'**eau minérale
*Jean is looking for mineral water*

**des** is used for both masculine and feminine nouns in the plural:

**Example:**

J'ai **des** sœurs; elle a **des** sœurs aussi
*I have sisters; she has sisters, too*

There are occasions when you use **de** or **d'** instead of these forms:

1. When your verb is negative:

**Examples:**

Je n'ai pas **de** fromage
*I haven't any cheese*
Elle ne mange pas **de** crème
*She doesn't eat (any) cream*
Elle ne cherche pas **d'**eau minérale
*She isn't looking for (any) mineral water*
Je n'ai pas **de** sœurs; il n'a pas **de** soeurs non plus
*I haven't any sisters; he hasn't any sisters either*

2. When, in the plural, the adjective you are using comes before the noun, you must use **de** instead of **des**:

**Examples:**

J'ai vu **de** petits magasins près de la gare
*I saw some small shops near the station*
Ce sont **de** bons amis.
*They are good friends*

3. When you are talking about specific quantities, use **de** or **d'**:

**Examples:**

Un kilo **de** pommes
*a kilo of apples*
500 grammes **de** jambon

*500 grams of ham*
Beaucoup **de** pommes
*a lot of apples*
beaucoup **d'**oranges
*a lot of oranges*

Other words which use **de/d'** in this way include:

| | |
|---|---|
| combien **de**...? | *how many?* |
| trop **de**... | *too many* |
| un peu **de**... | *a little* |
| assez **de**... | *enough* |

**Examples:**

Il y a **combien d'**enfants ici?
*How many children are there here?*
Il y a **trop d'**insectes
*There are too many insects*
J'ai **un peu de** sucre
*I've got a little sugar*
As-tu **assez de** pommes frites?
*Have you got enough chips?*

## Leaving out the article

There are times when the article is **not** needed in French where we would use it in English:

1. When stating a person's job:

**Example:**

Il est facteur
*He is a postman*

2. Before numbers such as **cent** or **mille**:

**Examples:**

Il y a **cent** élèves ici
*There are a hundred pupils here*
J'ai **mille** francs
*I have a thousand francs*

3. With words such as **sans**, **plusieurs**, **quelques**:

**Examples:**

Il est arrivé **sans** baggage
*He arrived without any luggage*
**Quelques** secondes
*A few seconds*

4. In exclamations where you would need the article in English:

**Examples:**

Quel dommage!
*What a shame!*
Quelle bonne idée!
*What a good idea!*

# COMPARISONS

Adverbs and adjectives can be used in **comparative** (e.g. bigger, faster, more beautiful) and **superlative** (e.g. biggest, fastest, most beautiful) forms.

## Comparatives of adjectives and adverbs

To compare one thing with another, add **plus** (more) **moins** (less) **aussi** (as ... as) before the adjective, which agrees as usual.

**Examples:**

Ma mère est **plus** intelligente que mon père
*My mother is* ***more*** *intelligent than my father*
Ma mère est **moins** intelligente que mon père
*My mother is* ***less*** *intelligent than my father*
Ma mère est **aussi** intelligente que mon père
*My mother is* ***as*** *intelligent as my father*

Comparatives of adverbs work in much the same way.

**Examples:**

Ma mère court **plus** vite que mon père
*My mother runs* ***faster*** *than my father*
Ma mère court **moins** vite que mon père
*My mother runs* ***less*** *fast than my father*
Ma mère court **aussi** vite que mon père
*My mother runs* ***as*** *fast as my father*

There are two irregular adjectival forms:

**bon** becomes **meilleur**
**mauvais** becomes **pire**

**Examples:**

Cette équipe est **meilleure** que l'autre
*This team is* ***better*** *than the other one*
Cette équipe est **pire** que l'autre
*This team is* ***worse*** *than the other one*

Where these are adverbs, they work like this:

**bien** becomes **mieux**
**mal** becomes **moins bien**

**Examples:**

Cette équipe joue **mieux** que l'autre
*This team plays* ***better*** *than the other one*
Cette équipe joue **moins bien** que l'autre
*This team plays* ***worse*** *than the other one*

## Superlatives of adjectives and adverbs

To say what is the biggest, best, greatest, etc., use **le plus** **la plus** **les plus** plus the adjective or the adverb.

**Examples:**

Le Centre Pompidou est le musée **le plus amusant** de Paris
*The Pompidou Centre is the most entertaining musuem in Paris*
La tapisserie de Bayeux est **la plus vieille** du monde
*The Bayeux tapestry is the oldest in the world*
Les Renaults sont les voitures françaises **les plus vendues**
*Renaults are the French cars with the highest sales*

The same can be done with **le/la/les moins**:

**Examples:**

Le français est la langue **la moins difficile** pour moi
*French is the least difficult language for me*
Annette chante **le moins bien**
*Annette sings the least well*

There are irregular forms:

| | |
|---|---|
| **bon** gives | **le meilleur/la meilleure** |
| **mauvais** gives | **le pire/la pire** |
| **bien** gives | **le mieux** |
| **mal** gives | **le moins bien** |

**Examples:**

Cette équipe est **la meilleure**
*This team is the best*
Cette équipe est **la pire**
*This team is the worst*
L'équipe écossaise a joué **le mieux**
*The Scottish team played the best*
Cette équipe a joué **le moins bien**
*This team played worst*

# CONJUNCTIONS

Conjunctions are words which join two clauses, such as 'and', 'that', 'because'.

French has the following common conjunctions which you need to know in Key Stage 3:

| | |
|---|---|
| alors | *so, for that reason* |
| comme | *as* |
| depuis que | *since* |
| dès que | *as soon as* |
| donc | *therefore, so* |
| et | *and* |
| mais | *but, however,* |
| ou | *or* |
| parce que | *because* |
| pendant que | *while* |
| quand | *when* |
| si | *if* |

# DAYS, MONTHS, DATES AND TIMES

## Dates

Like times, days and dates are very common in Listening and Reading exercises. Make sure you can do them!

### Days of the week

| | |
|---|---|
| lundi | *Monday* |
| mardi | *Tuesday* |
| mercredi | *Wednesday* |
| jeudi | *Thursday* |
| vendredi | *Friday* |
| samedi | *Saturday* |
| dimanche | *Sunday* |

***Point to watch:*** In French, days of the week are not written with capital letters!

### Months of the year

| | |
|---|---|
| janvier | *January* |
| février | *February* |
| mars | *March* |
| avril | *April* |
| mai | *May* |
| juin | *June* |
| juillet | *July* |
| août | *August* |
| septembre | *September* |
| octobre | *October* |
| novembre | *November* |
| décembre | *December* |

***Point to watch:*** Months don't have captial letters in French either!

### The year

It is usually acceptable to write dates in figures, so they need to be known only for recognition and for Speaking. There are usually two possible ways of giving the year. Learn whichever one suits you.

| | |
|---|---|
| **1982** | mille neuf cent quatre-vingt-deux<br>dix-neuf cent quatre-vingt-deux |
| **1983** | mille neuf cent quatre-vingt-trois<br>dix-neuf cent quatre-vingt-trois |
| **1984** | mille neuf cent quatre-vingt-quatre<br>dix-neuf cent quatre-vingt-quatre |
| **1985** | mille neuf cent quatre-vingt-cinq<br>dix-neuf cent quatre-vingt-cinq |
| **1986** | mille neuf cent quatre-vingt-six<br>dix-neuf cent quatre-vingt-six |
| **1996** | mille neuf cent quatre-vingt-seize<br>dix-neuf cent quatre-vingt-seize |
| **1997** | mille neuf cent quatre-vingt-dix-sept<br>dix-neuf cent quatre-vingt-dix-sept |
| **1998** | mille neuf cent quatre-vingt-dix-huit<br>dix-neuf cent quatre-vingt-dix-huit |
| **1999** | mille neuf cent quatre-vingt-dix-neuf<br>dix-neuf cent quatre-vingt-dix-neuf |
| **2000** | deux mille |
| **2001** | deux mille un |
| **2002** | deux mille deux |

### Giving the date

Use the following patterns:

Quel jour sommes-nous?
*What is the date?*
Nous sommes le vingt février
*It's the 20th of February*

Quelle est la date?
*What is the date?*
C'est le vingt février.
*It's the 20th of February*

jeudi le 20 février
*Thursday 20th February*

In letters, the date is written on the top right of the page:

Nantes, le 1.10.98

## Times

### Telling the time

**Hours**

| | |
|---|---|
| Il est une heure | *It's one o'clock* |
| Il est cinq heures | *It's five o'clock* |

**Quarters and half hours**

| | |
|---|---|
| Il est deux heures et quart | *It's quarter past two* |
| Il est deux heures et demie | *It's half past two* |
| Il est trois heures moins le quart | *It's quarter to three* |

**Minutes past and to the hour**

| | |
|---|---|
| Il est huit heures dix | *It's ten past eight* |
| Il est huit heures moins dix | *It's ten to eight* |

**Midnight and midday**

| | |
|---|---|
| Il est minuit | *It's midnight* |
| Il est midi | *It's midday* |
| Il est midi cinq | *It's five past twelve* |
| Il est midi moins dix | *It's ten to twelve* |
| Il est midi et demi | *It's half past twelve* |

**24-hour clock**

| | |
|---|---|
| dix-huit heures | 18h |
| dix-huit heures quinze | 18h15 |
| dix-huit heures trente | 18h30 |
| dix-huit heures quarante-cinq | 18h45 |
| dix-huit heures cinquante-neuf | 18h59 |
| dix-neuf heures deux | 19h02 |

# NOUNS

Nouns are the names of people, places and things.

## Gender

All nouns in French are either masculine (**un, le or l'**) or feminine (**une, la or l'**). You need to know the gender of each noun in order to write French accurately. Sometimes the gender is important to pronunciation, too.

## Gender rules

Knowing which gender a noun is presents major difficulties for English learners of French. The following rules and their exceptions may be helpful.

*(a)* The following categories of nouns are masculine:

1. Names of male people.
   Exception: la personne *person*
2. Days of the week, months, seasons, points of the compass.
3. The metric system.
   Exception: la tonne *ton*
4. Names of countries not ending in -e.

*(b)* Masculine word endings:

Nouns which end in the following ways are usually masculine:

| ending | example | Meaning |
|---|---|---|
| **-acle** | le spectacle | *show* |
| **-age** | le fromage, le village | *cheese, village* |
| **-ail** | le travail | *work* |
| **-ain** | le copain | *friend* |
| **-eau** | le château, le gâteau | *castle, cake* |
| Exceptions: | l'eau | *water* |
| | la peau | *skin* |
| **-ège** | le collège | *secondary school* |
| **-eil** | le soleil | *sun* |
| **-ème** | le problème | *problem* |
| **-ent** | l'argent | *money* |
| **-et** | le guichet | *ticket office* |
| **-ien** | le chien | *dog* |
| **-ier** | le papier | *paper* |
| **-isme** | le cyclisme | *cycling* |
| **-ment** | l'appartement | *flat* |
| **-oir** | le couloir | *corridor* |
| **-our** | l'amour | *love* |
| Exception: | la tour | *tower* |

*(c)* The following categories of nouns are feminine:

1. Names of most female people.
2. Names of countries ending in *-e*.
3. Names of fruits, flowers and vegetables ending in *-e*.
   Exception: le légume *vegetable*

*(d)* Feminine word endings:

Nouns which end in the following ways are usually feminine:

| ending | example | Meaning |
|---|---|---|
| **-aison** | la maison | *house* |
| **-ance** | la chance, les vacances | *chance, holidays* |
| **-anse** | la danse | *dance* |
| **-ée** | la journée | *day* |
| Exceptions: | le lycée | *secondary school* |
| | le musée | *museum* |
| **-ence** | l'essence | *petrol* |
| **-ette** | la chaussette | *sock* |
| **-ie** | la sortie | *exit* |
| **-ille** | la famille | *family* |
| **-ise** | la gourmandise | *greediness* |
| **-itude** | l'habitude | *habit* |
| **-tion** | la natation | *swimming* |
| **-rice** | une institutrice | *primary school teacher* |
| **-sion** | une excursion | *excursion* |
| **-xion** | une connexion | *connection* |

## Plural forms

### Number

It is particularly important to take note of whether nouns are singular or plural in order to make sure of adjective agreements and verb forms. Make a habit of it!

### Plurals

Where nouns are plural, most French nouns add an **-s**, as in English.

**Example:**

une voiture deux voiture**s**

There are a few groups of nouns which do not do this:

1. Those ending in *-s*, *-x*, and *-z* remain unchanged.

   **Examples:**

   | | | |
   |---|---|---|
   | le fils | les fils | *son* |
   | la voix | les voix | *voice* |
   | le prix | les prix | *price* |

2. Those ending in *-al* change it to *-aux* in the plural.

   **Example:**

   le cheval les chevaux *horse*

3. Those ending in *-eau*, *-eu* or *-ou* add an *-x* in the plural.

   **Examples:**

   | | | |
   |---|---|---|
   | le château | les châteaux | *castle* |
   | le feu | les feux | *light, fire* |
   | un genou | des genoux | *knee* |

4. Common exceptions include:

| | | |
|---|---|---|
| l'oeil | les yeux | *eye* |
| la pomme de terre | les pommes de terre | *potato* |
| le pneu | les pneus | *tyre* |
| le timbre-poste | les timbres-poste | *postage stamp* |
| le travail | les travaux | *work(s)* |

Note also:

| | | |
|---|---|---|
| monsieur | messieurs | *sirs* |
| mademoiselle | mesdemoiselles | *misses* |
| madame | mesdames | *ladies* |

Surnames do not change in the plural in French.

**Example:**

Nous sommes invités par les Janneau
*We've been invited by the Janneaus*

## NUMBERS

There are two sorts of numbers: **cardinal numbers** which are counting numbers (ordinary numbers); and **ordinal numbers** which say which order things come in.

### Cardinal numbers

| | |
|---|---|
| 0 | zéro |
| $^{1}/_{4}$ | un quart |
| $^{1}/_{3}$ | un tiers |
| $^{1}/_{2}$ | un demi |
| $^{2}/_{3}$ | deux tiers |
| $^{3}/_{4}$ | trois quarts |
| 1 | un, une |
| 2 | deux |
| 3 | trois |
| 4 | quatre |
| 5 | cinq |
| 6 | six |
| 7 | sept |
| 8 | huit |
| 9 | neuf |
| 10 | dix |
| 11 | onze |
| 12 | douze |
| 13 | treize |
| 14 | quatorze |
| 15 | quinze |
| 16 | seize |
| 17 | dix-sept |
| 18 | dix-huit |
| 19 | dix-neuf |
| 20 | vingt |
| 21 | vingt et un |
| 22 | vingt-deux, etc. |
| 30 | trente |
| 31 | trente et un |
| 32 | trente-deux, etc. |
| 40 | quarante |
| 41 | quarante et un |
| 42 | quarante-deux, etc. |
| 50 | cinquante |
| 51 | cinquante et un |
| 52 | cinquante-deux, etc. |
| 60 | soixante |
| 61 | soixante et un |
| 62 | soixante-deux, etc. |
| 70 | soixante-dix |
| 71 | soixante et onze |
| 72 | soixante-douze, etc. |
| 80 | quatre-vingts |
| 81 | quatre-vingt-un |
| 82 | quatre-vingt-deux, etc. |
| 90 | quatre-vingt-dix |
| 91 | quatre-vingt-onze,etc. |
| 99 | quatre-vingt-dix-neuf |
| 100 | cent |
| 101 | cent un |
| 102 | cent deux, etc. |
| 200 | deux cents |
| 210 | deux cent dix |

1 000 mille
1 311 mille trois cent onze

3 000 trois mille

1 000 000 un million

1 000 000 000 un milliard

***Point to watch:***

1. $^{1}/_{2}$ = un demi only in arithmetic. Elsewhere it is *une moitié*.
   However, *demi* can be used as an adjective.
   Example:
   une **demi**-bouteille *half a bottle*
   une **demi**-heure *half an hour*
2. For 1, use either **un** or **une**, depending on the gender of the object.
3. There are no hyphens in *vingt et un, trente et un,* etc.
   *Quatre-vingt-un* and *quatre-vingt-onze* do have hyphens, but *soixante et onze* doesn't.
4. *Mille* does not have an *s* in the plural.
5. Telephone numbers are read out in groups of two or three digits, written, e.g., 40.46.92.17.

## Ordinal numbers

1st premier, première (1er)*
2nd deuxième (2e) (second, seconde)**
3rd troisième (3e)
4th quatrième (4e),
5th cinquième (5e)
6th sixième (6e)
7th septième (7e)
8th huitième (8e)
9th neuvième (9e)
10th dixième (10e)
11th onzième (11e)
12th douzième (12e)
13th treizième (13e)
14th quatorzième (14e)
15th quinzième (15e)
16th seizième (16e)
17th dix-septième(17e)
18th dix-huitième (18e)
19th dix-neuvième (19e)
20th vingtième (20e)
21st vingt et unième (21e) etc.

*For 1st, use either premier or première, depending on the gender of the object.

**Seconde is used where there is no mention of any other numbers in the same sentence.

**Example:**

Je suis en seconde.
*I am in Year 11.*

## PREPOSITIONS

Prepositions show a relationship between one noun and another, often of position, which accounts for the name.

The use of prepositions in French is not always easy. This is because there is often no direct, once-and-for-all translation of the English equivalent. The French version will vary according to circumstances.

I have given below examples of the use of various prepositions, not all of which behave as you might expect. So study these carefully and imitate them as well as you can.

| | |
|---|---|
| à | **à** Paris<br>*in Paris* |
| | **à** la maison<br>*at home* |
| | **à** droite<br>*on the right* |
| | **à** bicyclette<br>*by bike* |
| à + le becomes au | **au** collège<br>*at secondary school* |
| | **au** magasin<br>*at the shop* |
| à + les becomes aux | **aux** magasins<br>*at the shops* |
| à côté de | **à côté de** moi<br>*next to me, beside me* |
| au-dessus de | **au-dessus de** la cuisine<br>*above the kitchen* |

**Example:**

Le ballon est passé **au-dessus de** ma tête
*The ball passed over my head*

| | |
|---|---|
| après | **après** l'école<br>*after school* |
| avant | **avant** minuit<br>*before midnight* |
| | **avant** d'arriver<br>*before arriving* |
| avec | **avec** mes amis<br>*with my friends* |
| chez | **chez** mon correspondant<br>*at my penfriend's house* |
| | **chez** moi<br>*at my house* |
| | **chez** C & A<br>*at C & A's* |
| dans | **dans** le placard<br>*in the cupboard* |

**Example:**

Alban entre **dans** le salon
*Alban comes into the living-room*

| | |
|---|---|
| de | la clé **de** la voiture<br>*the key of the car* |
| | la plume **de** ma tante<br>*my aunt's pen* |
| de + le becomes du | **du** fromage<br>*some cheese* |
| de + les becomes des | **des** magazines<br>*some magazines* |

**Examples:**

| | |
|---|---|
| depuis | J'habite ici **depuis** deux ans<br>*I have been living here for two years* |
| | **Depuis** Pâques il n'a rien fait<br>*He has done nothing since Easter* |

| | |
|---|---|
| derrière | **derrière** le café<br>*behind the café* |
| | **derrière** toi<br>*behind you* |
| devant | **devant** le café<br>*in front of the café* |
| | pas **devant** les enfants<br>*not in front of the children* |
| en | **en** voiture<br>*by car* |
| | **en** avance<br>*in advance* |
| en face de | **en face de** la gare<br>*opposite the station* |
| entre | **entre** le café et la gare<br>*between the café and the station* |
| | **entre** midi et deux heures<br>*between midday and two o'clock* |

**Examples:**

**Entre** nous, c'est un idiot
*Between you and me, he's a fool*

Nous sommes **entre** amis
*We are among friends*

jusqu'à — Nous jouerons **jusqu'à** trois heures
*We shall play till three o'clock*

par — **par** le train
*by train*

**Example:**

Elles regardent **par** la fenêtre
*They are looking out of the window*

parmi — **parmi** les fleurs
*among the flowers*

pendant — **pendant** l'après-midi
*during the afternoon*

**Example:**

J'ai travaillé **pendant** quatre heures
*I have worked for four hours*

plus de — J'ai **plus de** vingt livres d'Astérix
*I have over 20 Asterix books*

pour — c'est **pour** toi
*it's for you*

**Example:**

Nous serons en France **pour** deux jours
*We shall be in France for two days*

près de — **près de** Londres
*near London*

**près de** la gare
*near the station*

**Example:**

Assieds-toi **près de** moi
*Sit by me*

sous — **sous** la table
*under the table*

sur — **sur** la table
*on the table*

**Example:**

Une personne **sur** cinq porte des lunettes
*One person in five wears glasses*

sans — **sans** mon sac
*without my bag*

**sans** doute
*without a doubt*

**sans** hésiter
*without hesitating*

vers — **vers** trois heures
*at about three o'clock*

**vers** Paris
*towards Paris*

# PRONOUNS

Pronouns stand in the place of a noun, and are used to avoid repeating a noun or a proper name. Pronouns take the place of a noun which has been referred to earlier.

## Subject pronouns

| | |
|---|---|
| je | *I* |
| tu | *you* |
| il | *he, it* |
| elle | *she, it* |
| on | *one, we, they, you* |
| nous | *we* |
| vous | *you* |
| ils | *they* |
| elles | *they* |

## Use of subject pronouns

*Tu* is used in talking to one person who is

- a good friend
- a member of the family or a pet
- a young person

*Vous* is used in talking to two or more people who are

- good friends
- members of the family or pets
- young people

or to one person who is an adult who doesn't fit any of the categories above.

*Il* and elle can mean *'it'* when they refer to masculine or feminine nouns.

*On* has a variety of meanings.

- we

  **Example:**

  **On** rentre?
  *Shall we go home?*

- one

  **Example:**

  **On** est obligé de porter une cravate
  *One has to wear a tie*

- you (where the meaning could be rendered more poshly by 'one'.)

  **Example:**

  **On** est obligé de porter une cravate
  *You have to wear a tie*

- they (where 'they' are unspecified people in authority)

  **Example:**

  **On** n'accepte pas de chèques chez Montrichard
  *They don't take cheques at Montrichard's*

*Ils* is used for 'they' where

- all the nouns referred to are masculine
- there is a group of nouns referred to of which one is masculine.
  (It makes no difference how many feminine ones there are!)

*Elles* is used for 'they' where all the nouns referred to are feminine.

## Object pronouns

Direct object pronouns

me *me*
te *you*
le *him, it (masculine)*
la *her, it (feminine)*
se *oneself*

nous *us*
vous *you*
les *them*
se *themselves*

## Position of pronouns

Object pronouns come immediately before the verb, or, in the perfect and pluperfect tenses, immediately before the auxiliary.

**Example:**

Je **les** vois *I see them*
Je **les** ai vus *I have seen them*

In command forms, where the command is straightforward, the object pronouns follow the verb.

**Example:**

Donnez-**le**-moi!
*Give it to me*

***Point to watch:*** Note the hyphens!

## Emphatic pronouns (also known as stressed or disjunctive pronouns)

moi *me, I*
toi *you*
lui *him, he*
elle *her, she*

nous *us, we*
vous *you*
eux *them (masculine), they*
elles *them (feminine), they*

## Use of emphatic pronouns

1. After prepositions

**Examples:**

chez **moi** at my house
devant **eux** in front of them
avec **nous** with us

2. With c'est and ce sont

**Examples:**

Ah, c'est **toi**, Eric!
*Ah, it's you, Eric*
Ce sont **eux**
*It's them*

3. To emphasize the subject pronoun

**Examples:**

Tu as de la chance, **toi**!
*You're lucky, you are!*

4. As a one-word answer to a question.

**Example:**

Qui a mangé mon sandwich? – **Lui**
*Who ate my sandwich? – Him*

5. In comparisons.

**Example:**

Napoléon était plus petit que **toi**
*Napoleon was smaller than you*

6. Combined with -même(s):

moi-même *myself*
toi-même *yourself*, etc.
soi-même, *oneself*, also exists

**Examples:**

Vous l'avez vu **vous-mêmes**
*You saw it youselves*
On peut faire la lessive **soi-même**
*One can do the washing oneself*

## Relative pronouns

Relative pronouns introduce a clause giving more information about a noun. The correct relative pronoun is determined by its grammatical function within the relative clause.

Relative pronoun as the subject of the clause: *qui.*

**Examples:**

La personne **qui** est arrivée est ma mère
*The person who has arrived is my mother*
L'avion **qui** vole le plus vite s'appelle Concorde
*The plane which flies fastest is called Concorde*

Relative pronoun as the object of the clause: *que.* Clauses of this type will contain another subject.

**Examples:**

Les personnes **que** j'aime sont importantes pour moi
*The people I like are important to me*
Le travail **que** je fais est ennuyeux
*The work I am doing is boring*

## Indefinite pronouns

There are numbers of these in French. It's probably best to learn them as vocabulary.

autre

**Example:**

Je n'ai pas vu Jean, mais j'ai vu les **autres**
*I didn't see Jean, but I saw the others*

chacun

**Example:**

J'ai vu beaucoup de ses films. **Chacun** est agréable
*I've seen lots of his films. Each one is pleasant*

*n'importe* can be combined with various other words to mean 'any ... at all'

**Examples:**

**n'importe** quel(le) *no matter which*
**n'importe** qui *anybody at all*
**n'importe** quoi *anything at all*

plusieurs

**Example:**

As-tu des livres d'Astérix? Oui, j'en ai **plusieurs**
*Have you got any Asterix books? Yes, I've got several*

quelqu'un

**Examples:**

J'attends **quelqu'un**
*I am waiting for someone*
**Quelques-unes** de ces photos sont amusantes
*Some of these photos are entertaining*

tous

**Example:**

Il était aimé de **tous**
*He was liked by everyone*

tout

**Example:**

Il sait **tout**
*He knows everything*

tout le monde

**Example:**

**Tout le monde** est là
*Everyone is here*

***Point to watch:*** *tout le monde* is singular, despite its meaning!

# VERBS

A verb is a 'doing word'. It gives information about what is done, who or what does it, and when the action happened, happens, or will happen.

## Persons

The form of all verbs in French (as in English) is determined in part by the 'subject'. This is generally the person or thing which performs the action of the verb.

The subject can be one of three possible 'persons'.

The **first** person is used when the speaker performs the action of the verb, e.g.*je, nous.*

The **second** person is used when the person being spoken to performs the action of the verb, e.g. *tu, vous*

The **third** person is used when neither the speaker nor the person being spoken to is performing the action of the verb – i.e. the action is being performed by someone else, e.g. *il, elle, on, ils, elles, Sam, les enfants.*

## Different verb types

In French there are various sorts (or conjugations) of verbs which are named after the last letters of the infinitive. Each conjugation contains verbs which are regular (verbs which follow a pattern) and verbs which are irregular (verbs which do not follow a pattern). Many parts of irregular verbs have to be looked up in verb tables.

## Tenses

These are the different forms of verbs which describe mainly when something takes place, took place, will take place, etc.

There are some differences in the use of tenses between French and English, but future tenses refer to the future, present tenses refer to now or to regular events which are still going on, and past tenses such as the perfect refer to events which have already taken place. The conditional is used for conditions, actual or possible.

## Forms of French verbs

When a verb is listed in a dictionary, it is given in the infinitive.

**Examples:**

jouer — *to play*
répondre — *to reply*
choisir — *to choose*

In describing how tenses are formed, the infinitive will normally be the starting point.

French verbs are often seen as tricky. Many of the common ones are irregular – that is, they do not follow a rule. In all verbs, the spelling changes according to who is speaking, although the pronunciation does not always change to match. If you can master verbs, you have the key to success. So do make every attempt to get to grips with verbs. Take a few at a time. Make a point of checking the spelling, including the accents.

## Present tense

There is only one form of the present tense for each French verb. In English there are three: *I eat, I am eating* and *I do eat*. The French form *je mange* is used as an equivalent for all three.

### Use of the present tense

The present tense is used:

- to describe events that happen *regularly*

  **Example:**

  Je mange beaucoup de bonbons
  *I eat a lot of sweets*

- to describe what is happening *now*

  **Example:**

  Je lis un excellent livre
  *I am reading an excellent book*

- after depuis (see below, page 31)

### Formation of the present tense

Regular verbs are identified by the last two letters of their infinitive: *-er, -ir,* and *-re.* They form the present tense in different ways.

**- er verbs**

Regular *-er* verbs in French follow this pattern:

parler: *to talk or speak*

| | |
|---|---|
| je parl**e** | *I speak/I am speaking* |
| tu parl**es** | *you (singular) speak/you are speaking* |
| il parl**e** | *he speaks/he is speaking* |
| elle parl**e** | *she speaks/she is speaking* |
| on parl**e** | *we speak/we are speaking (one speaks, etc.)* |
| nous parl**ons** | *we speak/we are speaking* |
| vous parl**ez** | *you speak/you are speaking* |
| ils parl**ent** | *they speak/they are speaking* |
| elles parl**ent** | *they (feminine) speak/they are speaking* |

The endings for *-er* verbs are:

| | |
|---|---|
| je | -e |
| tu | -es |
| il/elle/on | -e |
| nous | -ons |
| vous | -ez |
| ils/elles | -ent |

These are added to the stem of the verb, that is the infinitive, **parler,** minus its **-er** ending.

Other common regular *-er* verbs include:

| | |
|---|---|
| aider | *to help* |
| aimer | *to like* |
| arriver* | *to arrive* |
| casser | *to break* |
| chercher | *to look for* |
| compter | *to count* |
| danser | *to dance* |
| déjeuner | *to eat lunch* |
| désirer | *to wish to* |
| dessiner | *to draw* |
| détester | *to detest* |
| donner | *to give* |
| durer | *to last* |
| écouter | *to listen to* |
| entrer* | *to enter* |
| fumer | *to smoke* |
| gagner | *to win* |
| inviter | *to invite* |
| jouer | *to play* |
| laver | *to wash* |
| louer | *to rent, hire* |
| marcher | *to walk* |
| monter* | *to climb* |
| montrer | *to show* |
| oublier | *to forget* |
| penser | *to think* |
| pleurer | *to cry* |
| porter | *to wear* |
| poser | *to put down* |
| pousser | *to push* |
| quitter | *to leave* |
| préparer | *to prepare* |
| regarder | *to look at* |
| rencontrer | *to meet* |
| rentrer* | *to go back* |
| réserver | *to reserve* |
| réparer | *to repair* |
| rester* | *to stay* |
| retourner* | *to return* |
| rouler | *to roll, travel by car* |
| sauter | *to jump* |
| sonner | *to ring (doorbell, etc.)* |
| tomber* | *to fall (down)* |
| toucher | *to touch* |
| tourner | *to turn* |
| trouver | *to find* |
| travailler | *to work* |
| traverser | *to cross* |
| visiter | *to visit* |
| voler. | *to steal* |

Verbs marked * take *être* in the perfect tense.

### B Irregular -er verbs

The most irregular *-er* verb is aller: *to go:*

| | |
|---|---|
| je vais | *I go, I am going* |
| tu vas | *you (familiar) go, you are going* |
| il va | *he goes, he is going* |
| elle va | *she goes, she is going* |
| on va | *one goes, people go, one is going, people are going* |
| nous allons | *we go, we are going* |
| vous allez | *you go, you are going* |
| ils vont | *they go, they are going* |
| elles vont | *they (feminine) go, they are going* |

### -er verbs with spelling changes

A number of common *-er* verbs have very slight spelling changes in some forms. Their endings are **not**, however, irregular.

*(a)* *Manger* and other verbs ending *-ger* have an extra **e** in the **nous** form for phonetic reasons (to make the *g* soft by following it with an *e*).

**Example:**

manger: *to eat*
nous mang**e**ons

Other verbs which behave like this include:

| | |
|---|---|
| bouger | *to move* |
| changer | *to change* |
| échanger | *to exchange* |
| loger | *to lodge with, stay with* |
| nager | *to swim* |
| obliger | *to oblige* |
| partager | *to share* |
| ranger | *to tidy up, arrange neatly* |
| voyager | *to travel* |

*(b)* *Commencer* and other verbs ending in *-cer* have a *ç* in the 'nous' forms to make the *ç* soft.

**Example:**

commencer: *to begin*
nous commençons

Other verbs which behave like this include:

| | |
|---|---|
| avancer | *to advance* |
| lancer | *to throw* |
| menacer | *to threaten* |
| prononcer | *to pronounce* |
| remplacer | *to replace* |

*(c)* Verbs ending in *-eler* and *-eter* double the *-l* or the *-t* in some persons of the verb.

s'appeler: *to be called*

je m'appe**ll**e
tu t'appe**ll**es
il s'appe**ll**e
elle s'appe**ll**e
on s'appe**ll**e

nous nous appelons
vous vous appelez
ils s'appe**ll**ent
elles s'appe**ll**ent

jeter: *to throw*
je je**tt**e
tu je**tt**es
il je**tt**e
elle je**tt**e
on je**tt**e

nous jetons
vous jetez
ils je**tt**ent
elles je**tt**ent

Other verbs which behave like this include:

appeler *to call*

Note that *acheter* and *geler* follow the same pattern as *lever.*

*(d)* Verbs ending in *-e...er* follow this pattern:

lever: *to lift*

je l**è**ve

tu l**è**ves
il l**è**ve
elle l**è**ve
on l**è**ve

nous levons
vous levez
ils l**è**vent
elles l**è**vent

Other verbs which behave like this include:

| | |
|---|---|
| acheter | *to buy* |
| geler | *to freeze* |
| mener | *to lead* |
| peser | *to weigh* |
| se promener | *to go for a walk* |

*(e)* Verbs ending in *-é-...er* follow this pattern:

considérer: *to consider*

je considère
tu considères
il consid**è**re
elle consid**è**re
on consid**è**re

nous considérons
vous considérez
ils consid**è**rent
elles consid**è**rent

Other verbs which behave like this include:

| | |
|---|---|
| espérer | *to hope* |
| s'inquiéter | *to be worried* |
| préférer | *to prefer* |
| répéter | *to repeat* |
| révéler | *to reveal* |

*(f)* Verbs ending in *-yer* follow this pattern. The *y* becomes an *i* where it is followed by an *e*.

nettoyer: *to clean*

je netto**i**e
tu netto**i**es
il netto**i**e
elle netto**i**e
on netto**i**e

nous nettoyons
vous nettoyez
ils netto**i**ent
elles netto**i**ent

Other verbs which behave like this include:

| | |
|---|---|
| appuyer | *to press* |
| balayer | *to sweep* |
| employer | *to use, to employ* |
| ennuyer | *to bore* |
| envoyer | *to send* |
| essayer | *to try* |
| essuyer | *to wipe* |
| payer | *to pay* |

**- ir verbs**

Regular *-ir* verbs in French follow this pattern:

finir: *to finish*

| | |
|---|---|
| je fin**is** | *I finish/I am finishing* |
| tu fin**is** | *you (singular)finish/you are finishing* |
| il fin**it** | *he finishes/he is finishing* |
| elle fin**it** | *she finishes/she is finishing* |
| on fin**it** | *we finish/we are finishing (one finishes, etc.)* |
| nous fin**issons** | *we finish/we are finishing* |
| vous fin**issez** | *you finish/you are finishing* |
| ils fin**issent** | *they finish/they are finishing* |
| elles fin**issent** | *they (feminine) finish/they are finishing* |

The endings for *-ir* verbs are:

| | |
|---|---|
| je | -is |
| tu | -is |
| il/elle/on | -it |
| nous | -issons |
| vous | -issez |
| ils/elles | -issent |

These are added to the stem of the verb, that is the infinitive, *finir*, minus its *-ir* ending.

Other common regular *-ir* verbs include:

| | |
|---|---|
| agrandir | *to enlarge* |
| applaudir | *to applaud, to clap* |
| atterrir | *to land (a plane)* |
| bâtir | *to build* |
| choisir | *to choose* |
| démolir | *to demolish* |
| remplir | *to fill (in, up)* |
| se sentir* | *to feel* |

Irregular *-ir* verbs include a group which have a present tense just like an *-er* verb.

couvrir: *to cover*

je couvre
tu couvres
il couvre
elle couvre
on couvre

nous couvrons
vous couvrez
ils couvrent
elles couvrent

Other verbs which behave like this include:

| | |
|---|---|
| découvrir | *to discover* |
| offrir | *to offer* |
| ouvrir | *to open* |
| souffrir | *to suffer* |

Check the verb table for other tenses of these verbs.

There are many other irregular *-ir* verbs. The following are also included in the verb table:

| | |
|---|---|
| contenir | *to contain* |
| convenir | *to be socially acceptable* |
| courir | *to run* |
| devenir* | *to become* |
| dormir | *to sleep* |
| s'endormir | *to go to sleep* |
| entretenir | *to maintain* |
| mourir* | *to die* |
| obtenir | *to obtain* |
| partir* | *to leave* |
| prévenir | *to warn* |
| repartir | *to set off again* |
| retenir | *to keep, retain* |
| revenir* | *to return, come back* |
| se sentir* | *to feel* |
| servir | *to serve* |
| sortir* | *to go out* |
| tenir | *to hold* |

| | |
|---|---|
| venir*. | to come |

Verbs marked * take être in the perfect tense.

#### -re verbs

Regular *-re* verbs in French follow this pattern:

vendre: *to sell*

| | |
|---|---|
| je vend**s** | *I sell/I am selling* |
| tu vend**s** | *you (singular) sell/you are selling* |
| il vend | *he sells/he is selling* |
| elle vend | *she sells/she is selling* |
| on vend | *we sell/we are selling (one sells, etc.)* |
| nous vend**ons** | *we sell/we are selling* |
| vous vend**ez** | *you sell/you are selling* |
| ils vend**ent** | *they sell/they are selling* |
| elles vend**ent** | *they (feminine) sell/they are selling* |

The endings for *-re* verbs are:

| | |
|---|---|
| je | -s |
| tu | -s |
| il/elle/on | - |
| nous | -ons |
| vous | -ez |
| ils/elles | -ent |

These are added to the stem of the verb, that is the infinitive, *vendre*, minus its *-re* ending.

Other common regular *-re* verbs include:

| | |
|---|---|
| attendre | *to wait for* |
| descendre | *to go down* |
| entendre | *to hear* |
| perdre | *to lose* |
| rendre | *to return, render* |
| répondre | *to answer* |

There are many irregular *-re* verbs. The following are included in the verb table:

| | |
|---|---|
| apprendre | *to learn* |
| battre | *to beat* |
| boire | *to drink* |
| comprendre | *to understand* |
| conduire | *to drive* |
| connaître | *to know (a person)* |
| construire | *to construct* |
| coudre | *to sew* |
| craindre | *to fear* |
| croire | *to believe* |
| détruire | *to destroy* |
| dire | *to say* |
| disparaître | *to disappear* |
| écrire | *to write* |
| entendre | *to hear* |
| éteindre | *to extinguish* |
| être | *to be* |
| faire | *to do* |
| lire | *to read* |
| mettre | *to put* |
| naître* | *to be born* |
| paraître | *to seem, appear* |
| prendre | *to take* |
| reconnaître | *to recognize* |
| reprendre | *to take (up) again* |
| rire | *to laugh* |
| suivre | *to follow* |
| surprendre | *to surprise* |
| vivre | *to live* |

Verbs marked * take *être* in the perfect tense.

#### -oir verbs

There is a group of verbs ending in *-oir* which are all irregular. The following are included in the verb table:

| | |
|---|---|
| s'asseoir* | *to sit down* |
| avoir | *to have* |
| devoir | *to be obliged to, to have to, 'must'* |
| falloir | *to be necessary* |
| pleuvoir | *to rain* |
| pouvoir | *to be able to, 'can'* |
| recevoir | *to receive* |
| savoir | *to know (a fact or how to)* |
| voir | *to see* |
| vouloir | *to want to* |

Verbs marked * take *être* in the perfect tense.

## Perfect tense (also known as the passé composé)

In French, the perfect tense is used to express the English 'have done' and 'did'. So 'j'ai mangé une pomme' could mean:

- *I ate an apple*

or
- *I have eaten an apple*

or
- *I did eat an apple*

### Use of the perfect tense

The perfect tense is used in conversation and letters:

- to describe an action in the past which is completed and is no longer happening
- to describe an action in the past which happened once only

### Formation of the perfect tense

The perfect tense is made up of two parts: the auxiliary verb, which is the present tense of either *avoir* or *être,* and the past participle. Most verbs have *avoir* as their auxiliary.

#### 1. Perfect tense with *avoir* – regular verbs

The past participles of regular verbs (including those *-er* verbs with minor changes in spelling in the present tense) are formed by removing *-er*, *-ir* or *-re* from the infinitive, and adding *-é*, *-i*, or *-u*.

**Examples:**

| | |
|---|---|
| parler | parl**é** |
| finir | fin**i** |
| vendre | vend**u** |

The past participles are then combined with the auxiliary, the present tense of *avoir,* as follows:

j'ai parlé
*I spoke/I have spoken/I did speak*
tu as parlé
*You spoke/you have spoken/you did speak*
il a parlé
*He spoke/he has spoken/he did speak*
elle a parlé
*She spoke/she has spoken/she did speak*
on a parlé
*One spoke/one has spoken/one did speak*

nous avons parlé
*We spoke/we have spoken/we did speak*
vous avez parlé
*You spoke/you have spoken/you did speak*

ils ont parlé
*They spoke/they have spoken/they did speak*
elles ont parlé
*They spoke/they have spoken/they did speak*

j'ai fini
*I finished/I have finished/I did finish*
tu as fini
*You finished/you have finished/you did finish*
il a fini
*He finished/he has finished/he did finish*
elle a fini
*She finished/she has finished/she did finish*
on a fini
*One finished/one has finished/one did finish*

nous avons fini
*We finished/we have finished/we did finish*
vous avez fini
*You finished/you have finished/you did finish*
ils ont fini
*They finished/they have finished/they did finish*
elles ont fini
*They finished/they have finished/they did finish*

j'ai vendu
*I sold/I have sold/I did sell*
tu as vendu
*You sold/you have sold/you did sell*
il a vendu
*He sold/he has sold/he did sell*
elle a vendu
*She sold/she has sold/she did sell*
on a vendu
*One sold/one has sold/one did sell*

nous avons vendu
*We sold/we have sold/we did sell*
vous avez vendu
*You sold/you have sold/you did sell*
ils ont vendu
*They sold/they have sold/they did sell*
elles ont vendu
*They sold/they have sold/they did sell*

### 2. Perfect tense with *avoir* – irregular verbs

Many common verbs are irregular. The formation of the perfect tense follows the same principle as for regular verbs: that there is an auxiliary, the present tense of *avoir,* and the past participle. The only problem is that the past participles have to be learned, as irregular verbs don't obey set rules (which is why they are irregular).

**Example:**

lire – lu

| | |
|---|---|
| j'ai lu | *I read/I have read/I did read* |
| tu as lu | *You read/you have read/you did read* |
| il a lu | *He read/he has read/he did read* |
| elle a lu | *She read/she has read/she did read* |
| on a lu | *One read/one has read/one did read* |
| nous avons lu | *We read/we have read/we did read* |
| vous avez lu | *You read/you have read/you did read* |
| ils ont lu | *They read/they have read/they did read* |
| elles ont lu | *They read/they have read/they did read* |

Here are 25 of the most commonly used verbs with their past participles. These and other irregular verbs can be checked in the verb table. If you don't know them already, make it a top priority to master them.

| Infinitive | Meaning | Past participle | Meaning |
|---|---|---|---|
| avoir | *to have* | eu | *had, have had* |
| boire | to drink | bu | *drank, have drunk* |
| comprendre | *to understand* | compris | *understood, have understood* |
| conduire | *to drive* | conduit | *drove, have driven* |
| connaitre | *to know (a person)* | connu | *knew, have known* |
| courir | *to run* | couru | *ran, have run* |
| croire | *to believe* | cru | *believed, have believed* |
| devoir | *to have to, 'ought'* | dû | *had to, have had to* |
| dire | *to say, tell* | dit | *said, told, have said, have told* |
| écrire | *to write* | écrit | *wrote, have written* |
| être | *to be* | été | *was, have been* |
| faire | *to do* | fait | *did, have done* |
| lire | *to read* | lu | *read, have read* |
| mettre | *to put* | mis | *put, have put* |
| ouvrir | *to open* | ouvert | *opened, have opened* |
| pleuvoir | *to rain* | plu | *rained, has rained* |
| pouvoir | *to be able to, 'can'* | pu | *was able to, have been able to* |
| prendre | *to take* | pris | *took, have taken* |
| recevoir | *to receive* | reçu | *received, have received* |
| rire | *to laugh* | ri | *laughed, have laughed* |
| savoir | *to know (a fact, how to)* | su | *knew, have known* |
| tenir | *to hold* | tenu | *held, have held* |
| vivre | *to live* | vécu | *lived, have lived* |
| voir | *to see* | vu | *saw, have seen* |
| vouloir | *to want to* | voulu | *wanted, have wanted* |

### 3. Perfect tense with être reflexive verbs

All reflexive verbs have the present tense of *être* as their auxiliary. Their past participles may be either regular or irregular – check the verb table. The past participle agrees (like an adjective) with the subject.

**Example:**

se laver: *to wash oneself*

je me suis lavé(e)
*I washed, I have washed myself*
tu t'es lavé(e)
*you washed, you have washed yourself*
il s'est lavé
*he washed, he has washed himself*
elle s'est lavée
*she washed, she has washed herself*
on s'est lavé(e)(s)
*one washed, one has washed oneself*

nous nous sommes lavé(e)s
*we washed, we have washed ourselves*
vous vous êtes lavé(e)(s)
*you washed, you have washed yourself*
ils se sont lavés
*they washed, they have washed themselves*
elles se sont lavées
*they washed, they have washed themselves*

If the (*e*) is in brackets, it is added only if the subject is feminine. If the (*s*) is in brackets, it is added only if the subject is plural.

Where an irregular past participle ends in *-s*, (example: *assis*) no further *s* is required for the masculine plural agreement.

**Example:**

Les garçons se sont assis
*The boys sat down*

### 4. Perfect tense with *être* – 16 verbs

Sixteen common verbs which are not reflexive also form the perfect tense with *être* as the auxiliary.

Most of them can be remembered in 6 pairs which are (or are nearly) opposite in meaning. Make it a top priority to master them.

| Infinitive | Meaning | Past participle | Meaning |
|---|---|---|---|
| aller | *to go* | allé | *went, have gone* |
| venir | *to come* | venu | *came, have come* |
| arriver | *to arrive* | arrivé | *arrived, have arrived* |
| partir | *to depart* | parti | *departed, have departed* |
| entrer | *to enter* | entré | *entered, have entered* |
| sortir | *to go out* | sorti | *went out, have gone out* |
| monter | *to climb* | monté | *climbed, have climbed* |
| descendre | *to descend* | descendu | *descended, have descended* |
| rester | *to stay* | resté | *stayed, have stayed* |
| tomber | *to fall (down)* | tombé | *fell (down), have fallen (down)* |
| naître | *to be born* | né | *was born, have been born* |
| mourir | *to die* | mort | *died, has died* |

The others are:

| | | | |
|---|---|---|---|
| retourner | *to return* | retourné | *returned, has returned* |
| revenir | *to come back* | revenu | *came back, has come back* |
| devenir | *to become* | devenu | *became, has become* |
| rentrer | *to go back* | rentré | *gone back, has gone back* |

As with reflexive verbs, the past participles of these verbs have to agree with the subject.

**Example:**

retourner: *to return*

je suis retourné(e)
*I returned, I have returned*
tu es retourné(e)
*you returned, you have returned*
il est retourné
*he returned, he has returned*
elle est retournée
*she returned, she has returned*
on est retourné(e)(s)
*one returned, one has returned*

nous sommes retourné(e)s
*we returned, we have returned*
vous êtes retourné(e)(s)
*you returned, you have returned*
ils sont retournés
*they returned, they have returned*
elles sont retournées
*they returned, they have returned*

If the (*e*) is in brackets, it is added only if the subject is feminine. If the (*s*) is in brackets, it is added only if the subject is plural.

## Imperfect Tense

The imperfect tense refers to events in the past. It is usually found in combination with the perfect tense.

### Use of the imperfect tense:

The inperfect tense in French is used:

- to set the scene in the past (to say what was happening when something else happened)

  **Example:**

  Il **traversait** la rue quand une voiture l'a tué
  *He was crossing the road (imperfect tense) when a car killed him (perfect tense)*

- for description in the past

  **Example:**

  Il **faisait** beau. Le soleil brillait. Jeanne était contente
  *The weather was good. The sun was shining. Jeanne was happy*

- for something that happened frequently in the past, or used to happen

  **Example:**

  Quand j'**habitais à** Londres, j'**allais** acheter mes cadeaux chez Harrods
  *When I lived in London I used to buy my presents at Harrods*

- in reported speech (also known as indirect speech) to report the present tense.

  **Example:**

  What the person actually said:
  'Je viens d'Angleterre'
  *I come from England (present tense)*

  Reported speech:
  Il a dit qu'il **venait** d'Angleterre
  *He said (perfect tense) he came (imperfect tense) from England*

### Formation of the imperfect tense

1. Nearly all verbs, *-er*, *-ir*, *-re* and *-oir*, form the imperfect tense in the following way:

   First find the *nous* form of the present tense
   Then remove the *-ons* to leave the imperfect stem
   Finally add the imperfect endings:

   | | |
   |---|---|
   | je | -ais |
   | tu | -ais |
   | il | -ait |
   | elle | -ait |
   | on | -ait |
   | nous | -ions |
   | vous | -iez |
   | ils | -aient |
   | elles | -aient |

   **Example:**

   faire: *to make/do*

| | | |
|---|---|---|
| *Nous* form of present tense: | faisons | |
| Imperfect stem (faisons minus *-ons*): | fais- | |
| Imperfect tense: | je fais**ais** | *I was doing* |
| | tu fais**ais** | *you were doing* |
| | il fais**ait** | *he was doing* |
| | elle fais**ait** | *she was doing* |
| | on fais**ait** | *one was doing* |
| | nous fais**ions** | *we were doing* |
| | vous fais**iez** | *you were doing* |
| | ils fais**aient** | *they were doing* |
| | elles fais**aient** | *they were doing* |

2. There is one irregular verb in the imperfect tense:
   *être: to be*

| | |
|---|---|
| j'étais | *I was* |
| tu étais | *you were* |
| il était | *he was* |
| elle était | *she was* |
| on était | *one was* |
| nous étions | *we were* |
| vous étiez | *you were* |
| ils étaient | *they were* |
| elles étaient | *they were* |

If you look carefully, you will see that it is only the imperfect stem, *ét-*, which is irregular. The endings are what you would expect.

### Future using *aller* + infinitive

This is the simplest way of talking about events in the future, and is similar to the English 'I am going to ...'

### Use of the future with *aller* + infinitive

- to talk about events in the immediate future

**Example:**

Je vais regarder la télévision ce soir.
*I am going to watch TV tonight*

### Formation of the future with *aller* + infinitive

Take the present tense of *aller*. Add the infinitive of any verb, regular or irregular.

**Example:**

acheter: *to buy*

| | |
|---|---|
| je vais acheter | *I am going to buy* |
| tu vas acheter | *you are going to buy* |
| il va acheter | *he is going to buy* |
| elle va acheter | *she is going to buy* |
| on va acheter | *one is going to buy* |
| nous allons acheter | *we are going to buy* |
| vous allez acheter | *you are going to buy* |
| ils vont acheter | *they are going to buy* |
| elles vont acheter | *they are going to buy* |

## Future tense

### Use of the future tense

- to express firm intention.

**Example:**

Je regarderai la télévision ce soir
*I shall watch TV this evening*

- to refer to events further ahead than the short term

**Example:**

Dans 5 ans j'aurai 18 ans
*I shall be 18 in 5 years' time*

### Formation of the future tense

#### 1. Regular -er and -ir verbs

Add the following endings to the infinitive:

| | |
|---|---|
| je | -ai |
| tu | -as |
| il | -a |
| elle | -a |
| on | -a |
| nous | -ons |
| vous | -ez |
| ils | -ont |
| elles | -ont |

**Examples:**

| | |
|---|---|
| je parler**ai** | *I shall/will speak* |
| tu parler**as** | *you will speak* |
| il parler**a** | *he will speak* |
| elle parler**a** | *she will speak* |
| on parler**a** | *one will speak* |
| nous parler**ons** | *we shall/will speak* |
| vous parler**ez** | *you will speak* |
| ils parler**ont** | *they will speak* |
| elles parler**ont** | *they will speak* |
| je finir**ai** | *I shall/will finish* |
| tu finir**as** | *you will finish* |
| il finir**a** | *he will finish* |
| elle finir**a** | *she will finish* |
| on finir**a** | *one will finish* |
| nous finir**ons** | *we shall/will finish* |
| vous finir**ez** | *you will finish* |
| ils finir**ont** | *they will finish* |
| elles finir**ont** | *they will finish* |

#### 2. Regular *-re* verbs

Remove the *e* from the infinitive. Add the same endings as for all other verbs.

**Example:**

| | |
|---|---|
| je vendr**ai** | *I shall/will sell* |
| tu vendr**as** | *you will sell* |
| il vendr**a** | *he will sell* |
| elle vendr**a** | *she will sell* |
| on vendr**a** | *one will sell* |
| nous vendr**ons** | *we shall/will sell* |
| vous vendr**ez** | *you will sell* |
| ils vendr**ont** | *they will sell* |
| elles vendr**ont** | *they will sell* |

#### 3. Irregular verbs

Irregular verbs have the same future endings as all other verbs. However, the future stem needs to be learned. Listed below are the future tenses of some of the most common irregular future tenses. Note that this contains some *-er* verbs which are not irregular in other parts.

| **Infinitive** | **Future tense** | **Meaning** |
|---|---|---|
| acheter | j'achèterai | *I shall buy* |
| aller | j'irai | *I shall go* |
| appeler | j'appellerai | *I shall call* |

| | | |
|---|---|---|
| s'asseoir | je m'assiérai | *I shall sit down* |
| avoir | j'aurai | *I shall have* |
| courir | je courrai | *I shall run* |
| devoir | je devrai | *I shall be obliged to* |
| envoyer | j'enverrai | *I shall send* |
| être | je serai | *I shall be* |
| faire | je ferai | *I shall do* |
| falloir | il faudra | *it will be necessary* |
| jeter | je jetterai | *I shall throw* |
| mourir | je mourrai | *I shall die* |
| pleuvoir | il pleuvra | *it will rain* |
| pouvoir | je pourrai | *I shall be able to* |
| recevoir | je recevrai | *I shall receive* |
| savoir | je saurai | *I shall know* |
| tenir | je tiendrai | *I shall hold* |
| venir | je viendrai | *I shall come* |
| voir | je verrai | *I shall see* |

## Reflexive verbs

These are verbs where the person does the action to herself or himself. These verbs have *se* or *s'* in front of the infinitive when you look them up.

### Use of reflexive verbs

- they are part of the normal vocabulary of French. They can be used in any way a normal verb can be. There are many more in French than there are in English, and some of the meanings are, at first, confusing.
- they are often used when referring to a part of the body.

**Examples:**

Je **me** suis coupé le doigt
*I have cut my finger*
Elle **se** lave les dents
She is *cleaning* her teeth

### Formation of reflexive verbs

1. Add the reflexive pronoun between the subject and the verb.

   This applies in all tenses. If in doubt, check the verb table.

   **Example:**

   se laver: *to wash oneself*

   je **me** lave
   *I wash myself/I am washing myself*
   tu **te** laves
   *you wash yourself/you are washing yourself*
   il **se** lave
   *he washes himself/he is washing himself*
   elle **se** lave
   *she washes herself/she is washing herself*
   on **se** lave
   *one washes oneself/one is washing oneself*
   nous **nous** lavons
   *we wash ourselves/we are washing ourselves*
   vous **vous** lavez
   *you wash yourself(yourselves)/you are washing yourself(yourselves)*
   ils **se** lavent
   *they wash themselves/they are washing themselves*
   elles **se** lavent
   *they wash themselves/they are washing themselves*

2. Where the reflexive verb is used as an infinitive, the reflexive pronoun agrees with the subject of the verb.

   **Examples:**

   **Je** suis obligé de **me** laver après le sport
   *I have to go to wash **myself** after sport*
   **Nous** sommes obligés de **nous** laver après le sport
   *We have to go to wash **ourselves** after sport*
   **On** est obligé de **se** laver après le sport
   *One has to go to wash **oneself** after sport*

3. In the perfect and pluperfect tenses:
   - all reflexive verbs have *être* as the auxiliary verb
   - the past participles of reflexive verbs agree with the subject.

   **Example:**

   se laver: *to wash oneself*

   je me suis lavé(e)
   *I washed myself/I have washed myself*
   tu t'es lavé(e)
   *you washed/you have washed yourself*
   il s'est lavé
   *he washed/he has washed himself*
   elle s'est lavée
   *she washed/she has washed herself*
   on s'est lavé(e)(s)
   *one washed/one has washed oneself*
   nous nous sommes lavé(e)s
   *we washed/we have washed ourselves*
   vous vous êtes lavé(e)(s)
   *you washed/you have washed yourself*
   ils se sont lavés
   *they washed/they have washed themselves*
   elles se sont lavées
   *they washed/they have washed themselves*

   If the *(e)* is in brackets, it is added only if the subject is feminine. If the *(s)* is in brackets, it is added only if the subject is plural.
   Where an irregular past participle ends in *-s*, example:

   *assis*, no further *s* is required for the masculine plural agreement.

   **Example:**

   Les garçons se sont assis
   *The boys sat down*

#### Common reflexive verbs

| | |
|---|---|
| s'amuser | *to enjoy oneself* |
| s'appeler | *to be called* |
| s'approcher de | *to approach* |
| s'arrêter | *to stop* |
| se baigner | *to bathe* |
| se brosser (les cheveux) | *to brush (one's hair)* |
| se coucher | *to go to bed* |
| se débrouiller | *to manage, to get on with (something)* |
| se dépêcher | *to hurry* |
| se déshabiller | *to undress* |
| se disputer avec | *to have an argument with* |
| s'entendre avec | *to get on with (someone)* |
| se fâcher | *to get angry* |
| se faire mal | *to hurt oneself* |
| s'habiller | *to get dressed* |
| s'intéresser à | *to be interested in* |
| se mettre à | *to begin* |
| se laver | *to get washed* |
| se lever | *to get up* |

| | |
|---|---|
| se peigner | *to comb one's hair* |
| se promener | *to go for a walk* |
| se raser | *to shave* |
| se reposer | *to rest* |
| se réveiller | *to wake up* |
| se sauver | *to run away* |
| se sentir | *to feel* |
| se taire | *to be silent* |
| se trouver | *to be situated* |

Verbs not in the above list can be made reflexive to express the idea of 'each other'. They then behave like reflexives in the perfect tense.

**Examples:**

Quand est-ce qu'on va **se** voir?
*When shall we see **each other**?*
Quand est-ce que nous **nous** sommes vu(e)s la dernière fois?
*When did we last see **each other?***

## Question forms

There are four ways of asking a question in French.

1. By tone of voice.

   A rising tone of voice at the end of a statement turns it into a question.

   **Example:**

   Ton frère habite à Londres?
   *Does your brother live in London?*

If you are writing, you obviously can't use tone of voice, so you must remember to use a question mark.

2. By beginning with *Est-ce que*

   Add *Est-ce que* to the beginning of any statement to convert it into a question.

   **Example:**

   Est-ce que ton frère habite à Londres?
   *Does your brother live in London?*

3. By inverting the subject and verb

   **Example:**

   Habites-tu à Londres?
   *Do you live in London?*

If the verbs ends in a vowel in the 3rd person singular you should add an extra *-t-* to make it easier to pronounce.

**Example:**

Votre frère, habite-**t**-il à Londres?
*Does your brother live in London?*

4. Question words can be used in front of methods 1 & 2 (statement and *est-ce que*)

   **Example:**

   Où habite ton frère?
   Où est-ce que ton frère habite?
   *Where does your brother live?*

Here is a list of question words:

| | |
|---|---|
| Combien? | *How much?* |
| Comment? | *How? (sometimes: What?)* |
| Où? | *Where?* |
| D'où? | *Where from?* |
| Lequel*? | *Which one?* |
| Pourquoi? | *Why?* |
| Quand? | *When?* |
| Qu'est-ce que..? | *What?* |
| Quel* | *Which, what?* |
| Qui? | *Who?* |
| Quoi? | *Pardon?, What? (used only on its own)* |

**Lequel* and *quel* are adjectives and agree with the noun being asked about.

**Example:**

Quel**les** chaussettes as-tu perdues?
*Which socks have you lost?*

5. By adding *n'est-ce pas*

   Add *n'est-ce pas* to the end of any statement to convert it into a question. It's similar to *isn't it?, doesn't he?,* etc., in English. There is only one French form for all the English ones.

   **Example:**

   Ton frère habite à Londres, **n'est-ce pas**?
   *Your brother lives in London, doesn't he?*

## Command forms (also known as imperatives)

The command forms of verbs are used in telling people to do something. They include the 'Let's ...' sort of command, which is a way of telling yourself and one or more other people to do something.

French verbs have three command forms, which are derived from *tu, vous* and *nous* forms of the present tense in most cases.

### Use of command forms

The form derived from the *tu* form is used when talking to one person who is

- a good friend
- a member of the family or a pet
- a young person

The form derived from the *vous* form is used when talking to two or more people who are

- good friends
- members of the family or pets
- young people

or to one person who is an adult who doesn't fit any of the categories above.

The form derived from the *nous* form is used to translate 'Let's do something'.

### Formation of commands

**1. *-ir* and *-re* verbs**

Miss out *tu* or *vous* or *nous* and just use the verb itself.

**Examples:**

| | |
|---|---|
| Finis ce livre! | *Finish that book!* |
| Finissez ce livre! | *Finish that book!* |
| Finissons ce livre! | *Let's finish that book!* |
| Vends ce livre! | *Sell that book!* |
| Vendez ce livre! | *Sell that book!* |
| Vendons ce livre! | *Let's sell that book!* |

**2. -*er* verbs.**

The principle is the same, but miss the *-s* off the *tu* form.

**Example:**

Parle! *Talk!*
Parlez! *Talk!*
Parlons! *Let's talk!*

**3. Irregular forms**

The following verbs have irregular command forms:

| Infinitive | Meaning | tu | vous | nous |
|---|---|---|---|---|
| avoir | *to have* | aie | ayez | ayons |
| être | *to be* | sois | soyez | soyons |
| savoir | *to know a fact, or how to* | sache | sachez | sachons |
| vouloir | *to want to* | veuille | veuillez | |

*Aller* has a modified form in the phrase *Vas-y (go to it, on you go).*

**4. Reflexive verbs**

Reflexive verbs have the following command forms:

**Example:**

Réveille-toi! *Wake up!*
Réveillez-vous! *Wake up!*
Réveillons-nous! *Let's wake up!*

## The infinitive

The infinitive is the part of the verb listed in a dictionary, and means 'to ...'. It doesn't agree with a subject. Infinitives may be found in combination with other verbs, as described below.

In French there are often two verbs in a sentence, the second of which is in the infinitive form. This is often the case in English, too, e.g. *I prefer* ***to swim****.*

There are four ways in which French uses two verbs in a sentence. Unfortunately, you have to learn which way each verb operates.

**1. Verbs followed directly by the infinitive**

Some verbs are followed directly by the infinitive.

**Example:**

J'aime **jouer** au tennis
*I like playing tennis*

These verbs include:

adorer *to love*
aimer *to like, to love*
aller *to go*
désirer *to want, to wish*
détester *to hate*
devoir *to have to, ('must')*
espérer *to hope to*
il faut *you need to*
pouvoir *to be able to, ('can')*
préférer *to prefer*
savoir *to know how to*
vouloir *to want to*

**2. Verbs followed by *à* + infinitive**

Some verbs are followed by *à* and an infinitive.

**Example:**

Il s'est décidé **à acheter** une Renault
*He made up his mind to buy a Renault*

These verbs include:

commencer à *to begin to*
continuer à *to continue to*
se décider à *to decide to, make up ones mind*
demander à *to ask to*
s'intéresser à *to be interested in*
inviter quelqu'un à *to invite someone to*
se mettre à *to begin to*
obliger quelqu'un à *to make someone do something*

**3. Verbs followed by *de* + infinitive**

Some verbs are followed by *de* and an infinitive.

**Example:**

Il a cessé **de pleuvoir**
*It's stopped raining*

These verbs include:

cesser de *to stop doing something*
décider de *to decide to*
dire de *to tell to*
essayer de *to try to*
offrir de *to offer to do something*
oublier de *to forget to do something*
permettre de *to allow to*
refuser de *to refuse to*

**4. There are expressions with *avoir* which are followed by *de* + the infinitive.**

**Example:**

J'ai envie de manger
*I want to eat*

These expressions include:

avoir besoin de *to need to*
avoir l'intention de *to intend to*
avoir peur de *to be afraid of doing something*
avoir le droit de *to have the right to, to be allowed to*
avoir le temps de *to have time to*
avoir envie de *to feel like doing something*

The preposition *pour* can also be used to introduce an infinitive.

**Examples:**

Il est allé au café **pour** boire une bière
*He went to the café to drink a beer*
Il est trop jeune **pour** boire du vin
*He is too young to drink wine*

## Use of tenses with depuis

*Depuis,* meaning since, or for, uses different tenses in French than you might expect.

1. If the action is still continuing, the present tense is used after *depuis.*

**Example:**

J'**habite** à Londres **depuis** cinq ans.
*I have lived in London for five years (and I still do)*

2. If the action lasted for some time, but is now over, the imperfect tense is used after *depuis.*

**Example:**

J'**habitais** à Londres depuis cinq ans quand je me suis décidé à quitter la grande ville
*I had been living in London for five years when I decided to leave the big city*

## Negatives

There are various negatives in French. They have two parts: *ne* and one other which varies according to meaning.

| | |
|---|---|
| ne ... pas | *not* |
| ne ... jamais | *never* |
| ne ... rien | *nothing* |
| ne ... personne | *nobody* |
| ne ... aucun* | *no, not one* |
| ne ... nulle part | *nowhere* |
| ne ... plus | *no more, no longer* |
| ne ... guère | *hardly, scarely* |
| ne ... que | *only* |
| ne ... ni ... ni ... | *neither ... nor ... nor ...* |

**Aucun* agrees like an adjective.

### Word-order and negatives

1. Generally, the negative forms a 'sandwich' round the verb, the *ne* going before the verb and the second part of the negative following it.

   **Example:**

   Je **ne** parle **pas** italien
   *I don't speak Italian*

2. In the perfect tense, the 'sandwich' is made round the auxiliary verb.

   **Examples:**

   Je **ne** suis **pas** sorti ce matin
   *I didn't go out this morning*
   Je **n'**ai **pas** vu le journal
   *I haven't seen the newspaper*

3. With reflexive verbs, the reflexive pronoun is included within the "sandwich".

   **Examples:**

   Je **ne** me lave **pas** très souvent
   *I don't wash very often*
   Je **ne** me suis **pas** lavé très souvent
   *I didn't wash very often*

4. If there is a pronoun or pronouns before the verb, they are included inside the 'sandwich'.

   **Examples:**

   Je **ne** les regarde **pas**
   *I don't look at them*
   Je **ne** les ai **pas** regardés
   *I didn't look at them*
   Je **ne** les lui ai **pas** donnés
   *I didn't give them to him*

#### Other features of negatives

1. Negatives are usually followed by *de*, in the same way as "any" follows negatives in English.

   **Examples:**

   Je n'ai pas **de** fromage
   *I haven't got **any** cheese*
   Je n'ai pas mangé **de** fromage
   *I haven't eaten **any** cheese*

2. *Aucun, personne* and *rien* can be used as the subject of a sentence. They still require the *ne*.

   **Examples:**

   **Aucune** voiture **n'**est arrivée
   *No car arrived*
   **Personne n'**a acheté de gâteau
   *Nobody bought any cake*
   **Rien n'**est arrivé
   *Nothing has happened*

3. *Jamais, personne* and *rien* can be used on their own in answer to questions.

   **Examples:**

   Est-ce que tu joues au tennis? **Jamais**
   *Do you play tennis? Never*
   Qui est là? **Personne**
   *Who is there? No-one*
   Qu'est-ce que tu as acheté? **Rien**
   *What did you buy? Nothing*

4. More than one negative can be combined in the following pairs:

   *jamais* and *personne*

   **Example:**

   Je ne vois **jamais personne**
   *I never see anybody*

   *jamais* and *rien*

   **Example:**

   Je n'achète **jamais rien**
   *I never buy anything*

   *plus* and *personne*

   **Example:**

   Je ne vois **plus personne**
   *I don't see anybody any more*

   *plus* and *rien*

   **Example:**

   Jean ne fait **plus rien**
   *Jean doesn't do anything any more*

## Conditional

Some forms of the conditional, such as *je voudrais* will be well known to all learners of French.

### Use of the conditional

- as a more polite alternative to the present tense when making requests

  **Example:**

  Je **voudrais** une bière, s'il vous plaît
  *I would like a beer, please*

  **Contrast:**

  Je **veux** une bière
  *I want a beer*

- as a way of expressing what you would do if something else happened /of expressing conditions.

  **Example:**

  Si j'étais (imperfect) très riche, je ne **travaillerais** (conditional) plus
  *If I were very rich, I would not work any more*

### Formation of the conditional

The conditional is formed in the same way for all verbs. Take the future stem of the verb and add the imperfect endings.

Check the section on the future tense if you are unsure about the future stem. I have contrasted the future and the conditional of the same verb – *avoir* – below:

| **Future tense** | **Conditional** |
|---|---|
| j'aurai | j'aur**ais** |
| tu auras | tu aur**ais** |
| il aura | il aur**ait** |
| elle aura | elle aur**ait** |
| on aura | on aur**ait** |
| nous aurons | nous aur**ions** |
| vous aurez | vous aur**iez** |
| ils auront | ils aur**aient** |
| elles auront | elles aur**aient** |

### Use of tenses after si

The tenses used after *si* are as follows:

1. *Si* + present tense is followed by the future tense. This is the same as English.

   **Example:**

   S'il fait beau, j'irai au parc zoologique
   *If the weather's good I'll go to the zoo*

2. *Si* + imperfect tense is followed by the conditional. This is similar to English, too.

   **Example:**

   S'il faisait beau, j'irais au parc zoologique
   *If the weather was good I would go to the zoo*

# Section three

## Practice Exercises with Solutions

In this section we give you many opportunities to check your progress in the four key skills. You will find a range of questions for each of the skills, together with suggested solutions. In the case of listening, you will be instructed, where appropriate, to listen to the accompanying cassette.

The chart below will help you to see, at a glance, where you can find the various materials in this section.


**Listening:**

- Questions 35
- Answers 42

**Reading**

- Questions 52
- Answers 60

**Speaking:**

- Questions 62
- Answers 70

**Writing:**

- Questions 73
- Answers 89

# Listening: questions

## Exercice 1 C'est quel numéro?

Coche les cases des numéros que tu entends

*Tick the boxes of the numbers you hear*

**A**

| | | | | |
|---|---|---|---|---|
| 3 | 9 | | | 19 |
| | | 6 | 11 | |
| | 5 | | | 12 |
| 17 | | 13 | | 20 |

**B**

| | | | | |
|---|---|---|---|---|
| 30 | 29 | | | 69 |
| | | 60 | 40 | |
| | 50 | | | 45 |
| 27 | | 33 | | 23 |

## Exercice 2: Comment est-ce qu'on écrit ton nom?

L'alphabet français:

*The French alphabet:*

a b c d e f g h i j k l m n o p q r s t u v w x y z
accent aigu (´), accent grave (`), accent circonflexe (^), c cédille (ç), e tréma (ë), deux p (pp), deux l (ll), deux r (rr), deux s (ss)

**A** Ecris les noms de famille que tu vas entendre (1–5)

*Write the surnames you hear (1–5)*

**B** Ecris les noms des villes françaises où ces personnnes habitent

*Write the names of the French towns where the speakers live*

**1** Moi, j'habite __________

**2** Moi, j'habite __________

**3** Moi, j'habite __________

**4** Moi, j'habite __________ au sud de la France.

**5** __________c'est ma ville.

## Exercice 3 Quelle heure est-il?

Ecris l'heure en chiffres

*Write the time in figures*

1 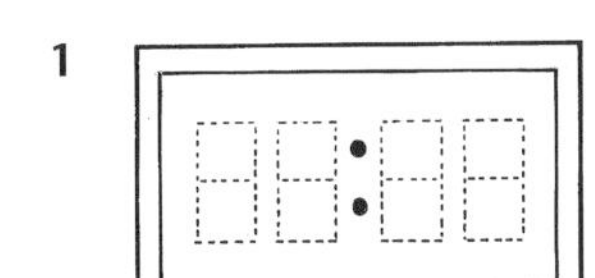

2 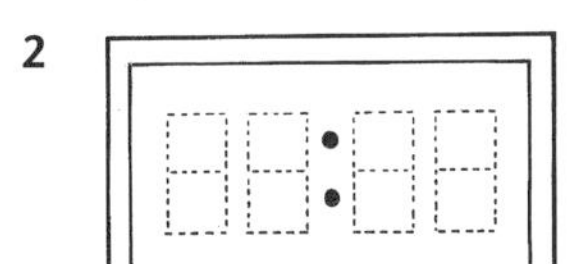

3 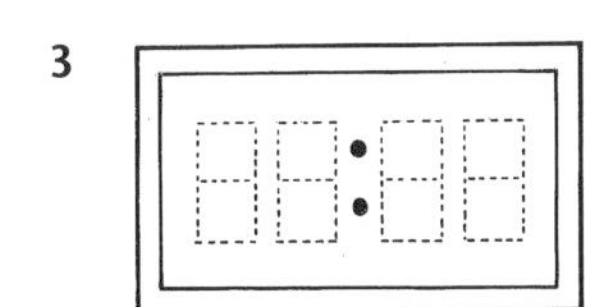

4 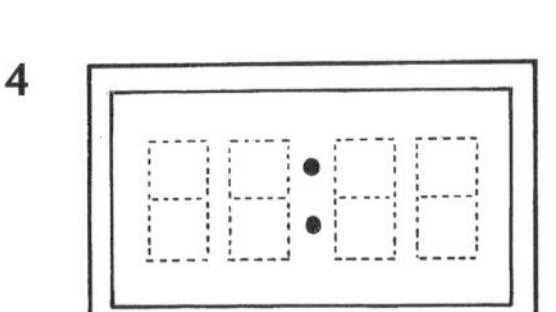

5 

6 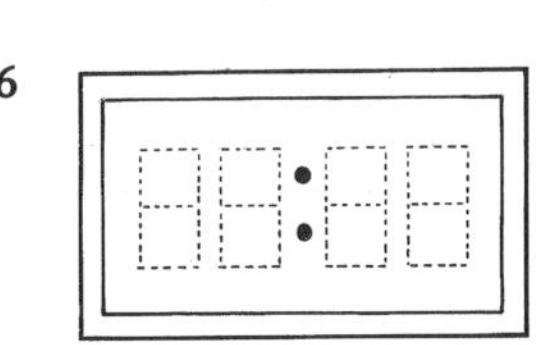

7 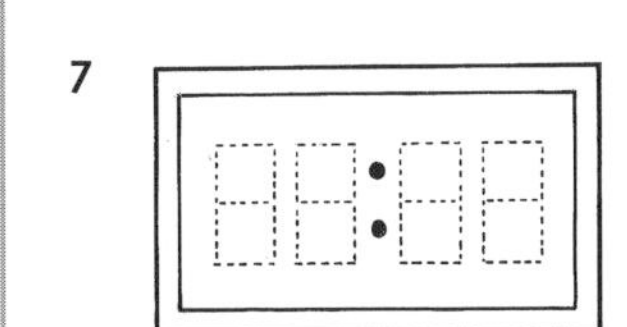

8 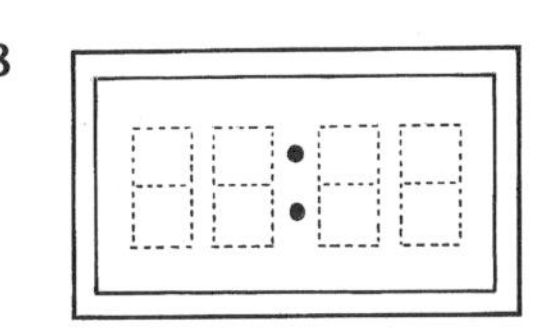

9 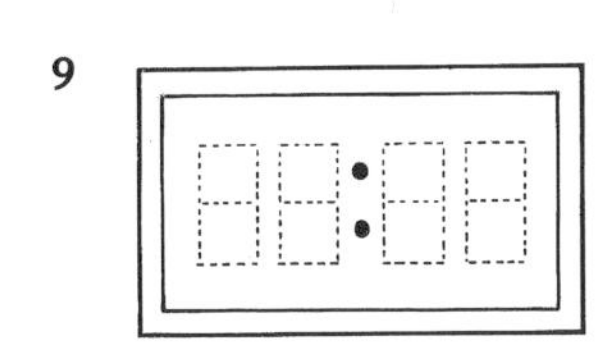

10 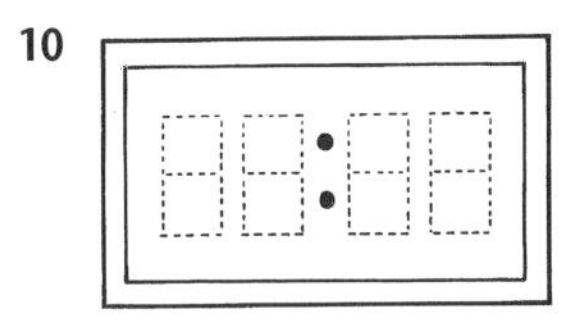

## Exercice 4 On se présente

Six personnes se présentent. Ecris leurs détails dans les cases

*Six people introduce themselves. Enter the information in the table below*

| Numéro | prénom | nom de famille | âge (ans) |
|---|---|---|---|
| 1 | | | |
| 2 | | | |
| 3 | | | |
| 4 | | | |
| 5 | | | |
| 6 | | | |

## Exercice 5 Les numéros de téléphone

Ecris les numéros de télephone que tu vas entendre

*Listen and enter the phone numbers in the table*

| | nom | numéro de téléphone |
|---|---|---|
| 1 | Vanessa Tillier | |
| 2 | Max Bertrand | |
| 3 | Marie Rodin | |
| 4 | Pierre Lemoine | |
| 5 | Sophie Girard | |
| 6 | Patrick Hervé | |

## Exercice 6 Quelle est la date de ton anniversaire?

Quelle est la date de leur anniversaire? Remplis le tableau

*When are their birthdays? Write the dates in the table*

| | nom | anniversaire |
|---|---|---|
| 1 | Vanessa Tillier | |
| 2 | Max Bertrand | |
| 3 | Marie Rodin | |
| 4 | Pierre Lemoine | |
| 5 | Sophie Girard | |
| 6 | Patrick Hervé | |

## Exercice 7 Ma famille et moi

Ecoute la cassette que tu as reçue de ton correspondant français. Complète le tableau

*You have received a cassette from your French exchange partner. Fill in the table*

| | |
|---|---|
| Nom | |
| Age | |
| Domicile | |
| Frère | |
| Sœur | |
| Animaux domestiques | |
| Passetemps | |

## Exercice 8 Les passetemps

Daniel parle maintenant de ses passetemps, et des passetemps de sa famille

*Now Daniel is talking about his free time and his family's hobbies*

Choisis la bonne expression pour faire une phrase. Coche la bonne case

*Choose the right expression to complete the sentences. Tick the right box*

**1** Daniel aime jouer au foot ☐
au rugby ☐
au volley ☐

**2** Il lit des magazines ☐
des romans de science-fiction ☐
le journal ☐

**3** Il a plus de 100 livres dans sa chambre ☐
200 ☐
300 ☐

**4** Son équipe est excellente ☐
assez bien ☐
nulle ☐

**5** Sa sœur joue de la trompette ☐
de la flûte ☐
du trombone ☐

**6** Son frère est sportif ☐
aime la musique ☐
est stupide ☐

**7** Ses parents aiment danser ☐
aiment aller au restaurant ☐
aiment aller au théâtre ☐

**8** Chez Daniel, c'est son père qui fait la cuisine ☐
sa mère ☐
sa sœur ☐

**9** Le responsable du jardin, c'est Daniel ☐
sa mère ☐
son père ☐

**10** C'est un jardin avec des fleurs ☐
des arbres ☐
des légumes ☐

## Exercice 9 La ville

Ton correspondant Damien a envoyé une brochure de sa ville. Il parle de la ville sur cassette

*Your exchange partner Damien has sent you a leaflet about his home town, St Herblain, and is now talking about the town on the cassette*

Vrai ou faux? Ecris V ou F dans les cases

*True or false? Write V or F in the boxes*

**1** Saint Herblain est près de Paris ☐

**2** Il y a beaucoup d'industries à Saint Herblain ☐

**3** Atlantis, c'est un grand centre commercial ☐

**4** On peut aller à Nantes en tramway ☐

**5** Les parents vont au cinéma à Nantes ☐

## Exercice 10 La météo

Tu es en vacances en France et tu écoutes la météo à la radio. Dessine les symboles météo sur la carte de la France

*You are on holiday in France and hear the weather forecast on the radio. Draw the weather symbols on to the map of France*

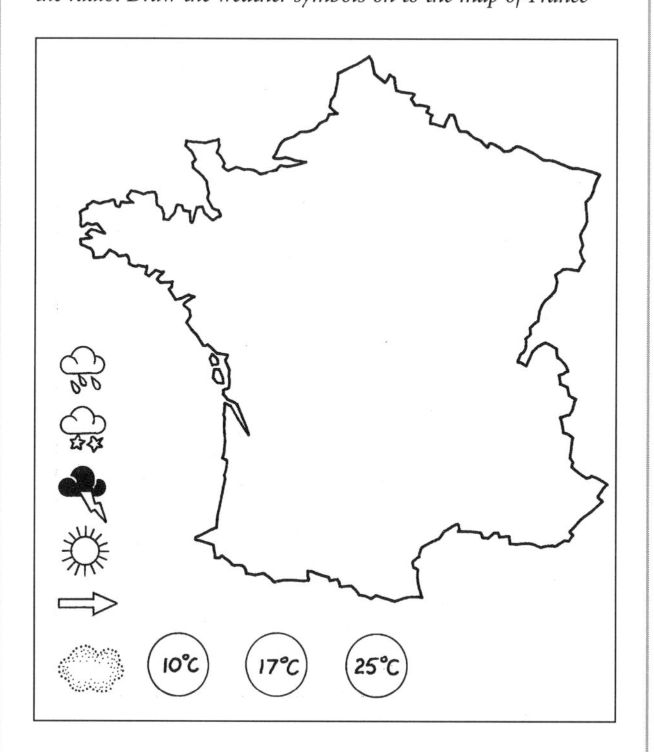


## Exercice 11 L'école

Julie va au collège à Nantes. Elle te parle de son collège

*Julie goes to the school in Nantes. She tells you about her school*

**A** Indique les phrases qui sont correctes

*Put a cross in the box next to the correct sentences:*

**1** Julie va au collège Jules Verne ☐

**2** Le collège est très moderne ☐

**3** Le collège est en centre ville ☐

**4** Le collège est petit ☐

**5** Le samedi, elle a des cours ☐

**6** Elle aime les mercredis ☐

**7** Elle aime beaucoup les maths ☐

**B** Ecoute encore une fois. Coche les cours qu'elle a

*Listen again. Tick the lessons she has*

| | |
|---|---|
| allemand | |
| chimie | |
| dessin | |
| français | |
| informatique | |
| instruction civique | |
| religion | |
| sport | |

## Exercice 12 Ma maison

Gabrielle parle de sa maison
*Gabrielle is talking about her house*

Dessine la maison de Gabrielle dans le jardin.
*Draw Gabrielle's house into the space in the picture*

## Exercice 13 Ma chambre

Gabrielle parle de sa chambre
*Gabrielle is talking about her room*

Quels meubles a Gabrielle dans sa chambre? Coche les cases
*Tick the items of furniture which Gabriele has in her room*

| | |
|---|---|
| un lit | |
| un fauteuil | |
| une table | |
| un canapé | |
| une armoire | |
| une chaise | |
| une table basse | |

## Exercice 14 Le ménage

Gabrielle aide ses parents
*Gabrielle helps her parents*

Qui fait quoi chez Gabrielle? Coche les cases
*Who does what in Gabrielle's family? Tick the boxes*

| | **Gabrielle** | **sa mère** | **son père** |
|---|---|---|---|
| la vaisselle | | | |
| mettre la table | | | |
| la cuisine | | | |
| le jardin | | | |
| la voiture | | | |
| passer l'aspirateur | | | |
| faire la poussière | | | |

## Exercice 15 L'argent de poche

Six jeunes personnes parlent de l'argent de poche. Complète le tableau

*Six teenagers are talking about pocket money. Fill in the table below*

| | **nom** | **argent de poche** | **gagne** | **achète** | **économise pour acheter** |
|---|---|---|---|---|---|
| 1 | Henri | | | | |
| 2 | Joëlle | | | | |
| 3 | Jean | | | | |
| 4 | Olivier | | | | |
| 5 | Chantal | | | | |
| 6 | Claudine | | | | |

## Exercice 16 Au camping

Tu travailles à la réception d'un camping. Remplis les fiches

*You are working on a campsite. Fill in the registration forms while your friend talks to the guests*

**1.**
*Nom* ______________________
*Durée du séjour:* ____ *nuits*
*Personnes:* ______________________
*Emplacement nº:* ______________________
*Tente* oui/non *Caravane* oui/non
*Electricité* oui/non

**2.**
*Nom* ______________________
*Durée du séjour:* ____ *nuits*
*Personnes:* ______________________
*Emplacement nº:* ______________________
*Tente* oui/non *Caravane* oui/non
*Electricité* oui/non

**3.**
*Nom* ______________________
*Durée du séjour:* ____ *nuits*
*Personnes:* ______________________
*Emplacement nº:* ______________________
*Tente* oui/non *Caravane* oui/non
*Electricité* oui/non

**4.**
*Nom* ______________________
*Durée du séjour:* ____ *nuits*
*Personnes:* ______________________
*Emplacement nº:* ______________________
*Tente* oui/non *Caravane* oui/non
*Electricité* oui/non

## Exercice 17 On prend rendez-vous

Ecoute ces personnes qui prennent rendez-vous au cabinet du médecin

*Listen to these people who are making appointments to see a doctor*

Ecris les rendez-vous dans l'agenda. C'est mardi aujourd'hui

*Enter the appointments into the diary. Today is Tuesday*

LUNDI

MARDI

MERCREDI

JEUDI

VENDREDI

SAMEDI

DIMANCHE

## Exercice 18 Au cabinet du médecin

Qu'est-ce qui ne va pas? Quels sont les remèdes recommandés par le médecin?
Joins les images et les remèdes

*What is wrong with the four patients and what does the doctor recomend?*
*Join the pictures and the remedies*

## Exercice 19 Au café

On commande à boire et à manger dans un café

*In a cafe people are ordering drinks and food*

Vrai ou faux? Ecris V ou F dans la case:

*True or False? Write V or F in the box*

**1** Le monsieur commande un café noir ☐
Il commande deux grands cafés ☐

**2** La dame commande un thé-citron ☐
Elle n'aime pas le jambon ☐

**3** La jeune fille commande de la limonade ☐
Elle commande une glace à la fraise et une glace au chocolat ☐

**4** La dame commande un chocolat chaud ☐
Elle n'a pas faim ☐

| personne | hors d'œuvre | plat principal | dessert |
|---|---|---|---|
| maman | | | |
| fille | | | |
| fils | | | |
| papa | | | |

## Exercice 20 Au restaurant

La famille Bertillon mange au restaurant

*The Bertillon family are eating in a restaurant*

Qu'est-ce qu'ils mangent? Remplis le tableau ci-dessus

*What do they eat? Complete the table above*

## Exercice 21 A la banque

Tu entends des conversations à la banque

*You hear various conversations in a bank*

Choisis la bonne réponse

*Choose the correct answer*

**1** Le premier client voudrait changer
- des dollars ☐
- des francs belges ☐
- des livres sterling ☐

**2** Le taux de change est de
- FF 5, 70 ☐
- FF 7, 50 ☐
- FF 9, 50 ☐

**3** Il y a une commission de
- FF 5 ☐
- FF 10 ☐
- zéro ☐

**4** Le second client veut
- changer de l'argent ☐
- toucher un chèque ☐
- changer des chèques de voyage ☐

**5** Il montre
- une photo ☐
- sa carte d'identité ☐
- son passeport ☐

**6** Le troisième client
- trouve la banque excellente ☐
- est obligé d'aller à la poste ☐
- a des francs suisses ☐

## Exercice 22 Dans le bus

Tu entends des passagers acheter des tickets de bus

*You hear passengers buying bus tickets*

Complète le tableau

*Complete the table*

| | Combien de personnes | Direction | Prix |
|---|---|---|---|
| 1 | | | |
| 2 | | | |
| 3 | | | |
| 4 | | | |

## Exercice 23 A la gare SNCF

Tu entends ces conversations au guichet de la gare SNCF

*You hear these conversations at the railway ticket office*

Réponds aux questions

*Answer the questions*

### Dialogue 1:

**1** Où est-ce que la dame veut aller?

**2** A quelle heure part le train?

**3** C'est quel quai?

### Dialogue 2:

**1** Où est-ce que le monsieur veut aller?

**2** A quelle heure arrive le train?

**3** Est-ce qu'il faut changer?

### Dialogue 3:

**1** Quand est-ce que le monsieur voyage à Clermont-Ferrand?

**2** Est-ce qu'il a déjà acheté son billet?

**3** Quelle place préfère-t-il?

## Exercice 24 Pour aller à ...

On demande le chemin. Marque sur la carte le chemin indiqué

*Various people are asking the way. Mark their routes on the map*

1.

×

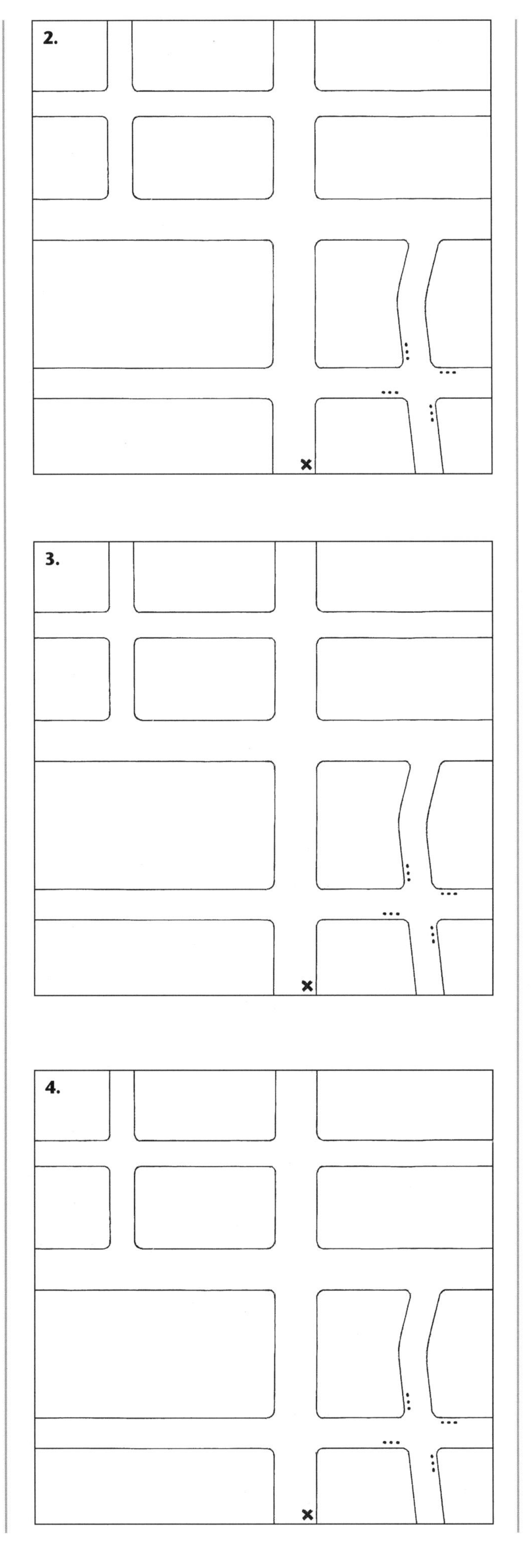


## Exercice 25 Au marché

Ecoute des conversations au marché

*Listen to some conversations at the market*

Remplis le tableau

*Fill in the table*

| | On achète | Prix |
|---|---|---|
| 1 | | |
| 2 | | |
| 3 | | |
| 4 | | |
| 5 | | |

## Exercice 26 La mode

Martine et Louise parlent de leurs vêtements préférés

*Martine and Louise are talking about their favourite clothes*

Fais la liste des vêtements mentionnés par les deux filles

*List the clothes mentioned by the two girls*

| Martine | Louise |
|---|---|
| | |

# Listening: *answers*

## Exercice 1 C'est quel numéro?

Eventually all the numbers on each card are called.

### Transcript (each number is repeated once):

**A**

trois, cinq, un, deux, dix-sept, vingt, dix, onze, treize, douze, quinze, seize, sept, neuf, quatre, dix-neuf, six

**B**

trente, cinquante, vingt, vingt-deux, vingt-trois, quarante et un, soixante-neuf, quarante-deux, quarante-quatre, quarante-cinq, vingt-neuf, trente-trois, cinquante-neuf, soixante, vingt-six, vingt-sept, vingt-huit, trente-huit, trente-neuf, quarante

## Exercice 2 Comment est-ce qu'on écrit ton nom?

L'alphabet français:

*The French alphabet*

### Transcript:

a b c d e f g h i j k l m n o p q r s t u v w x y z accent aigu (´), accent grave(`), accent circonflexe(^), c cédille(ç), e tréma (ë), deux p (pp), deux l (ll), deux r (rr), deux s (ss)

**A** Ecris les noms de famille que tu vas entendre

### Transcript:

**1** Legrand
**2** Jaulin
**3** Girard
**4** Daugé
**5** Dubois

**B** Ecris les noms des villes françaises où ces personnnes habitent

### Transcript:

**1** Moi, j'habite Dieppe, D I E P P E
**2** Moi, j'habite Nancy, N A N C Y
**3** Moi, j'habite Lille. Ça s'écrit L I L L E
**4** Moi, j'habite Avignon, au sud de la France. Ça s'écrit A V I G N O N
**5** Auxerre, c'est ma ville. Ça s'écrit A U X E R R E

### Answers:

**1** Dieppe
**2** Nancy
**3** Lille
**4** Avignon
**5** Auxerre

## Exercice 3 Quelle heure est-il?

Ecris l'heure en chiffres

### Transcript:

**1** Il est une heure
**2** Il est trois heures
**3** Il est neuf heures
**4** Il est onze heures et demie
**5** Il est cinq heures cinq
**6** Il est six heures vingt
**7** Il est une heure et quart
**8** Il est trois heures moins le quart
**9** Il est huit heures moins dix
**10** Il est midi

### Answers:

**1** 1.00
**2** 3.00
**3** 9.00
**4** 11.30
**5** 5.05
**6** 6.20
**7** 1.15
**8** 2.45
**9** 7.50
**10** 12.00

## Exercice 4 On se présente

Six personnes se présentent. Ecris leurs détails dans les cases

### Transcript:

**1** Je m'appelle Vanessa Tillier T I L L I E R. J'ai 12 ans.
**2** Bonjour! Je m'appelle Max Bertrand B E R T R A N D. J'ai 13 ans
**3** Salut, je m'appelle Marie Rodin. Ça s'écrit R O D I N. Moi, j'ai 20 ans
**4** Bonjour! Je me présente. Je m'appelle Pierre Lemoine L E M O I N E. J'ai 14 ans
**5** Je m'appelle Sophie Girard. G I R A R D. Moi, j'ai 16 ans
**6** Je m'appelle Patrick Hervé H E R V E avec e accent aigu à la fin. J'ai 11 ans

### Answers:

| Numéro | prénom | nom de famille | âge (ans) |
|---|---|---|---|
| 1 | Vanessa | Tillier | 12 |
| 2 | Max | Bertrand | 13 |
| 3 | Marie | Rodin | 20 |

| Numéro | prénom | nom de famille | âge (ans) |
|---|---|---|---|
| 4 | Pierre | Lemoine | 14 |
| 5 | Sophie | Girard | 16 |
| 6 | Patrick | Hervé | 11 |

## Exercice 5 Les numéros de téléphone

Ecris les numéros de télephone que tu vas entendre

### Transcript:

**1** – As-tu le téléphone, Vanessa?
– Oui, mon numéro, c'est le 43.14.05.04

**2** – Et toi, Max, quel est ton numéro de téléphone?
– C'est le 40.28.00.19

**3** – Marie, quel est ton numéro de téléphone?
– C'est le 31.44.08.51

**4** – Pierre, quel est ton numéro de téléphone?
– C'est le 33.25.25.46

**5** – As-tu le téléphone, Sophie?
– Oui, mon numéro, c'est le 51.19.11.39

**6** – Et toi, Patrick, quel est ton numéro de téléphone?
– C'est le 32.40.06.44

### Answers:

| | nom | numéro de téléphone |
|---|---|---|
| 1 | Vanessa Tillier | 43.14.05.04 |
| 2 | Max Bertrand | 40.28.00.19 |
| 3 | Marie Rodin | 31.44.08.51 |
| 4 | Pierre Lemoine | 33.25.25.46 |
| 5 | Sophie Girard | 51.19.11.39 |
| 6 | Patrick Hervé | 32.40.06.44 |

## Exercice 6 Quelle est la date de ton anniversaire?

Quelle est la date de leur anniversaire? Remplis le tableau

### Transcript:

1 Vanessa: Mon anniversaire, c'est le vingt février
**2** Max: Je suis né le trente novembre
**3** Marie: Mon anniversaire, c'est le seize juin
**4** Pierre: Je suis né le deux juillet
**5** Sophie: Je suis née le dix décembre
**6** Patrick: Mon anniversaire, c'est le dix-neuf mai

### Answers:

| | nom | anniversaire |
|---|---|---|
| 1 | Vanessa Tillier | 20 février |
| 2 | Max Bertrand | 30 novembre |
| 3 | Marie Rodin | 16 juin |
| 4 | Pierre Lemoine | 2 juillet |
| 5 | Sophie Girard | 10 décembre |
| 6 | Patrick Hervé | 19 mai |

## Exercice 7 Ma famille et moi

Ecoute la cassette que tu as reçue de ton correspondant français. Complète le tableau

### Transcript:

Bonjour. Je m'appelle Daniel et j'ai 13 ans. J'habite avec mes parents à Arcachon, assez près de Bordeaux. J'ai un frère, Michel et une sœur, Marlène. Mon frère a 17 ans et il prépare son bac au lycée. Ma sœur a 11 ans et elle va avec moi au collège. Mon père est employé de bureau, et maman est mère au foyer. A la maison nous avons un chat, un chien et un cochon d'Inde. J'aime jouer au volley, nager, lire et regarder la télé.

### Answers:

| | |
|---|---|
| Nom | Daniel |
| Age | 13 |
| Domicile | Arcachon, près de Bordeaux |
| Frère | (a) Michel: 17 ans – au lycée |
| Sœur | (b) Marlène: 11 ans – au collège |
| Animaux domestiques | chat, chien, cochon d'Inde |
| Passetemps | volley, nager, lire, regarder la télé |

## Exercice 8 Les passetemps

Daniel parle maintenant de ses passetemps, et des passetemps de sa famille

### Transcript:

Alors, mes passetemps, oui. J'aime jouer au volley, nager, et lire. Je lis des magazines et des romans d'aventure. J'ai plus de 200 livres dans ma chambre. Le mercredi je vais à la piscine avec mes amis. Le samedi après-midi je joue au volley dans un club sportif. Mon équipe joue bien. Cette année nous sommes les champions régionaux

Ma sœur n'aime pas le sport. Elle aime la musique. Elle joue de la flûte et du piano.

Mon frère aime la musique, lui aussi. Il joue de la trompette et de la guitare.

Mes parents aiment danser. Ils dansent deux fois par semaine dans un club de danse. C'est très sérieux, la danse, avec eux! Mon père aime se promener avec le chien, et il fait toujours la cuisine chez nous. Ma mère est responsable du jardin. Elle aime cultiver des légumes comme des carottes, des laitues, des pommes de terre, etc.

Choisis la bonne expression pour faire une phrase. Coche la bonne case

### Answers:

**1** Daniel aime jouer **au volley**
**2** Il lit **des magazines**
**3** Il a plus de **200** livres dans sa chambre
**4** Son équipe est **excellente**
**5** Sa sœur joue **de la flûte**

| | | |
|---|---|---|
| **6** | Son frère | **aime la musique** |
| **7** | Ses parents | **aiment danser** |
| **8** | Chez Daniel, c'est | **son père** qui fait la cuisine |
| **9** | Le responsable du jardin, c'est | **sa mère** |
| **10** | C'est un jardin avec | **des légumes** |

## Exercice 9 La ville

Ton correspondant Damien a envoyé une brochure de sa ville. Il parle de la ville sur cassette.

### Transcript:

Je t'ai déjà dit que j'habite Saint Herblain. C'est dans la banlieue de Nantes, dans l'ouest de la France. Il y a beaucoup de bureaux ici, beaucoup d'immeubles, et un grand centre commercial, Atlantis. On peut aller à Nantes en tramway. Mes parents vont souvent à Nantes au théâtre et au cinéma.

Vrai ou faux? Ecris V ou F dans les cases

### Answers:

| | | |
|---|---|---|
| **1** | Saint Herblain est près de Paris | **F** |
| **2** | Il y a beaucoup d'industries à Saint Herblain | **F** |
| **3** | Atlantis, c'est un grand centre commercial | **V** |
| **4** | On peut aller à Nantes en tramway | **V** |
| **5** | Les parents vont au cinéma à Nantes | **V** |

## Exercice 10 La météo

Tu es en vacances en France et tu écoutes la météo à la radio. Dessine les symboles météo sur la carte de la France

### Transcript:

Aujourd'hui nous sommes le dimanche 15 mai. La météo. Au nord de la France le matin il va faire du brouillard. Au centre de la France le soleil va briller et il va faire chaud avec des températures vers 25 degrés. Dans le sud de la France il va faire beau, mais le soir il va pleuvoir. Il va y avoir des orages. A l'ouest de la France il va faire plus froid avec des températures vers 10 degrés, et il va pleuvoir. A l'est il va y avoir du vent, mais les températures ne seront pas trop cruelles: vers 17 degrés.

### Answers:

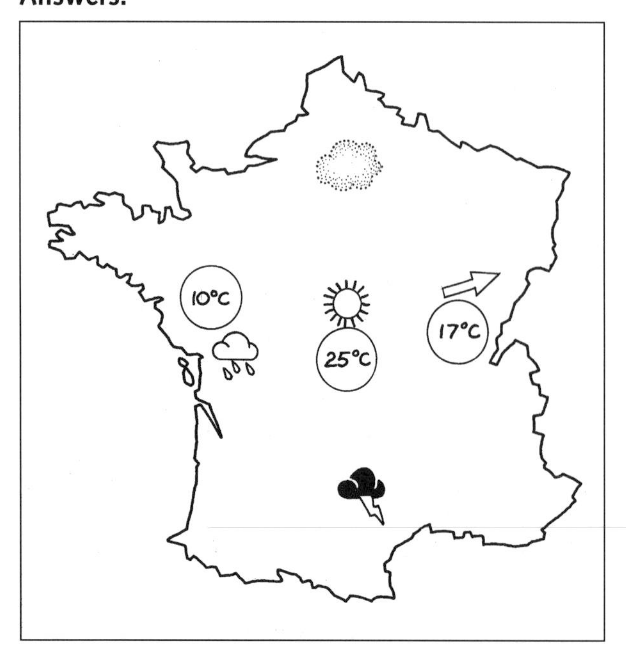


## Exercice 11 L'école

Julie va au collège Jules Verne à Nantes. Elle te parle de son collège

### Transcript:

Je suis en quatrième au collège à Nantes. Le collège est en centre ville.

J'y vais en bus. Le collège est grand, et très vieux. Il y a environ mille élèves et cent professeurs.

J'ai des classes le lundi, le mardi, le jeudi et le vendredi de huit heures à cinq heures. Nous avons une pause-déjeuner de deux heures. Le mercredi et le samedi il n'y a pas de classes l'après-midi. J'aime ça!

Je fais l'anglais en première langue vivante, et je fais aussi de l'espagnol. J'ai aussi des cours de français, de maths, de sciences naturelles, de biologie, d'histoire-géo, de musique, d'EMT, de sport et d'instruction civique. J'aime l'anglais et la musique, mais le reste, ce n'est pas très amusant, tu sais. Je suis forte en anglais et en français. Par contre je suis nulle en histoire-géo. Ça, c'est un désastre permanent pour moi.

**A** Indique les phrases qui sont correctes

### Answers:

| | | |
|---|---|---|
| **1** | Julie va au collège Jules Verne | **F** |
| **2** | Le collège est très moderne | **F** |
| **3** | Le collège est en centre ville | **V** |
| **4** | Le collège est petit | **F** |
| **5** | Le samedi, elle a des cours | **V** |
| **6** | Elle aime les mercredis | **V** |
| **7** | Elle aime beaucoup les maths | **F** |

**B** Ecoute encore une fois. Coche les cours qu'elle a

### Answers

| | |
|---|---|
| allemand | |
| chimie | |
| dessin | |
| français | ✓ |
| informatique | |
| instruction civique | ✓ |
| religion | |
| sport | ✓ |

## Exercice 12 Ma maison

Gabrielle parle de sa maison

### Transcript:

Mes parents et moi habitent une maison assez moderne. Il y a deux étages. Le garage est à gauche. A droite du garage il y a la porte d'entrée. A côté de la porte il y a une petite fenêtre pour les toilettes et une très grande fenêtre: c'est la salle de séjour. La cuisine et la salle à manger sont à l'arrière de la maison. Au premier étage il y a la fenêtre de la salle de bain à gauche, puis les fenêtres de deux chambres à droite. A l'arrière de la maison il y a les fenêtres des autres chambres à coucher.

Dessine la maison de Gabrielle dans le jardin

**Answer:**

## Exercice 13 Ma chambre

Gabrielle parle de sa chambre

**Transcript:**

Ma chambre est très belle et très grande. Il y a une moquette bleue et les murs sont bleus aussi. Les meubles sont en bois: un lit, une armoire, une table avec mon ordinateur et une table de nuit. J'ai aussi un vieux canapé de mes grands-parents et une table basse. La vue de la fenêtre est très jolie: on voit le jardin et, au loin, les montagnes.

Quels meubles a Gabrielle dans sa chambre? Coche les cases

**Answers:**

| | |
|---|---|
| un lit | ✓ |
| un fauteuil | |
| une table | ✓ |
| un canapé | ✓ |
| une armoire | ✓ |
| une chaise | |
| une table basse | ✓ |

## Exercice 14 Le ménage

Gabrielle aide ses parents

**Transcript:**

Je suis enfant unique. Je suis obligée d'aider mes parents avec le ménage. Je fais la vaisselle, je mets la table et je fais la cuisine le mercredi et le samedi. Mon père s'occupe de la voiture et de la cuisine. Ma mère travaille au jardin, et c'est elle qui passe l'aspirateur et qui fait la poussière. J'aime aider mes parents: c'est normal. Mais j'ai horreur de passer l'aspirateur: ça me donne des vibrations dans les bras!

Qui fait quoi chez Gabrielle? Coche les cases

**Answers:**

| | Gabrielle | sa mère | son père |
|---|---|---|---|
| la vaisselle | ✓ | | |
| mettre la table | ✓ | | |
| la cuisine | ✓ | | ✓ |
| le jardin | | ✓ | |
| la voiture | | | ✓ |
| passer l'aspirateur | | ✓ | |
| faire la poussière | | ✓ | |

## Exercice 15 L'argent de poche

Six jeunes personnes parlent de l'argent de poche. Complète le tableau

**Transcript:**

**1** Henri: Je m'appelle Henri. J'ai 20F d'argent de poche chaque semaine. J'achète des bonbons et des cadeaux, et je fais des économies pour acheter un ordinateur.

**2** Joëlle: Bonjour, je suis Joëlle. J'ai dix-sept ans. Mes parents ne me donnent pas d'argent de poche. Alors je gagne de l'argent dans un supermarché. Je travaille le samedi après-midi. Je gagne 250F. Je fais des économies pour me payer une voiture, mais je vais quelquefois au cinéma avec mon copain.

**3** Jean: Je m'appelle Jean. J'ai 10F par semaine. J'achète des magazines et des bonbons. Je ne fais pas d'économies.

**4** Olivier: Je m'appelle Olivier. J'ai de la chance, parce que mes parents sont très généreux: ils me donnent 50F par semaine. J'achète des choses pour mon scooter, et j'achète des vêtements. J'aime être cool et à la mode.

**5** Chantal: Je m'appelle Chantal Gravrand. Mes parents me donnent 30F comme argent de poche et je gagne aussi 50F. Je travaille dans le jardin d'un voisin. Je fais des économies pour les vacances. Je voudrais voyager en Amérique cet été.

**6** Claudine: Je m'appelle Claudine. Malheureusement, mon père est au chômage, alors chez nous il y a des problèmes. Pour moi, il n'y est pas question d'argent de poche.

## Answers:

| | nom | argent de poche | gagne | achète | économise pour acheter |
|---|---|---|---|---|---|
| 1 | Henri | 20F | 0F | bonbons, cadeaux | ordinateur |
| 2 | Joëlle | 0F | 250F | billets pour cinéma | voiture |
| 3 | Jean | 10F | 0F | magazines, bonbons | non |
| 4 | Olivier | 50F | 0F | choses pour scooter, vêtements | |
| 5 | Chantal | 30F | 50F | | voyage en Amérique |
| 6 | Claudine | 0F | 0F | rien | |

## Exercice 16 Au camping

Tu travailles à la réception d'un camping. Remplis les fiches

### Transcript:

**1** – Avez-vous encore de la place, s'il vous plaît?
– Oui, monsieur. Vous êtes combien?
– Nous sommes quatre.
– Avez-vous une tente?
– Non, nous avons une caravane.
– Vous restez combien de temps?
– Deux nuits.
– Votre nom, s'il vous plaît?
– Duroy.
– Comment est-ce que ça s'écrit?
– D U R O Y.
– Merci. Avez-vous besoin d'électricité?
– Oui, s'il vous plaît.
– Alors, prenez l'emplacement nº 17.

**2** – Bonjour, madame. Nous voulons rester deux nuits.
– Avez-vous encore de la place, s'il vous plaît?
– Oui, monsieur. Vous êtes combien?
– Nous sommes quatre, deux adultes et deux enfants.
– Avez-vous une caravane?
– Oui, nous avons une caravane.
– Votre nom, s'il vous plaît?
– Léonin.
– Ça s'écrit comment?
– L E O N I N.
– Merci. Avez-vous besoin d'électricité?
– Oui, s'il vous plaît.
– Alors, prenez l'emplacement nº 23.

**3** – Bonjour, madame. Qu'y a-t-il pour votre service?
– Avez-vous encore de la place, pour une nuit, s'il vous plaît?
– Oui, madame. Vous êtes combien?
– Nous sommes six.
– Avez-vous une tente ou une caravane?
– Nous avons deux tentes.
– C'est à quel nom?
– Menaec.
– Comment est-ce que ça s'écrit?
– M E N A E C.
– Alors, prenez les emplacements nº 54 et 55.

**4** – Bonjour, monsieur. Avez-vous encore de la place, s'il vous plaît?
– Oui, monsieur. Vous restez combien de temps?
– Une semaine, si possible.
– Avez-vous une tente ou une caravane?
– Nous avons une caravane.
– Pour combien de personnes?
– Nous sommes deux adultes.
– C'est à quel nom, s'il vous plaît?
– Berger.
– Comment est-ce que ça s'écrit?
– B E R G E R.
– Merci. Avez-vous besoin d'électricité?
– Oui, s'il vous plaît.
– Alors, prenez l'emplacement nº 34.

### Answers:

**1.**
*Nom* **DUROY**
*Durée du séjour:* **2** *nuits*
*Personnes:* **4**
*Emplacement nº:* **17**
*Tente* oui/**non** *Caravane* **oui**/non
*Electricité* **oui**/non

**2.**
*Nom* **LÉONIN**
*Durée du séjour:* **2** *nuits*
*Personnes:* **4**
*Emplacement nº:* **23**
*Tente* oui/**non** *Caravane* **oui**/non
*Electricité* **oui**/non

**3.**
*Nom* **MENAEC**
*Durée du séjour:* **1** *nuits*
*Personnes:* **6**
*Emplacement nº:* **54 et 55**
*Tente* **oui**/non *Caravane* oui/**non**
*Electricité* oui/**non**

**4.**

*Nom* **BERGER**

*Durée du séjour:* **7** *nuits*

*Personnes:* **2**

*Emplacement nº:* **34**

*Tente* oui/**non** *Caravane* **oui**/non

*Electricité* **oui**/non

## Exercice 17 On prend rendez-vous

Ecoute ces personnes qui prennent rendez-vous au cabinet du médecin

**LUNDI**

**MARDI**

**MERCREDI**
15h
François Mulhouse

**JEUDI**
15h 30
Gisèle Lamartine

**VENDREDI**
8h 45
Marie Lenoir

**SAMEDI**
11h
Thomas Lazio

**DIMANCHE**

**Transcript:**

**1**
- Cabinet du Dr Meyer, bonjour.
- Bonjour. Je voudrais un rendez-vous, s'il vous plaît
- Oui, Pouvez-vous venir mercredi à 15h?
- Mercredi à trois heures, oui, ça va, merci.
- Votre nom, s'il vous plaît?
- François Mulhouse.
- Alors, M. Mulhouse, votre rendez-vous est mercredi à quinze heures.
- Au revoir, madame.

**2**
- Cabinet du Dr Meyer, bonjour.
- Allô. C'est Gisèle Lamartine. Je voudrais un rendez-vous jeudi après-midi. C'est possible?
- Oui, madame. Le docteur Meyer peut vous recevoir jeudi à trois heures et demie.
- Merci, c'est excellent. Alors, jeudi à trois heures et demie. Au revoir.
- Au revoir, madame.

**3**
- Cabinet du Dr Meyer, bonjour.
- Bonjour. J'ai besoin de voir un médecin d'urgence. C'est pour ma fille. Elle est malade. Elle a de la fièvre et elle est toute rouge. Elle s'appelle Marie Lenoir, et elle a dix ans.
- Bon, alors en principe nous ouvrons à neuf heures. Mais amenez votre fille Vendredi à neuf heures moins le quart. C'est le plus tôt possible.
- Merci. Nous venons alors à neuf heures moins le quart.

**4**
- Cabinet du Dr Meyer, bonjour.
- Bonjour, je m'appelle Thomas Lazio. Je voudrais voir le médecin. C'est à cause de mon dos.
- Oui, voyons, vendredi à 17h?
- Non, je travaille à 17 heures. Vous avez une possibilité le matin?
- Oui, c'est possible samedi à onze heures.
- C'est bon: samedi à onze heures. Merci, madame.
- Je vous en prie, monsieur. Au revoir, monsieur.

## Exercice 18 Au cabinet du médecin

Qu'est-ce qui ne va pas? Quels sont les remèdes recommandés par le médecin?

Joins les images et les remèdes

**Transcript:**

**1**
- Alors, où avez-vous mal?
- J'ai mal à la gorge depuis quatre jours. Je tousse beaucoup.
- Je vais regarder. Ouvrez la bouche, s'il vous plaît. Aha, c'est tout rouge. Je vous donne une ordonnance pour des antibiotiques. Vous les trouverez à la pharmacie.
- Merci, docteur.

**2**
- Bonjour, madame. Qu'est-ce que vous avez?
- C'est mon dos. J'ai horriblement mal au dos.
- Oui. Alors. Prenez de l'aspirine ou un autre analgésique et reposez-vous.
- Merci, docteur.

**3**
- Bonjour, monsieur. Qu'est-ce que vous avez?
- J'ai mal au ventre et j'ai la diarrhée.
- Aha. Je vais voir cela. Est-ce que ça fait mal ici?
- Oui, aïe! ouille!
- Ce n'est pas très grave. Mais je vous donne une ordonnance pour un sirop calmant. Vous le trouverez à la pharmacie.
- Merci, docteur.

**4** – Alors, Eric. Qu'est-ce que tu as fait?
– Je me suis coupé la main avec mon couteau de modellisme.
– Tu dois faire attention. Fais voir. Oui, tu t'es bien coupé. Je vais te mettre un pansement. Et je te donne une ordonnance pour une crème antiseptique. Tu la trouveras à la pharmacie.
– Merci, docteur.

## Exercice 19 Au café

On commande à boire et à manger dans un café

### Transcript:

**1** – Qu'y a-t-il pour votre service, monsieur?
– Deux cafés-crème, s'il vous plaît.
– Des grands ou des petits?
– Des grands, s'il vous plaît.

**2** – Qu'y a-t-il pour votre service, madame?
– Un thé-citron, s'il vous plaît, et un sandwich au jambon.
– Tout de suite.

**3** – Mademoiselle?
– Deux cocas, s'il vous plaît. Vous avez des glaces?
– Oui, mademoiselle. Nous avons vanille, fraise, chocolat, café, pistache.
– Alors, une glace au chocolat et une glace à la fraise, s'il vous plaît.
– Alors ça vous fait deux cocas, une glace au chocolat et une glace à la fraise.

**4** – Monsieur!
– Oui, madame. Qu'y a-t-il pour votre service?
– Un chocolat chaud et un croissant, s'il vous plaît.
– Tout de suite, madame.

Vrai ou faux? Ecris V ou F dans la case

### Answers:

| | | |
|---|---|---|
| **1** | Le monsieur commande un café noir | **F** |
| | Il commande deux grands cafés | **V** |
| **2** | La dame commande un thé-citron | **V** |
| | Elle n'aime pas le jambon | **F** |
| **3** | La jeune fille commande de la limonade | **F** |
| | Elle commande une glace à la fraise et une glace au chocolat | **V** |
| **4** | La dame commande un chocolat chaud | **V** |
| | Elle n'a pas faim | **F** |

## Exercice 20 Au restaurant

La famille Bertillon mange au restaurant

Qu'est-ce qu'ils mangent? Remplis le tableau

### Transcript:

– Vous avez choisi, messieurs-dames?
– Oui, madame.
– Qu'est-ce que vous prenez comme hors d'œuvre?
– Madame prend des crudités. Ma fille prend du pâté maison. Mon fils prend des œufs à la russe, et moi je prends des crudités, comme madame.
– Et ensuite?
– Madame prend du poulet, ma fille du poulet aussi. Mon fils et moi, nous prenons tous les deux du bœuf bourguignon.
– Comme dessert?
– Des glaces pour tout le monde, s'il vous plaît, madame.
– Et comme boisson?
– De l'eau minérale et un demi de vin rouge, s'il vous plaît.

**Answers:**

| personne | hors d'œuvre | plat principal | dessert |
|---|---|---|---|
| maman | crudités | poulet | glace |
| fille | pâté | poulet | glace |
| fils | œufs à la russe | bœuf bourguignon | glace |
| papa | crudités | bœuf bourguignon | glace |

## Exercice 21 A la banque

Tu entends des conversations à la banque

### Transcript:

1 – Bonjour, je voudrais changer de l'argent.
– Oui, monsieur. Qu'est-ce vous désirez changer?
– J'ai 50 livres sterling.
– C'est bon.
– Quel est le taux de change?
– La livre vaut 7,50 FF. Alors, ça vous fait 365 francs, c'est à dire 375 francs moins 10F de commission.

2 – Bonjour, madame. Je voudrais changer des chèques de voyage.
– Oui, monsieur. Avez-vous une pièce d'identité?
– Voilà mon passeport.
– Signez ici, s'il vous plaît.

3 – Bonjour, madame. Je voudrais changer des francs belges en francs français.
– Je regrette, monsieur, nous ne faisons pas de change ici. Le plus facile pour vous, c'est d'aller à la poste, c'est juste en face.

Choisis la bonne réponse

### Answers:

1 Le premier client voudrait changer
***des livres sterling***

2 Le taux de change est de
***FF7, 50***

3 Il y a une commission de
***FF10***

4 Le second client veut changer
***des chèques de voyage***

5 Il montre
***son passeport***

6 Le troisième client
***est obligé d'aller à la poste***

## Exercice 22 Dans le bus

Tu entends des passagers acheter des tickets de bus

Complète le tableau

### Transcript:

1 – Un ticket pour l'hôtel de ville, s'il vous plaît.
– Trois francs.
– Est-ce que je peux descendre à l'hôtel de ville?
– Oui, le bus s'arrête juste devant l'hôtel de ville.

2 – Deux tickets pour aller à la piscine, s'il vous plaît
– Sept francs. Merci.

3 – Un adulte et un enfant. Deux tickets pour aller à la gare SNCF, s'il vous plaît.
– Ça fait quatre francs cinquante, s'il vous plaît.

4 – Deux tickets pour le château, s'il vous plaît, monsieur.
– Vous avez quel âge?
– Moi j'ai dix-sept ans et ma sœur a treize ans.
– Alors, ça fait un adulte et un enfant, 4F 50.

### Answers:

| | Combien de personnes | Direction | Prix |
|---|---|---|---|
| 1 | 1 | hôtel de ville | FF3,00 |
| 2 | 2 | piscine | FF7,00 |
| 3 | 2 | gare SNCF | FF4,50 |
| 4 | 2 | château | FF4,50 |

## Exercice 23 A la gare SNCF

Tu entends ces conversations au guichet de la gare SNCF

### Transcript:

1 – Bonjour, monsieur. A quelle heure part le prochain train pour Calais?
– A 13h45.
– Un billet simple pour Calais, s'il vous plaît.
– En seconde?
– Oui, en seconde.
– 35 francs, s'il vous plaît, madame.
– C'est quel quai?
– N° 9.
– Merci, monsieur.

2 – Je voudrais aller à Genève, jeudi soir.
– Oui, monsieur, vous avez un train à 19h.
– Quand est-ce qu'il arrive à Genève?
– A 23h 5.
– Est-ce qu'il faut changer?
– Non, c'est direct.
– Merci, madame.

3 – Je voyage à Clermont-Ferrand vendredi matin. Est-ce que je peux réserver une place?
– Vous voyagez avec quel train, monsieur?.
– Avec le train de 10h. Voici mon billet.
– Oui, c'est bon.
– Préférez-vous une place près de la fenêtre ou une place centrale?
– Une place près de la fenêtre, s'il vous plaît.

– C'est bon, monsieur. Votre place est dans la voiture C, place nº 29.

Réponds aux questions

## Answers

### Dialogue 1:

**1** Où est-ce que la dame veut aller?
***Calais***

**2** A quelle heure part le train?
***13h45***

**3** C'est quel quai?
***nº9***

### Dialogue 2:

**1** Où est-ce que le monsieur veut aller?
***Genève***

**2** A quelle heure arrive le train?
***23h 45***

**3** Est-ce qu'il faut changer?
***non***

### Dialogue 3:

**1** Quand est-ce que le monsieur voyage à Clermont-Ferrand?
***vendredi, 10h***

**2** Est-ce qu'il a déjà acheté son billet?
***oui***

**3** Quelle place préfère-t-il?
***une place près de la fenêtre***

## Exercice 24 Pour aller à ...

On demande le chemin. Marque sur la carte le chemin indiqué

### Transcript:

**1** – Pardon, monsieur, pour aller à la gare SNCF, s'il vous plaît?
– La gare SNCF, voyons. Oui. Allez tout droit et prenez la deuxième rue à gauche. La gare SNCF est à droite.
– Merci, monsieur.
– De rien.

**2** – Pardon, madame, est-ce qu'il y a un café par ici?
– Un café? Oui, il y a un café place John F Kennedy.
– Et pour aller à la place John F Kennedy?
– Ce n'est pas loin. Tournez à droite au coin de la rue, puis tout droit aux feux: le café est en face.
– Merci, madame.
– Je vous en prie.

**3** – Bonjour, monsieur. Pouvez-vous me dire où se trouve le musée?
– Naturellement. C'est un peu compliqué. Allez tout droit et prenez la troisième rue à gauche, puis la première à droite.
– C'est loin d'ici?
– A environ deux kilomètres.
– Oh, bof, ça va. Merci monsieur.
– Bonne journée.

**4** – Bonjour, madame. Pour aller à l'hôtel de ville, s'il vous plaît?
– Oui. C'est tout près. Allez à droite, ici, et tournez à gauche aux feux. L'hôtel de ville est à droite à côté de la poste.
– Merci, madame.
– Je vous en prie, monsieur.

### Answers:

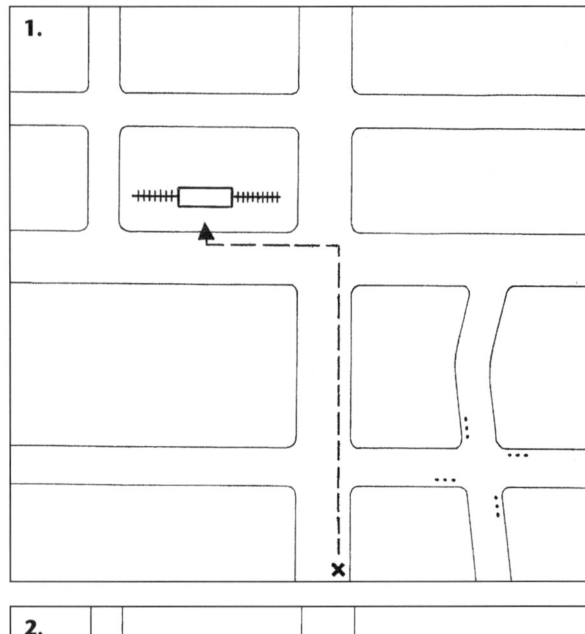

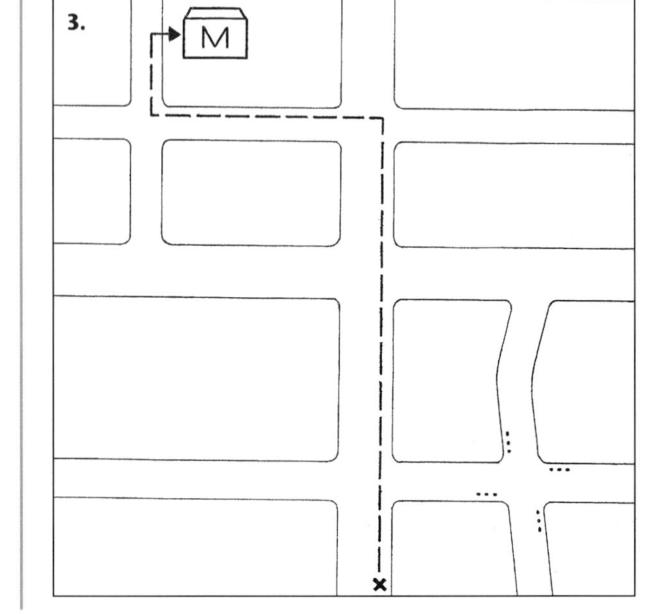

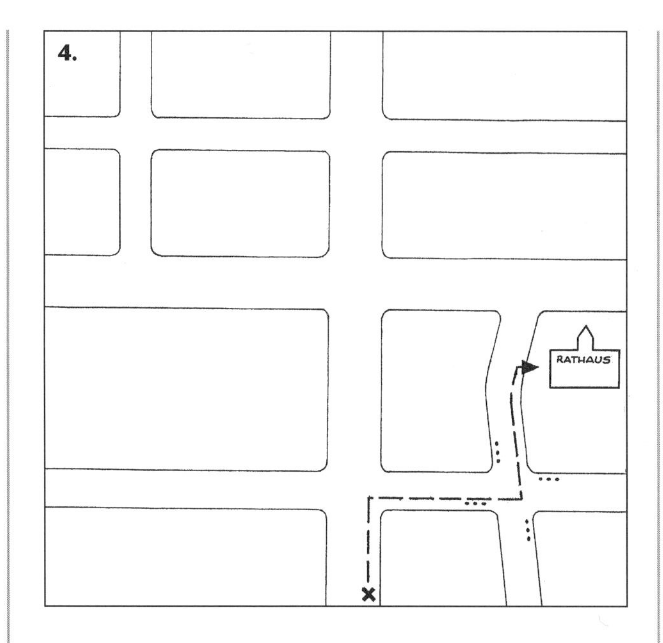


## Exercice 25 Au marché

Ecoute des conversations au marché

### Transcript:

**1** – Vous désirez?
– Trois pommes, s'il vous plaît.
– Et avec cela?
– Un kilo de pommes de terre et cinq cents grammes de tomates.
– Voilà, madame. Ça fait 15F, s'il vous plaît.

**2** – Bonjour, monsieur. Avez-vous des pêches?
– Oui, 4F le kilo.
– Alors un kilo de pêches, et six bananes.
– Et avec cela?
– C'est tout, merci.
– Ça fait 7F, s'il vous plaît.

**3** – Bonjour, madame.
– Bonjour, monsieur.
– Je voudrais trois melons, s'il vous plaît.
– C'est tout?
– Oui, c'est tout.
– Ça fait 15F, monsieur.

**4** – Bonjour, madame.
– Bonjour, Monsieur Paletot. Vous désirez?
– 250g de fraises, s'il vous plaît, et un citron.
– Et avec cela?
– Une grosse laitue bien fraîche.
– Voilà, Monsieur Paletot. Ça vous fait 19F.

**5** – Vous désirez, madame?
– Un kilo de haricots verts.
– Et avec ça?
– Une pastèque et 250 grammes de cerises.
– C'est tout?
– Oui, c'est tout.
– Merci. Ça fait 13F50.

Remplis le tableau:

### Answers:

| | On achète | Prix |
|---|---|---|
| 1 | pommes, pommes de terre, tomates | 15F |
| 2 | pêches, bananes | 7F |
| 3 | melons | 15F |
| 4 | fraises, citron, laitue | 19F |
| 5 | haricots verts, pastèque, cerises | 13F50 |

## Exercice 26 La mode

Martine et Louise parlent de leurs vêtements préférés

### Transcript:

**Martine:**

J'aime les vêtements confortables. Je porte souvent un jean bleu, ou un pantalon en velours. J'aime les T-shirts: c'est chic, c'est moderne, et ce n'est pas cher du tout. S'il fait froid je porte un pull. Mon pull favori est en laine écossaise. Je n'aime pas les collants et les jupes. Ce n'est pas pratique et l'hiver, ce n'est pas assez chaud.

**Louise:**

Pour moi, il est important d'avoir quelque chose de chic. Je porte de préférence une jupe bleu foncé avec un collant et des talons. Avec un chemisier en soie et une veste, c'est bien vu partout. Pour ne pas avoir froid l'hiver, il faut un bon manteau en laine et un copain avec une voiture. Un copain doit bien servir à quelque chose!

Fais la liste des vêtements mentionnés par les deux filles

### Answers:

| Martine | Louise |
|---|---|
| jean bleu, pantalon en velours, T-shirt, pull, collant, jupe | jupe bleu foncé, collant, talons, chemisier en soie, veste, manteau |

# Reading: *questions*

## Introduction

Reading tasks are perhaps one of the easiest in language-learning. Usually you will be able to understand more than you are able to use actively.

## Strategies for understanding

You need to develop strategies for helping you to work out what you don't understand at first. Many students forget that French and English are, in fact, related (1066 and all that). This means that there are many points of similarity between the two languages.

These include the following:

*(a)* most adverbs changing from *'-ment'* to *'-ly'* in English

**Examples:**
complètement, rarement

*(b)* verbs removing the final *'r'* to give the English

**Examples:**
admirer, compléter, arriver

*(c)* verbs ending in *'-er'* changing to *'-ate'* in English

**Example:**
décorer

*(d)* words ending in *'-el'* changing to *'-al'* in English

**Examples:**
officiel, individuel

*(e)* words ending in *'-aire'* changing to '-ar' or *'-ary'* in English

**Examples:**
populaire, militaire

*(f)* words ending in *'-e, -é* or *-ée'* changing to *'-y'* in English

**Examples:**
économie, partie, liberté, armée

*(g)* words ending in *'-e'* lose it in English

**Examples:**
branche, signe, vaste, uniforme

*(h)* words gain an *'-e'* in English

**Examples:**
pur, futur, féminin

If you analyse words a little more closely, you will find some equivalent prefixes (syllables put on the front of a word) and suffixes (syllables put on the end of a word) in French and English.

### French-English Examples

**Prefixes**

| | | | |
|---|---|---|---|
| dé- | *dis-* | décourager | *to discourage* |
| | | découvrir | *to discover* |
| | | déçu | *disappointed* |
| | | dégoûtant | *disgusting* |
| | | déguiser | *to disguise* |
| | | détruire | *to destroy* |
| dé(s)- | *de-, un-* | démolir | *to demolish* |
| | | se déshabiller | *to get undressed* |
| éc- | *sc-, sq-* | école | *school* |
| | | Ecosse | *Scotland* |
| | | échelle | *musical scale; ladder* |
| | | écran | *screen* |
| ép- | *sp-* | épeler | *to spell* |
| | | épice | *spice* |
| | | éponge | *sponge* |
| ét- | *st-* | établissement | *establishment* |
| | | état | *state* |
| | | étranger | *stranger* |
| | | étudiant | *student* |
| im-, in- | *un-, in-* | impoli | *impolite* |
| | | incroyable | *unbelievable* |
| pré- | *fore-* | prénom | *first name, forename* |
| | | prévoir | *to foresee* |
| re- | *re-, again* | recommencer | *to begin again* |
| | | rentrer | *to return* |
| | | retrouver | *to meet, find again* |
| | | revenir | *to come back* |
| sou-, sous- | *sub-, under-* | sous-sol | *basement* |
| | | souterrain | *underground* |
| | | sous-marin | *submarine* |

**Suffixes**

| | | | |
|---|---|---|---|
| -aine | *about* | dixaine | *about 10* |
| | | douzaine | *dozen (about 12)* |
| | | centaine | *about 100* |
| -é | *-ed* | enlevé | *removed* |
| | | fatigué | *tired* |
| | | situé | *situated* |
| -er, -ier | *profession/ classification* | boucher | *butcher* |
| | | pâtissier | *pastry-cook, confectioner* |
| | | vacancier | *holiday-maker* |
| | | voilier | *sailing-boat* |
| -er | *tree* | bananier | *banana tree* |
| | | cerisier | *cherry tree* |
| | | oranger | *orange tree* |
| | | pommier | *apple tree* |
| -eur | *-er, -or* | acteur | actor |
| | | chanteur | singer |

| | | | |
|---|---|---|---|
| | | directeur | *director* |
| | | mineur | *miner, minor* |
| -eur | *-ness* | blancheur | *whiteness* |
| | | douceur | *sweetness* |
| | | hauteur | *highness: height* |
| -eux | *-ous* | curieux | *curious* |
| | | désastreux | *disastrous* |
| | | ingénieux | *ingenious* |
| | | merveilleux | *marvellous* |
| | | précieux | *precious* |
| -ir | *-ish* | abolir | *abolish* |
| | | finir | *finish* |
| | | punir | *punish* |
| -oire | *-ory* | gloire | *glory* |
| | | laboratoire | *laboratory* |
| | | réfectoire | *refectory, canteen* |
| -té | *-ty* | beauté | *beauty* |
| | | cité | *city* |
| | | difficulté | *difficulty* |
| | | facilité | *facility* |

Finally, it may be worth noting that where there is a circumflex (^) in French, there is often an *-s-* in English. For example:

| | |
|---|---|
| août | *August* |
| coûter | *to cost* |
| dégoûtant | *disgusting* |
| forêt | *forest* |
| île | *isle, island* |
| intérêt | *interest* |
| pâte | *paste, pasta* |
| prêtre | *priest* |
| rôti | *roast* |

## False friends

There are many words in French which look like English ones, but which have different meanings. Make sure you are aware of them! Check the list below:

| **French word** | **English meaning** | |
|---|---|---|
| le car | *coach* | (**not** car) |
| la cave | *cellar* | (**not** cave) |
| complet | *full, no vacancies* | (**not** finished) |
| la correspondance | *place to change trains* | (**not** always letters) |
| un hôtel de ville | *town hall* | (**not** hotel) |
| la journée | *day* | (**not** journey) |
| la monnaie | *change* | (**not** always money) |
| le parfum | *flavour* | (**not** always perfume) |
| passer | *to spend time* | (**not** always to pass) |
| la place | *square* | (**not** always a place) |
| le quai | *platform* | (**not** always a jetty) |
| large | *wide* | (**not** large) |

## Varieties of reading exercises

Many of the passages you are asked to read will be short. Some of them will be very short. The sort of thing you can expect include (roughly arranged in order of difficulty):

*(a)* public signs and notices
*(b)* road signs
*(c)* tickets, town plans, road maps
*(d)* simple instructions
*(e)* menus, labels on food and drink
*(f)* timetables (school and public transport)
*(g)* notes left by other people
*(h)* advertisements and special offers; handbills
*(i)* guides and brochures concerning entertainment, sport, tourist attractions
*(j)* informal letters from a French-speaking person; invitations
*(k)* formal letters
*(l)* newspaper and magazine articles
*(m)* imaginative writing

## Dealing with longer texts

When you face a longer reading passage, take the time to read it through once without immediately looking up words in a dictionary or glossary. Try to work out the general gist of the piece, what it is about. Then take a look at the questions and make sure you understand them. Next, read the text again and see where you will find the answers to the questions. Usually the questions on a passage follow the sequence of the passage, so the first one will refer to the first paragraph, and so on.

You will see that in this way you can manage most texts without a dictionary. Don't start looking up every single new word, but just those which seem to be really necessary. When you use a dictionary, take care which translation or meaning is given. Often a word can have several meanings, depending on the context. So don't assume the first one given is the correct one. If you are not sure, look up the word in the other 'end' of the dictionary. If the word you are given is not the same as the one you started with: beware!

## Question words and likely answers

Many of the questions will be seeking an answer about:

Who?
What?
Where?
When?
How long?
How many?
How much?
Why?

These are the vocabulary topics which are most likely to be covered by each of those questions:

| | |
|---|---|
| Who? | • family and friends<br>• professions<br>• descriptions: physical appearance, size, age, etc. |
| What? | • covers virtually all objects, prices, and instructions and activities<br>• food and drink, and free time and entertainment |
| Where? | • positions and prepositions<br>• location of buildings in town and country<br>• countries<br>• directions and distances |
| When? | • time – by the 12- and 24-hour clock<br>• time in relation to other events |
| How long? | • time, especially duration |
| How many? | • numbers |
| How much? | • quantity<br>• numbers |
| Why? | • reasons |

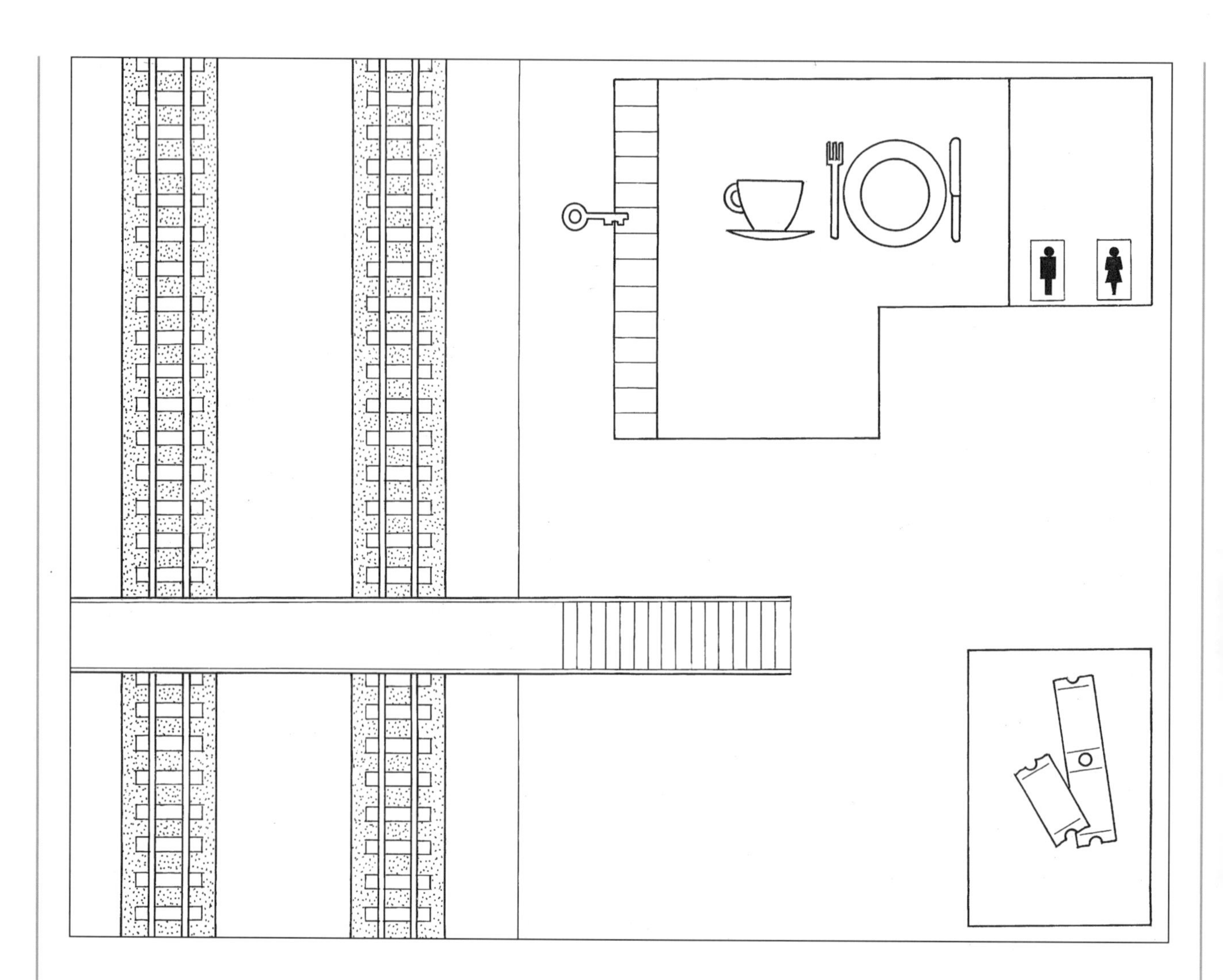

## Exercice 1 A la gare

Joins les panneaux avec les bons endroits sur le plan

*Match the signs to the correct places on the plan at the top of the page.*

**buffet les consignes automatiques**
**guichet quai les WC**

## Exercice 2 En ville

Où est-ce que je peux trouver...? Ecris la bonne lettre dans la case

*Where can I find...? Write the correct letter in the box*

1 de l'aspirine? ☐
2 du mouton? ☐
3 du pain? ☐
4 du fromage? ☐
5 une carte postale? ☐

## Exercice 3 Le plan de la ville

C'est quelle lettre?

*Which letter is it?*

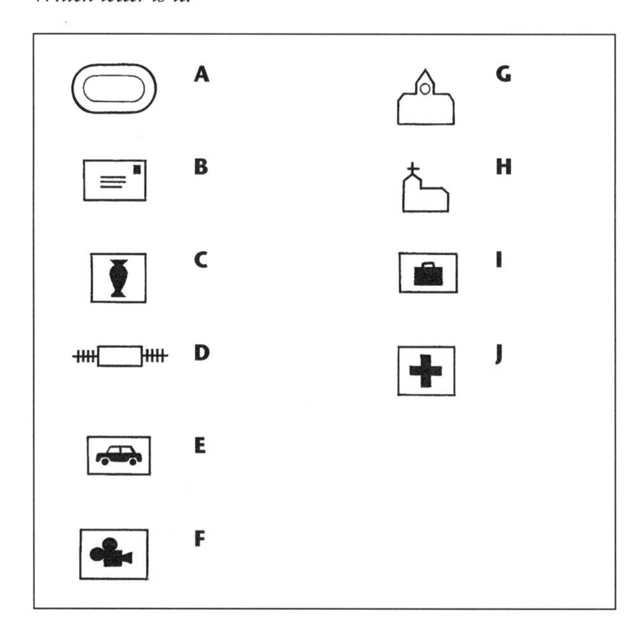


**1** le cinéma ☐
**2** l'église ☐
**3** la gare SNCF ☐
**4** l'hôpital ☐
**5** l'hôtel de ville ☐
**6** le musée ☐
**7** l'office de tourisme ☐
**8** le parking ☐
**9** la poste ☐
**10** le stade ☐

## Exercice 4 On fait des canapés

Mets dans le bon ordre

*Put the pictures in the right order*

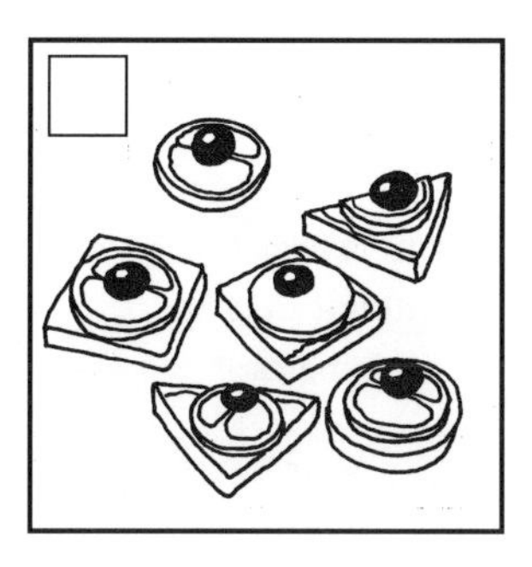

Garnissez les tranches de pain avec des tomates, des œufs durs, des radis, des carottes, des olives

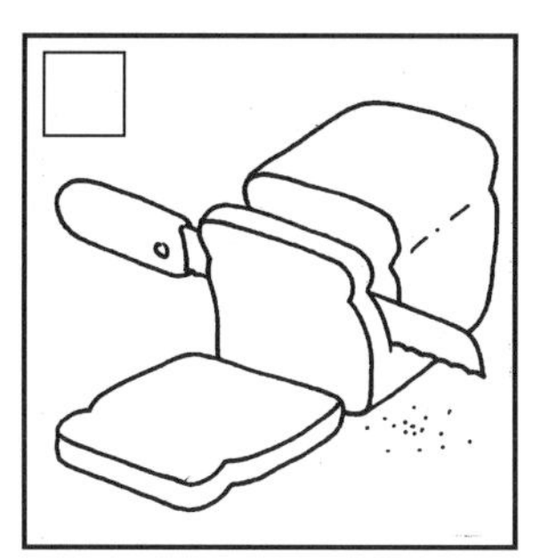

Coupez des tranches de pain de mie

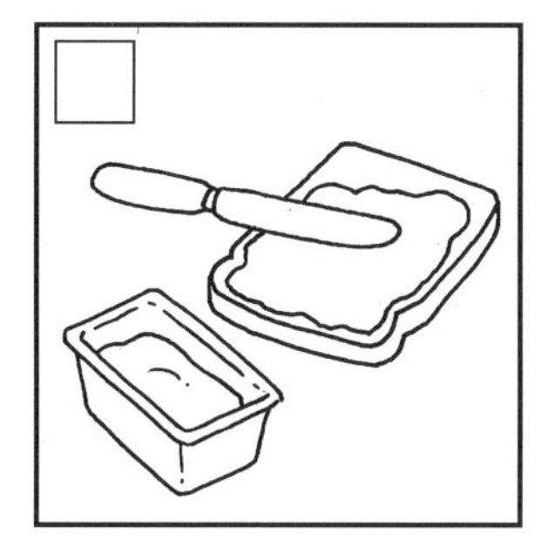

Tartinez-les avec du beurre

Coupez les tartines de pain en triangle, en rond, en rectangle

## Exercice 5 Un menu

Qu'est-ce que tu as commandé? Ecris en anglais les cinq choses que tu as commandées de ce menu

*What did you order? Write in English the five courses you have chosen from this menu*

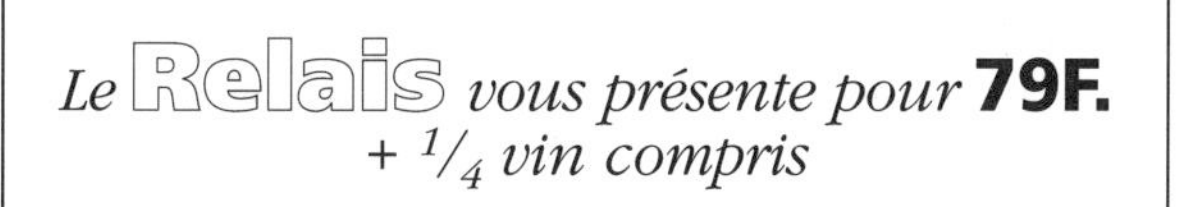


*Hors d'oeure varies*
*Salade de tomates*
*Sardines beurre*
*Oeuf au plat*
*Melon Suppl. 2F*
*Jambon de Paris*
*Pâté de campagne*
*Escargols de Bourgogne (les six) Suppl. 4F*

*Sole Frite*
*Haddock beurre*
*Colin froid mayonnaise*
*Steack grillé*
*Escalope de veau*
*Poulet roti*
*Assiette anglaise*
*$^1/_4$ de poulet froid mayonnaise*

*Liqumes au choix: Haricots verts • Petits pois*
*Riz • Frites • Salad de saison*

*Fromages: Camembert • Petits Suisses • Chévre*
*Yaourt*
*Patisseries: Tarte maison • Gâtëua au chocolat*
*Fruits: Pêche • Poire • Banane*
*Glaces: Pêche Melba • Cassatte aux fruits*
*Café express 2F*

Couvert compris Service non compris
Consultez notre carte des vins

## Exercice 6 L'emploi du temps de Joël

Regarde l'emploi du temps de Joël. Réponds aux questions en français

*Look at Joël's timetable. Answer the questions in French*

| | lundi | mardi | jeudi | vendredi | samedi |
|---|---|---|---|---|---|
| 8.30 – 9.25 | français | maths | anglais | maths | français |
| 9.25 – 10.20 | dessin | géographie | français | géographie | anglais |
| ← | | récréation | | | → |
| 10.35 – 11.30 | éducation physique | sciences physiques | maths | histoire | éducation physique |
| 11.30 – 12.25 | anglais | | anglais renforcé | étude | |
| ← | | déjeuner | | | → |
| 13.30 – 14.25 | maths | travaux pratiques | travaux pratiques | français | |
| 14.25 – 15.20 | étude | biologie | | anglais | |
| ← | | récréation | | | → |
| 15.35 – 16.30 | musique | français | histoire | anglais reinforcé | |

1 A quelle heure commencent les classes?
2 Combien de leçons de maths a-t-il par semaine?
3 Qu'est-ce qu'il a le vendredi après le déjeuner?
4 Combien de langues étrangères est-ce qu'il apprend?
5 Quels jours a-t-il de l'éducation physique?

## Exercice 7 Un message

Lis ce message

Read this message
Vrai ou faux?

Marlène a téléphoné à 2 h.
Elle demande : Est-ce que tu peux
jouer au tennis ce soir?
Si oui - vas la chercher chez
elle à 6 h !
Si non - Elle veut jouer au tennis
au parc public
Samedi à Cinq heures avec tout le
monde.

*True or false?*

1 Marlène a téléphoné à trois heures
2 Marlène veut jouer au tennis ce soir
3 Marlène veut jouer au tennis à cinq heures
4 Marlène joue au tennis au centre sportif
5 Tout le monde joue au tennis samedi

## Exercice 8 L'hôtel Fimotel

**HOTEL RESTAURANT * * NN**

**42 Chambres**
**tout confort**

**repas à partir de 55f**

**fimotel**

Parking commun avec hypermarché Continent
Centre Commercial Supermonde

Un hôtel agréable et confortable pour touristes et voyageurs. A 90 minutes du car-ferry au Havre, à 20 minutes du car-ferry Caen-Ouistreham.
Sans être de grand luxe, l'hôtel Fimotel vous offre de très belles chambres (douche, WC privé, télévision). Prix de la nuitée 110 F. Ce n'est vraiment pas cher.

Et pour nos amis britanniques, l'hypermarché Continent est en face pour rendre plus facile leurs achats.

Coche la bonne case

*Tick the right box*

1 L'hôtel Fimotel a une étoile ☐
deux étoiles ☐
trois étoiles ☐
quatre étoiles ☐

2 L'hôtel Fimotel est pour les touristes ☐
pour les soldats ☐
uniquement pour les Français ☐
uniquement pour les Britanniques ☐

3 L'hôtel Fimotel est très près de Paris ☐
très près de Caen-Ouistreham ☐
très près du Havre ☐
sur le car-ferry ☐

4 Les chambres à l'hôtel Fimotel sont de grand luxe ☐
ont le téléphone ☐
ont une douche ☐
sont chères ☐

5 L'hypermarché Continent est en face ☐
est fermé ☐
est uniquement pour les Britanniques ☐

## Exercice 9 Au camping

Lis cette brochure qui concerne les activités proposées par les animateurs du camping

*Read the brochure on the right concerning activities arranged on a campsite*

A quelle heure peut-on faire quoi?

*When can you do what?*

1. A quelle heure peut-on jouer à la pétanque?
2. A quelle heure peut-on s'exercer le matin?
3. A quelle heure peut-on danser?
4. A quelle heure peut-on voir de belles couleurs?
5. A quelle heure peut-on visiter quelque chose?

### Programme du 15 août

| | |
|---|---|
| *Entre 9h et 10h* | Aérobic sur la plage |
| *Entre 10h et 12h30* | Club des clowns: jeux et sports sur la plage pour enfants entre 5 et 9 ans |
| *Entre 14h30 et 17h* | Grand concours sportif des campeurs Tennis–Volley–Foot–Pétanque |
| *17h* | Visite guidée de la ville |
| *21h* | Grand bal |
| *23h* | Feu d'artifice |

## Exercice 10 Une lettre de Sophie

Lis la lettre et réponds aux questions

*Read the letter below and answer the questions*

1. Comment s'appelle la correspondante?
2. Comment s'appelle son frère aîné?
3. Où habitent-ils?
4. Bruno, quel âge a-t-il?
5. Donne une description du chat.

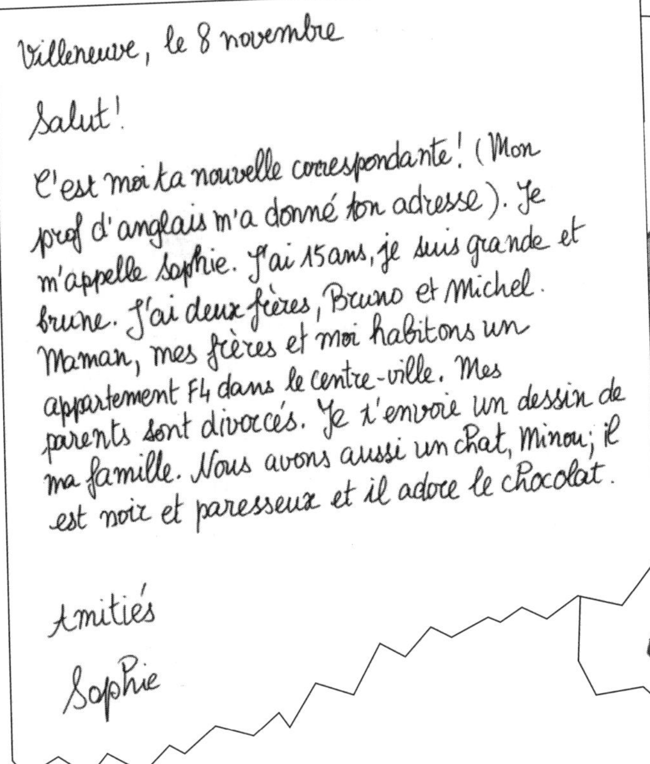

Villeneuve, le 8 novembre

Salut!

C'est moi ta nouvelle correspondante! (Mon prof d'anglais m'a donné ton adresse). Je m'appelle Sophie. J'ai 15 ans, je suis grande et brune. J'ai deux frères, Bruno et Michel. Maman, mes frères et moi habitons un appartement F4 dans le centre-ville. Mes parents sont divorcés. Je t'envoie un dessin de ma famille. Nous avons aussi un chat, Minou; il est noir et paresseux et il adore le chocolat.

Amitiés

Sophie

## Exercice 11
## Une réservation

Lis cette lettre

*Read the letter on the right*

Coche les cases contre les demandes de M. McKeane

*Tick the boxes against the things which Mr McKeane asks for*

M. McKeane demande

- une réservation pour deux nuits ☐
- une réservation pour quatre personnes ☐
- deux chambres pour deux personnes ☐
- une douche ☐
- la télévision ☐
- le petit déjeuner ☐
- une liste des garages ☐
- une voiture ☐

PO Bo
Mal
WR14
Tel: (01684) 577

Hôtel de l'Océan
1, place du marché
44700 THARON
France

le 5 juin

Messieurs,

Je voudrais faire une réservation pour trois nuits du 15 septembre au 17 septembre pour quatre personnes.

Pouvez-vous réserver deux chambres pour une personne et une chambre pour deux personnes avec petit déjeuner et dîner?

Je voudrais louer une voiture. Est-ce possible? Veuillez m'envoyer une liste des garages à Tharon, et, si possible, une liste des tarifs de location de voiture.

Je vous prie d'agréer, Messieurs, l'expression de mes sentiments distingués.

A McKeane

AR McKeane

# Grand-père attaque des hooligans

Caen, 11 septembre

Un monsieur âgé de 75 ans a attaqué des jeunes hier soir à Caen. Il a trouvé les deux hooligans dans la salle de séjour de son appartement. L'un des deux jeunes avait déjà le magnétoscope de M. Lefort sous le bras. L'autre jeune était en train de mettre le portefeuille et le carnet de chèques de l'ancien prof de gym dans sa poche. M. Lefort nous a dit qu'il était bien préparé. Dans sa chambre il a pris l'aspirateur - modèle très solide - et il a attaqué les deux jeunes. Ils étaient si surpris qu'ils sont partis en laissant le magnétoscope. On a retrouvé le portefeuille et le carnet de chèques dans l'escalier. M. Lefort était, en effet, le plus fort!

## Exercice 12 Grand-père attaque des hooligans

Lis cet article et réponds aux questions en anglais

*Read this article on the left and answer the questions in English*

1. How old is M. Lefort?
2. Where exactly did he find the hooligans?
3. What electrical item did they want to steal?
4. What two other items did they take?
5. What did M. Lefort attack them with?
6. Why might M. Lefort be so strong?
7. What did the thieves get away with?

## Exercice 13 Une excursion

Numérote les images pour les mettre dans le bon ordre

*Number the pictures to put them in the correct order*

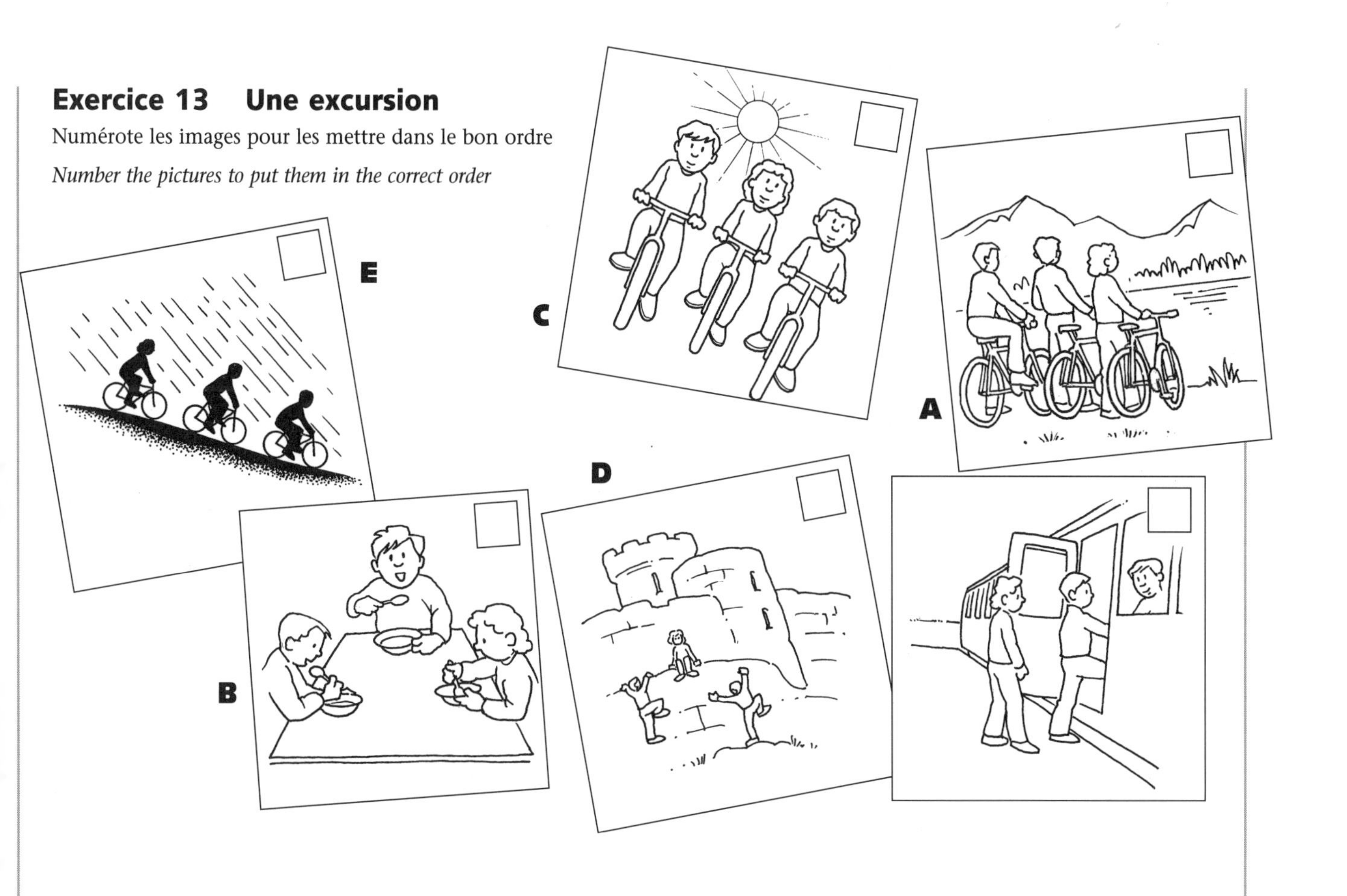


Avec deux amis j'ai fait une grande excursion. Nous sommes partis à vélo. Il faisait beau, le soleil brillait et il n'y avait pas de vent. Après une heure et demie de route nous sommes arrivés au lac. L'eau était froide, alors nous n'avons pas nagé. Nous avons mangé notre pique-nique: il était excellent.

Après le pique-nique nous avons fait encore 10 kilomètres pour visiter un château en ruine - c'est le château de Ranrouët, et c'est vraiment chouette.

Soudain il y a eu un orage. Nous n'avions pas d'anorak. Nous avons quitté le château et nous sommes allés à la gare de l'autre côté de la forêt. Nous étions tout mouillés, alors nous avons décidé de rentrer en train. Ma mère était contente de nous voir, et elle nous a fait de la soupe parce que nous avions très froid.

# Reading: *answers*

## Exercice 1 A la gare

**Answers:**

**A** quai
**B** buffet
**C** guichet
**D** les WC
**E** les consignes automatiques

## Exercice 2 En ville

**Answers:**

| | | | |
|---|---|---|---|
| **1** | de l'aspirine? | ***à la pharmacie*** | **F** |
| **2** | du mouton? | ***à la boucherie*** | **B** |
| **3** | du pain? | ***à la boulangerie*** | **A** |
| **4** | du fromage? | ***à la crémerie*** | **E** |
| **5** | une carte postale? | ***à la librairie*** | **C** |

## Exercice 3 Le plan de la ville

**Answers:**

| | | |
|---|---|---|
| **1** | le cinéma | *cinema* |
| **2** | l'église | *church* |
| **3** | la gare SNCF | *railway station* |
| **4** | l'hôpital | *hospital* |
| **5** | l'hôtel de ville | *town hall* |
| **6** | le musée | *museum* |
| **7** | l'office de tourisme | *tourist information office* |
| **8** | le parking | *car park* |
| **9** | la poste | *post office* |
| **10** | le stade | *stadium* |

## Exercice 4 On fait des canapés

**Answer:**

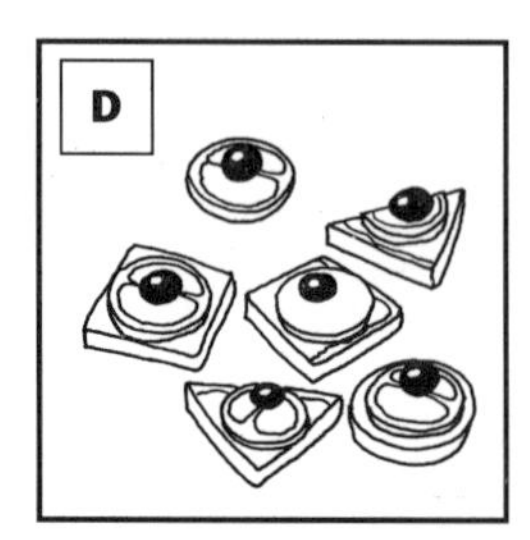


Garnissez les tranches de pain avec des tomates, des œufs durs, des radis, des carottes, des olives

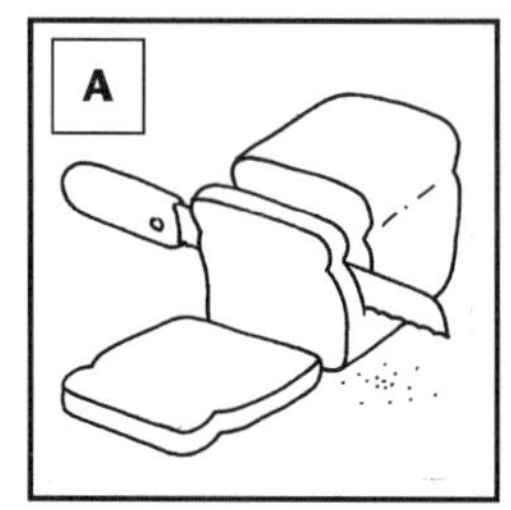


Coupez des tranches de pain de mie

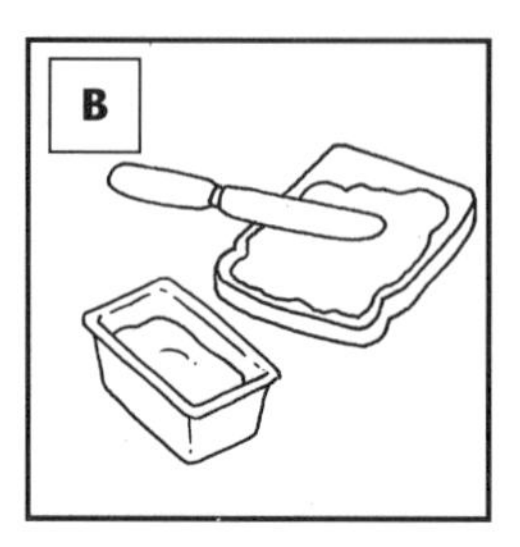


Tartinez-les avec du beurre

Coupez les tartines de pain en triangle, en rond, en rectangle

## Exercice 5 Un menu

**Answers:**

Your answers will vary according to your food preferences. However, a translation of the menu is as follows:

**Starters**

tomato salad
sardines
salami
fried egg
melon
ham
pâté
snails

**Fish**

sole
haddock
pollock in mayonnaise

**Meat**

steak
veal escalope
roast chicken
selection of cold meats
$\frac{1}{4}$ cold chicken with mayonnaise

**Vegetables**

French beans
peas
rice
chips
salad in season

**Cheeses**

Camembert
Petit Suisse
Goat

**Yoghurt**

**Pastries**

home-made tart
chocolate gateau

**Fruit**

peach
pear
banana

**Ices**

peach melba
fruit cup

## Exercice 6 L'emploi du temps de Joël

1. A quelle heure commencent les classes?
   ***8h30***
2. Combien de leçons de maths a-t-il par semaine?
   ***4***
3. Qu'est-ce qu'il a le vendredi après le déjeuner?
   ***français***
4. Combien de langues étrangères est-ce qu'il apprend?
   ***1***
5. Quels jours a-t-il de l'éducation physique?
   ***lundi et samedi***

## Exercice 7 Un message

| | | |
|---|---|---|
| 1 | Marlène a téléphoné à trois heures | ***FAUX*** |
| 2 | Marlène veut jouer au tennis ce soir | ***VRAI*** |
| 3 | Marlène veut jouer au tennis à cinq heures | ***FAUX*** |
| 4 | Marlène joue au tennis au centre sportif | ***FAUX*** |
| 5 | Tout le monde joue au tennis samedi | ***VRAI*** |

## Exercice 8 L'hôtel Fimotel

1. L'hôtel Fimotel a
   ***deux étoiles***
2. L'hôtel Fimotel est
   ***pour les touristes***
3. L'hôtel Fimotel
   ***est très près de Caen-Ouistreham***
4. Les chambres à l'hôtel Fimotel
   ***ont une douche***
5. L'hypermarché Continent
   ***est en face***

## Exercice 9 Au camping

1. A quelle heure peut-on jouer à la pétanque?
   ***14h30 – 17h***
2. A quelle heure peut-on s'exercer le matin?
   ***9h – 10h***
3. A quelle heure peut-on danser?
   ***21h***
4. A quelle heure peut-on voir de belles couleurs?
   ***23h***
5. A quelle heure peut-on visiter quelque chose?
   ***17h***

## Exercice 10 Une lettre de Sophie

1. Comment s'appelle la correspondante?
   ***Sophie***
2. Comment s'appelle son frère aîné?
   ***Michel***
3. Où habitent-ils?
   ***A Villeneuve, dans un appartement F4***
4. Bruno, quel âge a-t-il?
   ***13 ans***
5. Donne une description du chat.
   ***noir, paresseux, aime le chocolat***

## Exercice 11 Une réservation

M. McKeane demande

| | |
|---|---|
| une réservation pour deux nuits | ☐ |
| une réservation pour quatre personnes | ☑ |
| deux chambres pour deux personnes | ☐ |
| une douche | ☐ |
| la télévision | ☐ |
| le petit déjeuner | ☑ |
| une liste des garages | ☑ |
| une voiture | ☐ |

## Exercice 12 Grand-père attaque hooligans

1. How old is M. Lefort?
   ***75***
2. Where exactly did he find the hooligans?
   ***in the living-room of his flat***
3. What electrical item did they want to steal?
   ***video recorder***
4. What two other items did they take?
   ***wallet; cheque book***
5. What did M. Lefort attack them with?
   ***the hoover***
6. Why might M. Lefort be so strong?
   ***ex-gym teacher***
7. What did the thieves get away with?
   ***nothing***

## Exercice 13 Une excursion

The order of the picutures should be:

1. The three children cycling in the sun
2. Three children and their bikes having a picnic by a lake
3. The children climbing on the walls of an old castle
4. The children cycling through a forest in the rain, downhill
5. The children catching a train back home
6. Three children eating soup in a dining-room

# Speaking: *questions*

## Introduction

Many people find this aspect of French the easiest, because you don't have to be quite so accurate when speaking as compared to writing. It is always more important to get the message across than to be grammatically exact. So don't be shy – speak out!

Remember to speak clearly. French vowel sounds are sometimes a bit tricky for British people to produce, especially the **é**, **è**, **u**, **ou** and **eux** sounds. But don't give up. With practice you will improve without perhaps even noticing it.

In this section with speaking exercises, you'll find a number of rôle-plays to do.

Answers are given at the end of the section. The dialogues are recorded on the cassette. Use the pause or stop button on your cassette player to give you time to repeat the correct answers.

## Situation 1 Pour aller à...

Tu es en ville et tu demandes le chemin

*You are in town and ask the way*

**Example:**

Pardon monsieur/madame, pour aller à l'hôtel de ville, s'il vous plaît?

1  

2  

3 

4 

5 

6 

7 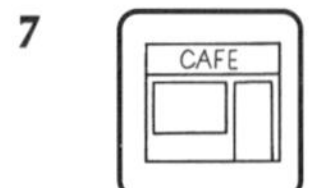


8 

9 

## Situation 2 Tu indiques le chemin

Maintenant, c'est toi qui donnes des indications

*Now you are describing the way:*

1 Pour aller à la piscine, s'il vous plaît?

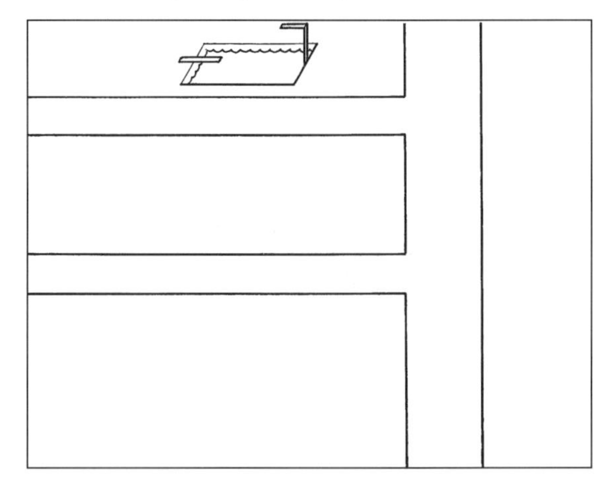

2 Pour aller à la cathédrale, s'il vous plaît?

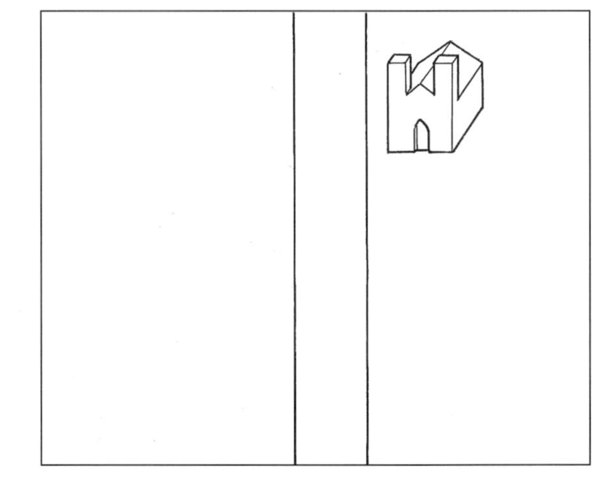

**3** Pour aller à l'hôtel "Mon Repos", s'il vous plaît?

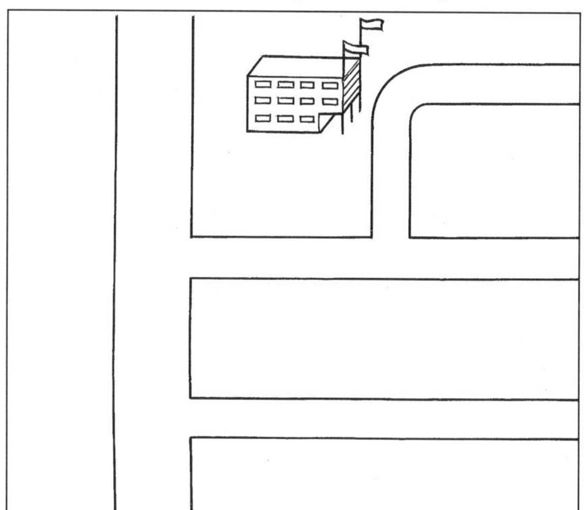

**4** Pardon, est-ce qu'il y a une boîte aux lettres par ici?

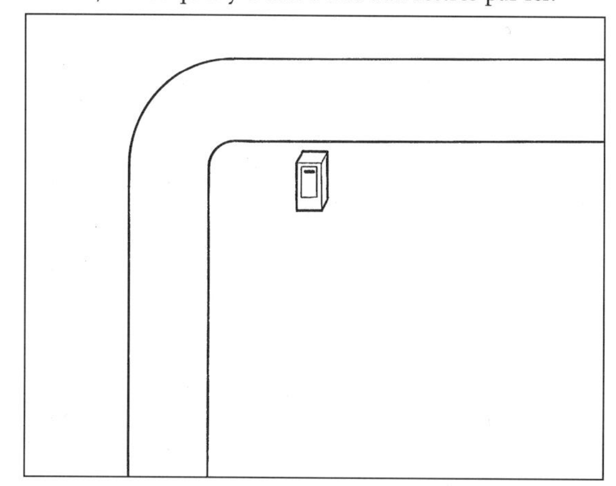

**5** Pardon, pour aller au stade, s'il vous plaît?

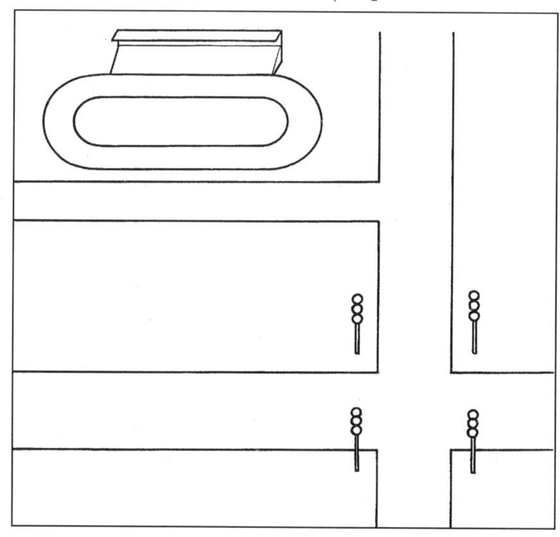

## Situation 3 Qu'est-ce qu'il a?

Regarde ce pauvre garçon. Peux-tu dire ce qu'il a?

*Look at this poor boy. Can you say what is wrong with him?*

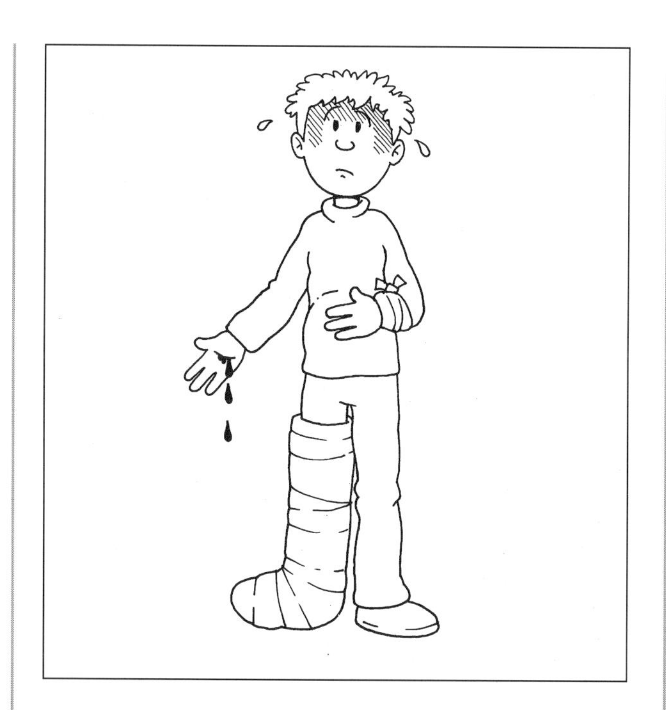

## Situation 4 Où est-ce que ça fait mal?

Regarde les dessins. Peux-tu dire où il/elle a mal?

*Look at the pictures. Can you say where it hurts?*

**1**

**2**

3

4

5

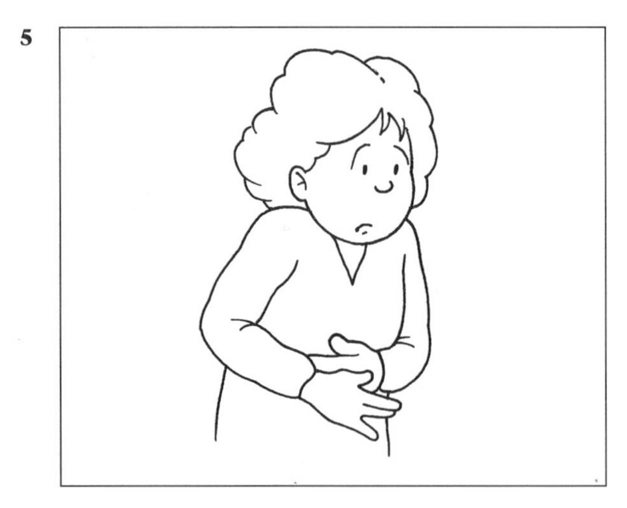

6

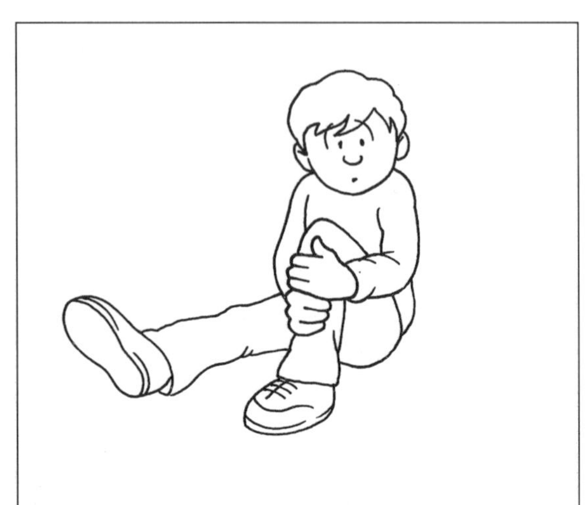

## Situation 5 Tu prends rendez-vous

Tu es en France et tu voudrais un rendez-vous chez le dentiste. Qu'est-ce que tu dis à la réceptionniste?

*You are in France and would like an appointment with the dentist. What do you say to the receptionist?*

– Allô. Cabinet du Dr Plomb. Qu'y a-t-il pour votre service?
– *Say you would like an appointment.*
– Jeudi, ça vous va?
– *Ask if they haven't got anything earlier.*
– Non, je n'ai rien avant jeudi.
– *Say that you will wait till then.*
– Alors, jeudi à 15h.
– *Say thank you and goodbye.*

## Situation 6 Qu'est-ce que tu commandes?

Tu es au café. Passe des commandes selon les dessins

*You are in a cafe giving your order. Look at the pictures. What do you order?*

1

2

3

4

5

## Situation 7 Au café

Complète le dialogue

*Complete the dialogue*

– Bonjour, messieurs-dames. Vous désirez?

– Tout de suite.

– Ça fait 35 francs, s'il vous plaît.

– *Say you have only a 100F note.*

– Ça ne fait rien. Alors trente-cinq, quarante, cinquante et cent francs.

– *Say goodbye.*

## Situation 8 Au restaurant

Regarde la carte. Choisis tes plats. Réponds aux questions de la serveuse.

*Look at the menu at the top of the page. Choose what you want to eat. Then answer the waitress's questions.*

La serveuse demande:

– Avez-vous déjà choisi?

–

– Qu'est-ce que vous prenez comme hors d'œuvre?

–

– Et comme plat principal?

–

– Est-ce que vous voulez déjà commander un dessert?

–

– Et qu'est-ce que vous prenez comme boissons?

–

– Merci, messieurs-dames. Ça vient tout de suite.

–

### Restaurant St Michel

### Menu

**Hors d'œuvre variés**

| | |
|---|---|
| Crudités | 7F |
| Pâté de campagne | 7F |
| Salade de tomates | 7F |

**Plats chauds**

| | |
|---|---|
| Omelette aux champignons | 20F50 |
| Poulet rôti | 23F50 |
| Steak grillé | 27F50 |
| Truite maison | 25F50 |

**Légumes au choix**

| | |
|---|---|
| Carottes | 7F |
| Frites | 7F |
| Haricots verts | 7F |
| Petits pois | 7F |

**Fromages**

| | |
|---|---|
| Camembert, Brie, Emmental | 12F |

**Desserts**

| | |
|---|---|
| Fruits: Pêche, Poire, Banane | 7F |
| Glaces: parfums au choix | 10F |
| Tarte Maison, Gâteau au chocolat | 12F |

## Situation 9 Au marché

Tu fais des courses au marché

*You are shopping in the market. What do you say?*

**1** – Bonjour, vous désirez?

– Et avec ça?

– Alors ça fait 15F en tout.

**2** – Bonjour, vous désirez?

– Et ensuite?

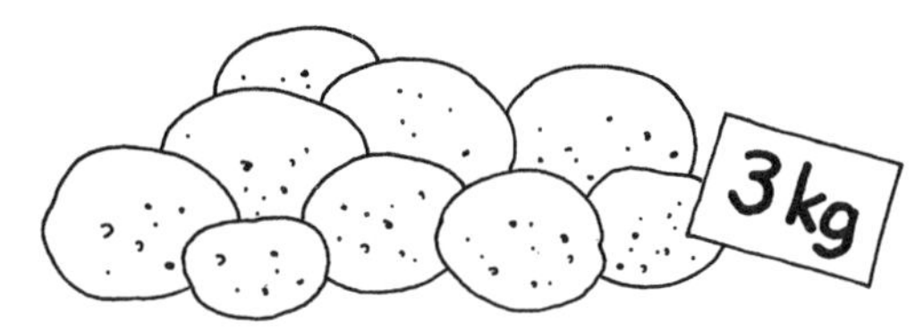


– Ça fait 9F .

**3** – Bonjour, vous désirez?

– C'est tout?

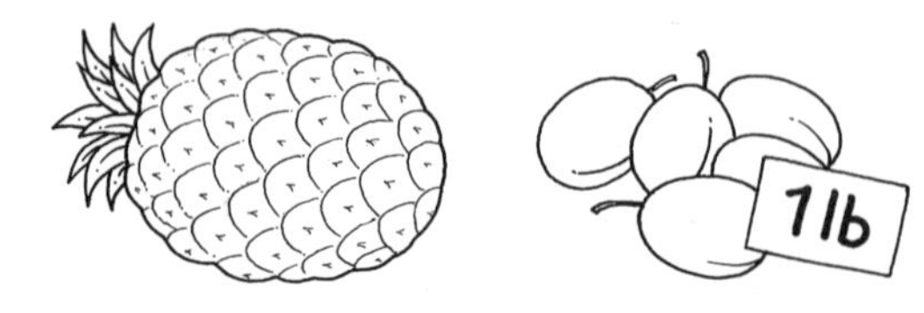


– Ça fait 16F.

**4** – Bonjour, vous désirez?

– Et avec cela?

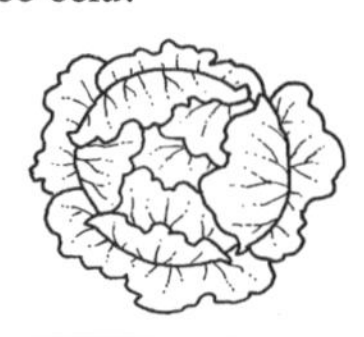

– Ça fait 7F.

## Situation 10 Des souvenirs

Tu cherches un cadeau pour ta sœur. Le vendeur te montre un livre, mais c'est trop cher. Tu n'as que 40F. Puis il te montre une poupée. Ta sœur n'aime pas les poupées. Enfin il te montre une écharpe verte. Tu veux acheter une écharpe, mais en rouge.

*You are looking for a present for your sister. The assistant shows you a book, but it is too expensive. You have only 40F. The assistant then shows you a doll You sister doesn't like dolls. In the end, he shows you a green scarf. You want to buy a scarf, but not a red one.*

– Bonjour. Vous désirez?

– *You want a present for your sister.*

– Un livre, par exemple. Celui-ci est très beau, et coûte 50F.

– *It is too expensive.*

– Une poupée, par exemple. Celle-ci est très jolie.

– *Your sister doesn't like dolls.*

– Une écharpe peut-être pour 30F. Celle-ci en vert est chouette.

– *You would like a scarf, but in red.*

– Pas de problème. Nous l'avons aussi en rouge.

## Situation 11 Ta correspondante achète une jupe

Tu fais du shopping dans un grand magasin avec ta correspondante. Elle cherche une jupe

*You are shopping in a department store with your exchange partner. You are helping her to find a skirt.*

– *Tell her to look over there. There are skirts on special offer.*

– Ah oui. Ces jupes sont super.

– *Ask her if she wants to try one on.*

– Bonne idée. Je vais essayer cette jupe noire.

[quelques minutes plus tard]

– Qu'en penses-tu? Elle me va?

– *You say it is a bit small.*

– Tu as raison. Je vais l'essayer dans une taille plus grande.

[quelques minutes plus tard]

– *You tell her that this skirt really suits her.*

– Merci. Je la prends.

## Situation 12 Tu achètes un pull

Tu cherches un pull pour toi.
*You are looking for a jumper for yourself*

– *Ask the shop assistant if they have any jumpers on special offer.*

– Oui, nous avons ceux-ci à 85F.

– *Say you would like to try one on.*

– Avec plaisir. Vous faites quelle taille?

– *Say you need size 40.*

– Dans cette taille nous en avons un en bleu foncé.

– *Say you'd like one in dark green.*

– Pas de problème. Voici le même pull en vert foncé.

– *Ask if you can try it on.*

– Les cabines sont par là.

[quelques minutes plus tard]

– *Say the jumper fits. Ask where the cash desk is.*

– La caisse est près de la sortie.

## Situation 13 A la banque

Tu es à la banque

*You are at the bank*

**1** – Bonjour, monsieur.

– *Say you'd like to change £50.*

– Pas de problème.

– *Ask what the exchange rate is.*

– Le taux de change est de FF7,50 la livre sterling.

– *Ask if there is a commission.*

– Oui, il y a une commission de 10F.

**2** – Say you would like to change a traveller's cheque.

– C'est pour des dollars?

– Say no, pounds sterling.

– Bon. Combien voulez-vous changer?

– Say £100.

– Avez-vous une pièce d'identité?

– Say you have got your passport.

– C'est bon. Signez ici, s'il vous plaît.

## Situation 14 A la poste

Tu achètes des timbres à la poste

*You are in the post office buying stamps*

**1** – Vous désirez?

–

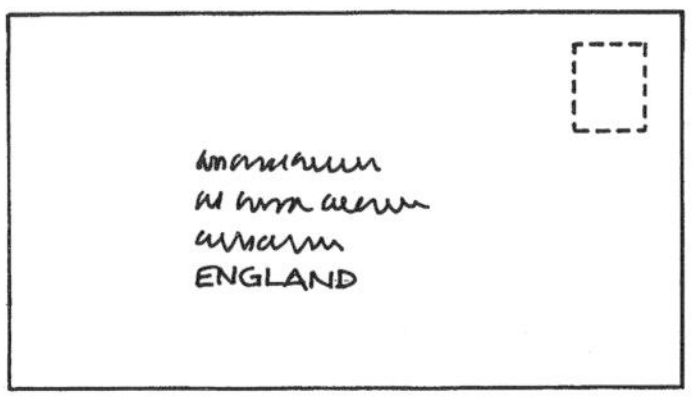


– 3F.

–

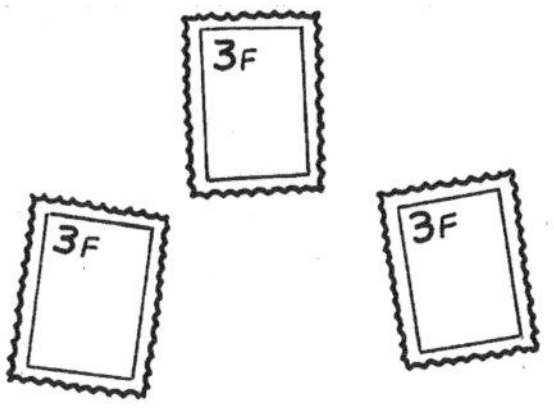


– 9F s'il vous plaît.

**2** –

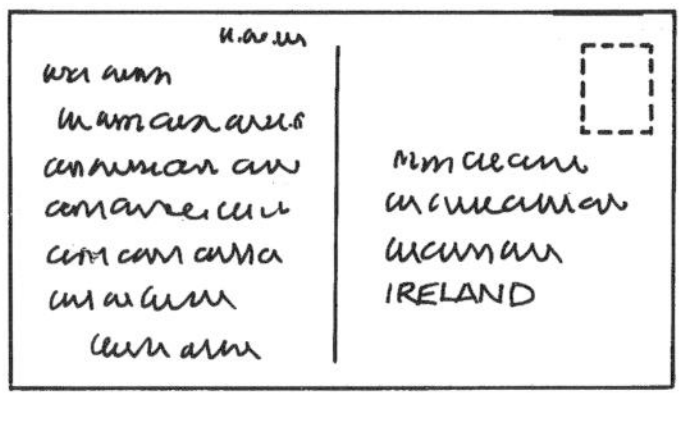


– 2F 80.

–

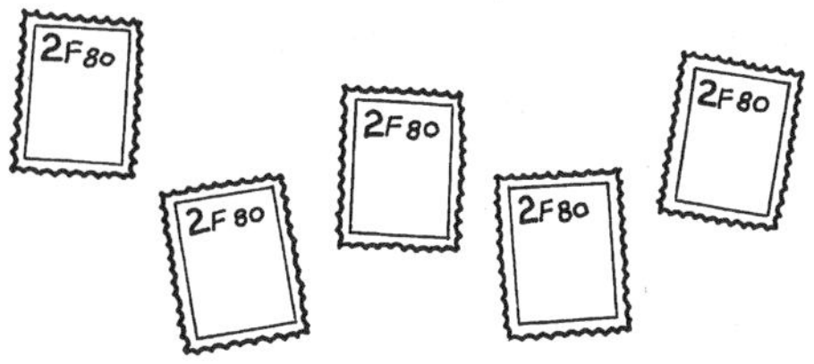


– 14F, s'il vous plaît.

**3** –

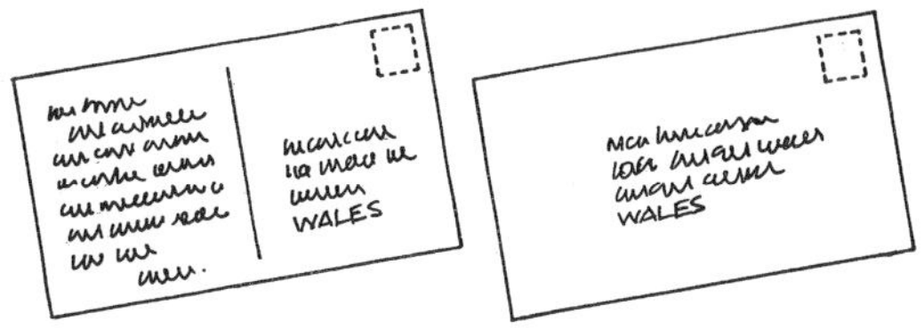


– 2F80 et 3F.

–

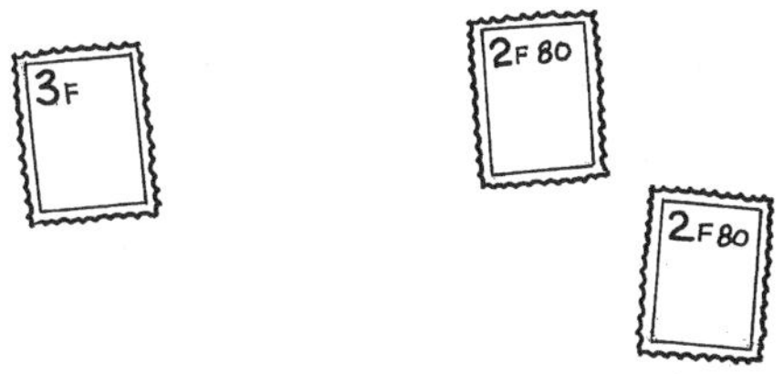


– Ça fait 8,60F.

**4** –

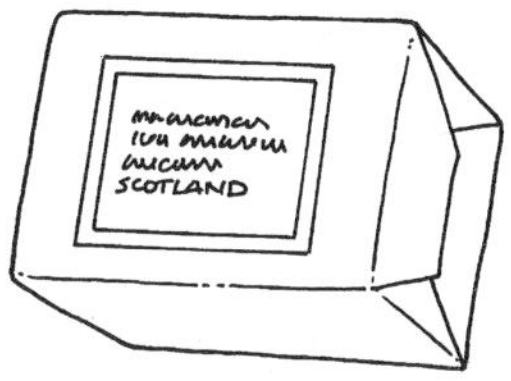


– Il faut le peser. Alors, ça fait 25F.

–

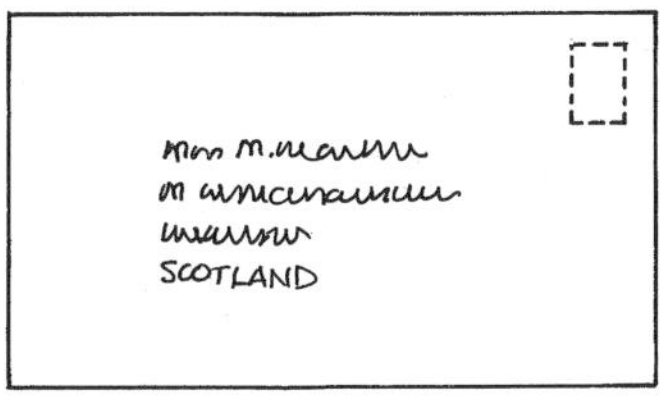


– 3F.

–

– Ça vous fait 28F en tout.

**5** –

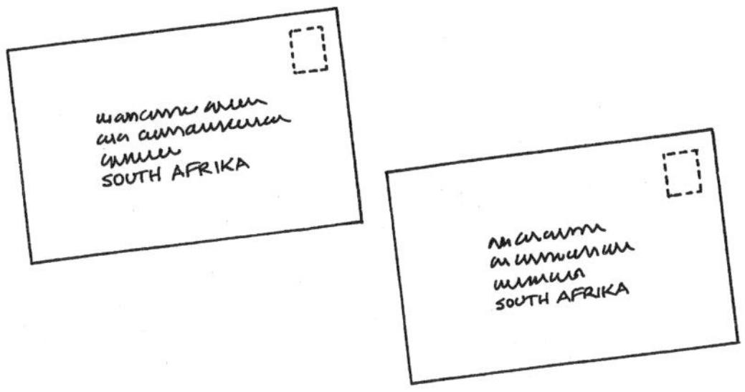


– Pour l'Afrique du Sud, ça fait 5F.

–

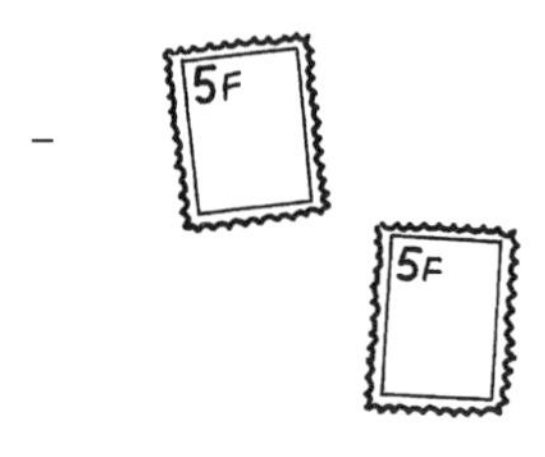


– Ça fait 10F.

## Situation 15 En autobus

Tu prends le bus dans une ville française. Qu'est-ce que tu dis au conducteur?

*You are travelling by bus in a French town. What do you say to the driver?*

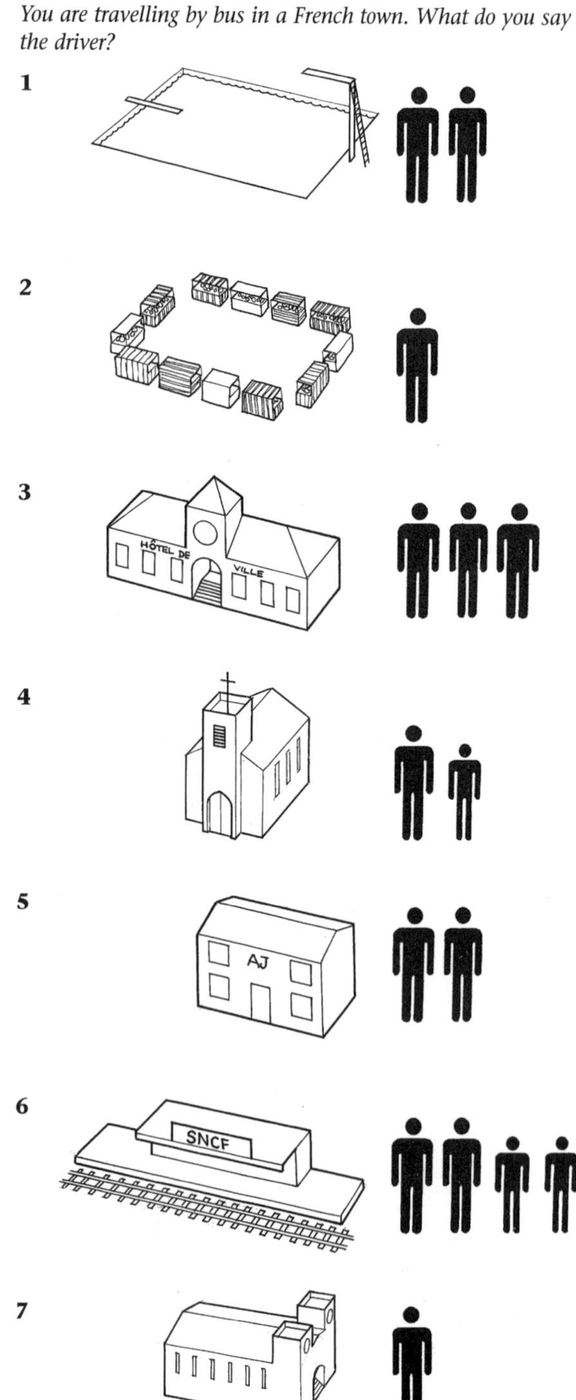


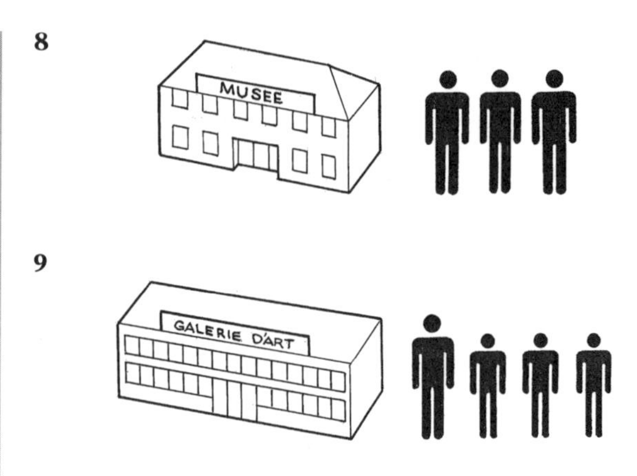


## Situation 16 En train

Tu es au guichet

*You are at the ticket office*

**1** – *Ask when the next train to Paris leaves.*
– A 15h45.
– *Ask where it leaves from.*
– Quai n° 3.
– *Ask when it will arrive in Paris.*
– Il arrive à 17h05.

**2** – *Say you want to travel to Bordeaux on Thursday morning. Is there a train?*
– Oui, il y a un train à 10h15.
– *Ask when it will arrive in Bordeaux.*
– A 12h15.
– *Ask what platform.*
– Quai 5a.
– *Ask if you have to change.*
– Non, c'est direct.

**3** – *Say you'd like a return ticket to Dijon.*
– En première classe?
– *Say no, second class.*
– 235F, s'il vous plaît.
– *Ask what time the train leaves.*
– Le prochain train part à 10h35.
– *Ask what time it will arrive in Dijon.*
– A 12h45.

**4** – *Say you'd like to reserve a seat.*
– C'est pour quel train?
– *For the train at 12.15 on Tuesday to Biarritz.*
– Quelle place préférez-vous?
– *Say you'd like a window seat.*
– C'est bon. Vous avez la place n° B12.

**5** – *Say you'd like two single tickets to Brussels.*
– Ça fait 450F.
– *Ask if the train goes direct.*
– Non, il faut changer à Lille.

**6** – *Say you'd like two returns to Clermont-Ferrand, one adult and one child.*
– 90F, s'il vous plaît.
– *Ask when the next train leaves.*
– A 20h40, quai numéro 7.

## Situation 17 Au cinéma

Tu vas au cinéma avec un ami/une amie

*You are going to the cinema in France with a friend.*

**1**
- Bonsoir, messieurs-dames.
- *Say you'd like two tickets for the film.*
- Où les voulez-vous?
- *Say in the balcony.*
- Ça fait 30F.
- *Ask when the show finishes.*
- Vers 22h.

**2**
- Bonsoir.
- *Ask if the film tonight has subtitles.*
- Non, il est en version originale
- *Ask for three tickets near the screen.*
- Ça fait 39F.
- *Ask when the show starts.*
- Dans une demi-heure.

**3**
- Bonsoir.
- *Say you'd like two tickets, one adult, one child.*
- 27F, s'il vous plaît.
- *Ask if the film is in English.*
- Non, il est doublé.
- *Say that doesn't matter.*

## Situation 18 Au théâtre

Tu vas au théâtre en France avec un ami/une amie

*You are going to the theatre in France with a friend.*

- Bonjour.
- *Say you'd like four tickets for the performance on Tuesday.*
- Au balcon, à l'orchestre. Où les voulez-vous?
- *Ask for seats near the front.*
- Nous avons encore quatre places, au neuvième rang. Ça vous convient?
- *Say, yes, that's fine.*
- Alors, ça vous fait 200F.
- *Ask if you can pay by credit card.*
- Bien sûr. Pas de problème.

# Speaking: *answers*

## Situation 1 Pour aller à...

**Exemple:**

Pardon monsieur/madame, pour aller à l'hôtel de ville?

1. *Pardon monsieur/madame, pour aller au musée?*
2. *Pardon monsieur/madame, pour aller à la rivière?*
3. *Pardon monsieur/madame, pour aller au parc?*
4. *Pardon monsieur/madame, pour aller à l'église?*
5. *Pardon monsieur/madame, pour aller au parking?*
6. *Pardon monsieur/madame, pour aller à l'auberge de jeunesse?*
7. *Pardon monsieur/madame, pour aller au café?*
8. *Pardon monsieur/madame, pour aller à la poste?*
9. *Pardon monsieur/madame, pour aller à la banque?*

## Situation 2 Tu indiques le chemin

1. Pour aller à la piscine, s'il vous plaît?

   *Allez tout droit. Prenez la deuxième rue à gauche. La piscine est dans cette rue.*

2. Pour aller à la cathédrale, s'il vous plaît?

   *Allez tout droit. La cathédrale est à droite.*

3. Pour aller à l'hôtel "Mon Repos", s'il vous plaît?

   *Allez tout droit. Prenez la première rue à droite, puis la première à gauche. L'hôtel est à gauche.*

4. Pardon, est-ce qu'il y a une boîte aux lettres par ici?

   *Allez tout droit. Au coin de la rue il y a une boîte à lettres.*

5. Pardon. Pour aller au stade, s'il vous plaît?

   *Allez tout droit. Aux feux, continuez tout droit, puis prenez la première rue à gauche.*

## Situation 3 Qu'est-ce qu'il a?

1. *Il s'est cassé la jambe.*
2. *Il s'est coupé la main.*
3. *Il s'est foulé le poignet.*
4. *Il a mal au ventre.*
5. *Il a de la fièvre.*

## Situation 4 Où est-ce que ça fait mal?

1. *J'ai mal à la tête.*
2. *J'ai mal à la gorge.*
3. *J'ai mal aux dents.*
4. *J'ai mal aux oreilles.*
5. *J'ai mal au ventre.*
6. *J'ai mal à la jambe.*

## Situation 5 Tu prends rendez-vous

– Allô. Cabinet du Dr Plomb. Qu'y a-t-il pour votre service?

– *Je voudrais prendre rendez-vous.*

– Jeudi, ça vous va?

– *Vous n'avez rien avant jeudi?*

– Non, je n'ai rien avant jeudi.

– *Alors j'attendrai.*

– Alors, jeudi à 15h.

– *Merci, madame. Au revoir, madame.*

## Situation 6 Qu'est-ce que tu commandes?

1. *Je voudrais deux cafés, s'il vous plaît.*
2. *Je voudrais un thé, s'il vous plaît.*
3. *Je voudrais deux limonades et une glace, s'il vous plaît.*
4. *Je voudrais un chocolat chaud et un croissant, s'il vous plaît.*
5. *Je voudrais un café, un thé au citron, un coca et trois glaces, s'il vous plaît.*

## Situation 7 Au café

– Bonjour, messieurs-dames. Vous désirez?

– *Je voudrais deux cafés, un coca et trois glaces, s'il vous plaît.*

– Tout de suite.

– *Combien je vous dois?*

– Ça fait 35 francs, s'il vous plaît.

– *Je n'ai qu'un billet de cent francs.*

– Ça ne fait rien. Alors trente-cinq, quarante, cinquante et cent francs.

– *Au revoir, monsieur.*

## Situation 8 Au restaurant

This is one set of possible answers.

– Avez-vous déjà choisi?

– *Oui, madame.*

– Qu'est-ce que vous prenez comme hors d'œuvre?

– *Un pâté de campagne.*

– Et comme plat principal?

– *Une truite maison avec des haricots verts et un poulet rôti avec des frites, s'il vous plaît.*

– Est-ce que vous voulez déjà commander un dessert?

– *Un gâteau au chocolat et des fruits, s'il vous plaît.*

– Et qu'est-ce que vous prenez comme boisson?

– *De l'eau minérale, s'il vous plaît.*

– Merci, messieurs-dames. Ça vient tout de suite.

## Situation 9 Au marché

1. – Bonjour, vous désirez?

   – *Un kilo de pommes, s'il vous plaît.*

   – Et avec ça?

- *Trois bananes et une livre de fraises, s'il vous plaît.*
- Alors ça fait 15F en tout.

**2** - Bonjour, vous désirez?
- *Cinq cents grammes de carottes, s'il vous plaît.*
- Et ensuite?
- *Trois kilos de pommes de terre, s'il vous plaît.*
- Ça fait 9F.

**3** - Bonjour, vous désirez?
- *Une livre de poires, s'il vous plaît.*
- C'est tout?
- *Un ananas et 500 grammes de prunes, s'il vous plaît.*
- Ça fait 16F.

**4** - Bonjour, vous désirez?
- *300 grammes de haricots verts.*
- Et avec cela?
- *Une laitue.*
- Ça fait 7F.

## Situation 10 Des souvenirs

- Bonjour. Vous désirez?
- *Je cherche un cadeau pour ma sœur.*
- Un livre, par exemple. Celui-ci est très beau, et coûte 50F.
- *C'est trop cher.*
- Une poupée, par exemple. Celle-ci est très jolie.
- *Ma sœur n'aime pas les poupées.*
- Une écharpe peut-être pour 30F. Celle-ci en vert est chouette.
- *Oui, j'aimerais une écharpe, mais en rouge.*
- Pas de problème. Nous l'avons aussi en rouge.

## Situation 11 Ta correspondante achète une jupe

- *Regarde! Il y des jupes en promotion.*
- Ah oui. Ces jupes sont super.
- *Est-ce que tu veux en essayer une?*
- Bonne idée. Je vais essayer cette jupe noire.

[quelques minutes plus tard]

- Qu'en penses-tu? Elle me va?
- *C'est un peu étroit.*
- Tu as raison. Je vais l'essayer dans une taille plus grande.

[quelques minutes plus tard]

- *La jupe te va très bien.*
- Merci. Je la prends.

## Situation 12 Tu achètes un pull

- *Avez-vous des pulls en promotion?*
- Oui, nous avons ceux-ci à 85F.
- *Je voudrais en essayer un.*
- Avec plaisir. Vous faites quelle taille?
- *Je fais du quarante.*
- Dans cette taille nous en avons un en bleu foncé.
- *Je voudrais un pull vert foncé.*
- Pas de problème, voici le même pull en vert foncé.
- *Est-ce que je peux l'essayer?*
- Les cabines sont par là.

[quelques minutes plus tard]

- *Le pull me va. Où est la caisse?*
- La caisse est près de la sortie.

## Situation 13 A la banque

**1** - Bonjour, monsieur.
- *Je voudrais changer cinquante livres sterling.*
- Pas de problème.
- *Quel est le taux de change?*
- Le taux de change est de FF7,50 la livre sterling.
- *Est-ce qu'il y a une commission?*
- Oui, il y a une commission de 10F.

**2** - *Je voudrais changer un chèque de voyage.*
- C'est pour des dollars?
- *Non, c'est en livres sterling.*
- Bon. Combien voulez-vous changer?
- *Cent livres.*
- Avez-vous une pièce d'identité?
- *Oui, j'ai mon passeport.*
- C'est bon. Signez ici, s'il vous plaît.

## Situation 14 A la poste

1 - Vous désirez?
- *C'est combien pour envoyer une lettre en Angleterre?*
- 3F.
- *Alors trois timbres à trois francs, s'il vous plaît.*
- 9F s'il vous plaît.

**2** - *C'est combien pour envoyer une carte postale en Irlande?*
- 2F80.
- *Alors, cinq timbres à deux francs quatre-vingts, s'il vous plaît.*
- 14F, s'il vous plaît.

**3** - *C'est combien pour envoyer une carte postale et une lettre au Pays de Galles, s'il vous plaît?*
- 2F80 et 3F.
- *Je voudrais un timbre à 3 francs et deux à deux francs quatre-vingts.*
- Ça fait 8,60F.

**4** - *Je voudrais envoyer ce paquet en Ecosse.*
- Il faut le peser. Alors, ça fait 25F.
- *C'est combien pour envoyer une lettre en Ecosse?*
- 3F.
- *Alors, un timbre à trois francs, s'il vous plaît.*
- Ça vous fait 28F en tout.

**5** - *C'est combien pour envoyer une lettre en Afrique du Sud?*
- Pour l'Afrique du Sud, ça fait 5F.

– *Alors, deux timbres à cinq francs, s'il vous plaît.*
– Ça fait 10F.

## Situation 15 En autobus

1 *Deux tickets pour aller à la piscine, s'il vous plaît.*
2 *Un ticket pour aller au marché, s'il vous plaît.*
3 *Trois tickets pour aller à l'hôtel de ville, s'il vous plaît.*
4 *A l'église, s'il vous plaît. Un adulte et un enfant.*
5 *Deux tickets pour aller à l'auberge de jeunesse, s'il vous plaît.*
6 *Au stade, s'il vous plaît. Deux adultes et deux enfants.*
7 *Un ticket pour aller à la cathédrale, s'il vous plaît.*
8 *Trois tickets pour aller au musée, s'il vous plaît.*
9 *A la galerie d'art, s'il vous plaît. Un adulte et trois enfants.*

## Situation 16 En train

1 – *A quelle heure part le prochain train pour Paris, s'il vous plaît?*
– A 15h45.
– *Il part de quel quai?*
– Quai nº 3.
– *A quelle heure est-ce qu'il arrive à Paris?*
– Il arrive à 17h05.

2 – *Je voudrais aller à Bordeaux jeudi matin. Y a-t-il un train?*
– Oui, il y a un train à 10h15.
– *A quelle heure est-ce qu'il arrive à Bordeaux?*
– A 12h15.
– *Il part de quel quai?*
– Quai 5a.
– *Est-ce qu'il faut changer?*
– Non, c'est direct.

3 – *Un aller-retour pour Dijon, s'il vous plaît.*
– En première classe?
– *Non, en seconde.*
– 235F, s'il vous plaît.
– *A quelle heure part le train?*
– Le prochain train part à 10h35.
– *A quelle heure est-ce qu'il arrive à Dijon?*
– A 12h45.

4 – *Je voudrais réserver une place.*
– C'est pour quel train?
– *Pour le train de 12h15, pour Biarritz mardi.*
– Quelle place préférez-vous?
– *Je préfère une place près de la fenêtre.*
– C'est bon. Vous avez la place nº B12.

5 – *Deux allers simples pour Bruxelles.*
– Ça fait 450F.
– *Est-ce que c'est direct?*
– Non, il faut changer à Lille.

6 – *Deux aller-retour pour Clermont-Ferrand, un adulte et un enfant, s'il vous plaît.*
– 90F, s'il vous plaît.
– *A quelle heure part le prochain train?*
– A 20h40, quai nº 7.

## Situation 17 Au cinéma

1 – Bonsoir, messieurs-dames.
– *Je voudrais deux places pour le film, s'il vous plaît.*
– Où les voulez-vous?
– *Au balcon.*
– Ça fait 30F.
– *A quelle heure finit la séance?*
– Vers 22h.

2 – Bonsoir.
– *Est-ce que le film de ce soir est sous-titré?*
– Non, il est en version originale.
– *Trois places devant, s'il vous plaît.*
– Ça fait 39F.
– *A quelle heure commence la séance?*
– Dans une demi-heure.

3 – Bonsoir.
– *Je voudrais deux places, un adulte et un enfant.*
– 27F, s'il vous plaît.
– *Est-ce que le film est en anglais?*
– Non, il est doublé.
– *Bon, ça ne fait rien.*

## Situation 18 Au théâtre

– Bonjour.
– *Je voudrais quatre places pour le spectacle mardi, s'il vous plaît.*
– Au balcon, à l'orchestre. Où les voulez-vous?
– *Je voudrais des places vers l'avant.*
– Nous avons encore quatre places, au neuvième rang. Ça vous convient?
– *Oui, c'est bien.*
– Alors, ça vous fait 200F.
– *Est-ce que je peux payer avec une carte de crédit?*
– Bien sûr. Pas de problème.

# Writing: questions

## Introduction

You will be asked to do a variety of writing tasks for your homework, apart from simply copying vocabulary or exercise sentences.

When you do written work in French there are a number of points to watch out for:

- **verb endings:** they are often not pronounced in French, which means you need to know which ending to use when (see verbs section in the grammar).
- **genders:** look up individual words you are not sure of
- **adjective agreements:** adjectives agree with (= change their spelling to match) the noun they refer to. You need to know if the noun is masculine or feminine, singular or plural (see adjectives section in the grammar)
- **accents:** many letters in French have accents; it is quite important to make sure you have them correctly and clearly written, pointing the right way

## Writing letters

Often you will be asked to write letters or postcards.

### Letters to friends

Letters to friends are nearly always written in the *tu* form. Your letter will begin with *Cher* if it is addressed to a boy and with *Chère* if it is for a girl. *Chers* is also used in most cases when you write to two or more people.

Your letter will look like this:

> Harlow, le 20 mars
>
> Chère Hélène,
>
> Comment vas-tu?

You can finish a letter to a penfriend with one or more of the following phrases:

écris-moi bientôt — *write soon*
à bientôt — *see you soon*
amitiés — *best wishes*
grosses bises — *love and kisses*

If you are a boy, finish with one of:

ton ami — *your friend*
ton correspondant — *your penfriend*

Then sign your name.

If you are a girl, finish with one of:

ton amie — *your friend*
ta correspondante — *your penfriend*

Then sign your name.

### Formal business letters

Business letters are always written in the *vous* form. If you write to an information office, campsite, hotel, etc., you begin your letter with the more formal: Messieurs.

Your letter will look like this:

> Harlow, le 20 mars
>
> Hôtel Les Briards
> 1, place du marché
> 56213 Balleroy
> France
>
> Messieurs,

You can finish a formal letter with one or other of more of the following *formules*, both of which amount to *Yours Sincerely:*

> Je vous prie d'agréer, Messieurs, l'expression de mes sentiments distingués.
> Veuillez agréer, Messieurs, l'expression de mes sentiments distingués.

You then sign your name.

## Exercice 1 Mon arbre généalogique

Complète ton arbre généalogique
*Complete your family tree in French*

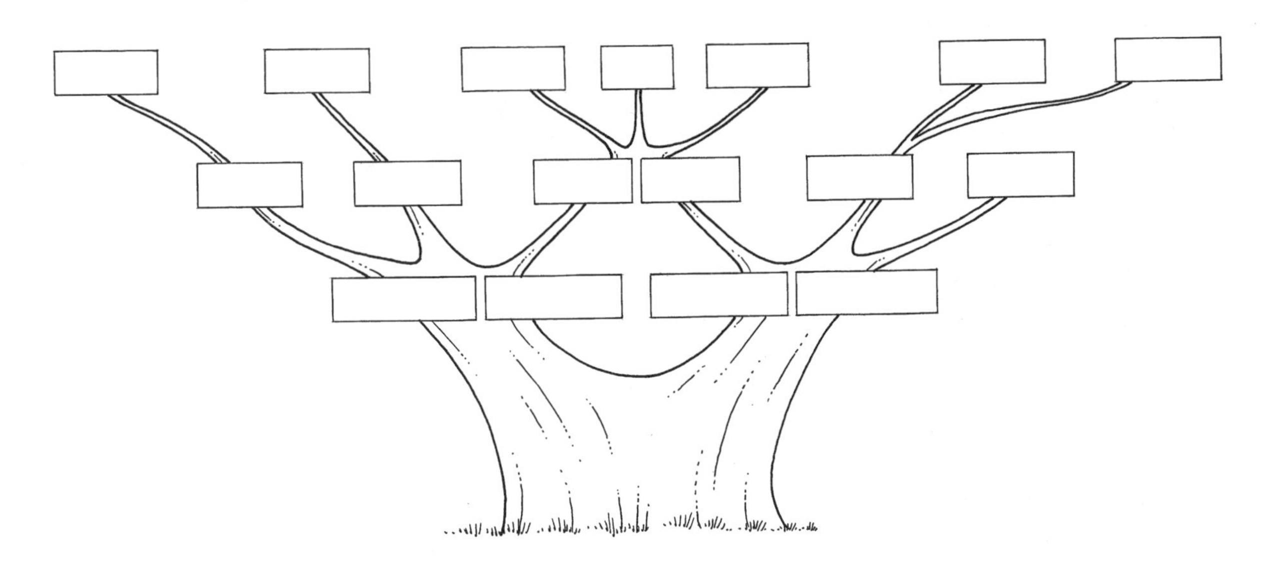

## Exercise 2 Mon identité

Complète ta fiche d'identité

*Complete your identity details*

Attaché votre photo ici

Je m'appelle

Nom

Prénom

Adresse

Ville

Code Postal

Téléphone

## Exercise 3 Dans la salle de classe

Ecris le nom des articles dans la salle de classe

*Write the names of the classroom objects on the page opposite*

| | |
|---|---|
| le | bureau |
| le | cahier |
| la | chaise |
| un | élève |
| une | élève |
| une | étagère |
| la | fenêtre |
| une | image |
| le | magnétophone |
| le | manuel |
| le | mur |
| un | ordinateur |
| le | placard |
| le | plafond |
| le | plancher |
| la | porte |
| le | poster |
| le | rétro-projecteur |
| la | table |
| le | tableau |

## Exercise 4 Mots croisés: mon matériel scolaire

Qu'est-ce que c'est en français?

*What are these in French?*

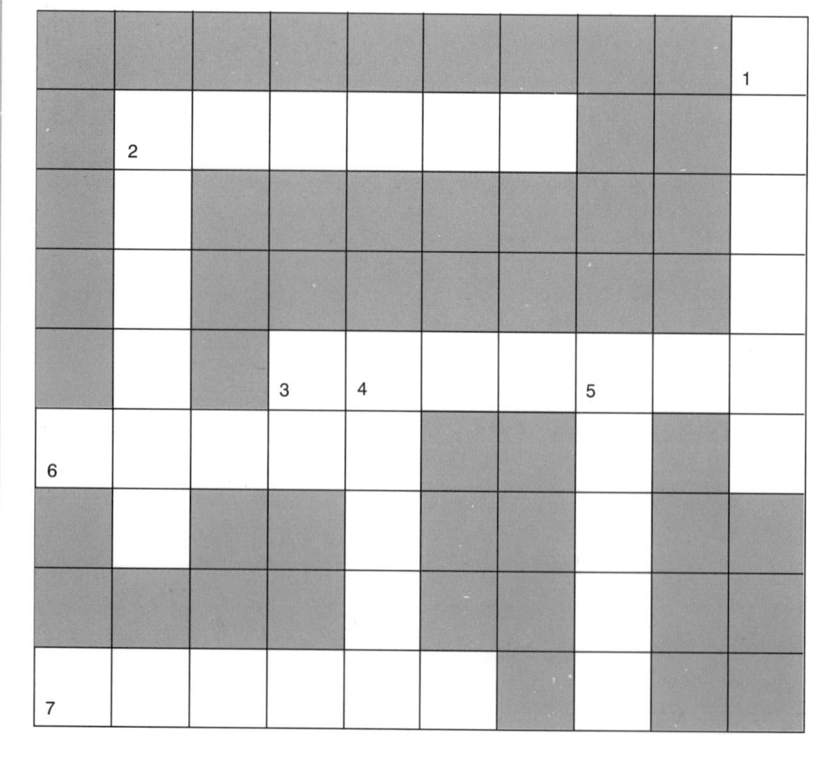

**Horizontalement:**

2

3

6

7 

**Verticalement:**

1 

2

4

5

## Exercice 5 Une lettre de Sophie

**A** Copie la lettre. Remplace les images par des mots

*Copy out the letter, inserting the correct words for the pictures:*

Basingstoke, le 10 octobre

Chère Gisèle

Je suis ta nouvelle correspondante anglaise. Je m'appelle Sophie Clarke et j'ai douze ans. J'habite Basingstoke. Basingstoke, c'est au de l'Angleterre . Nous habitons une . J'ai deux et une

 .

Nous avons un  et une .

J'aime et j'ai mon  . Comme mon père, j'aime regarder l'équipe de foot de Liverpool. Je vais au  tous les samedis.

A bientôt

Sophie

**B** Ecris la lettre en changeant les détails pour parler de toi.

*Write out this letter again changing the details to make it about you.*

## Exercice 6 A la maison

Regarde le plan de la maison. Ecris le nom des pièces dans les cases

*Look at the picture of a house. Write the names of the rooms into the correct boxes*

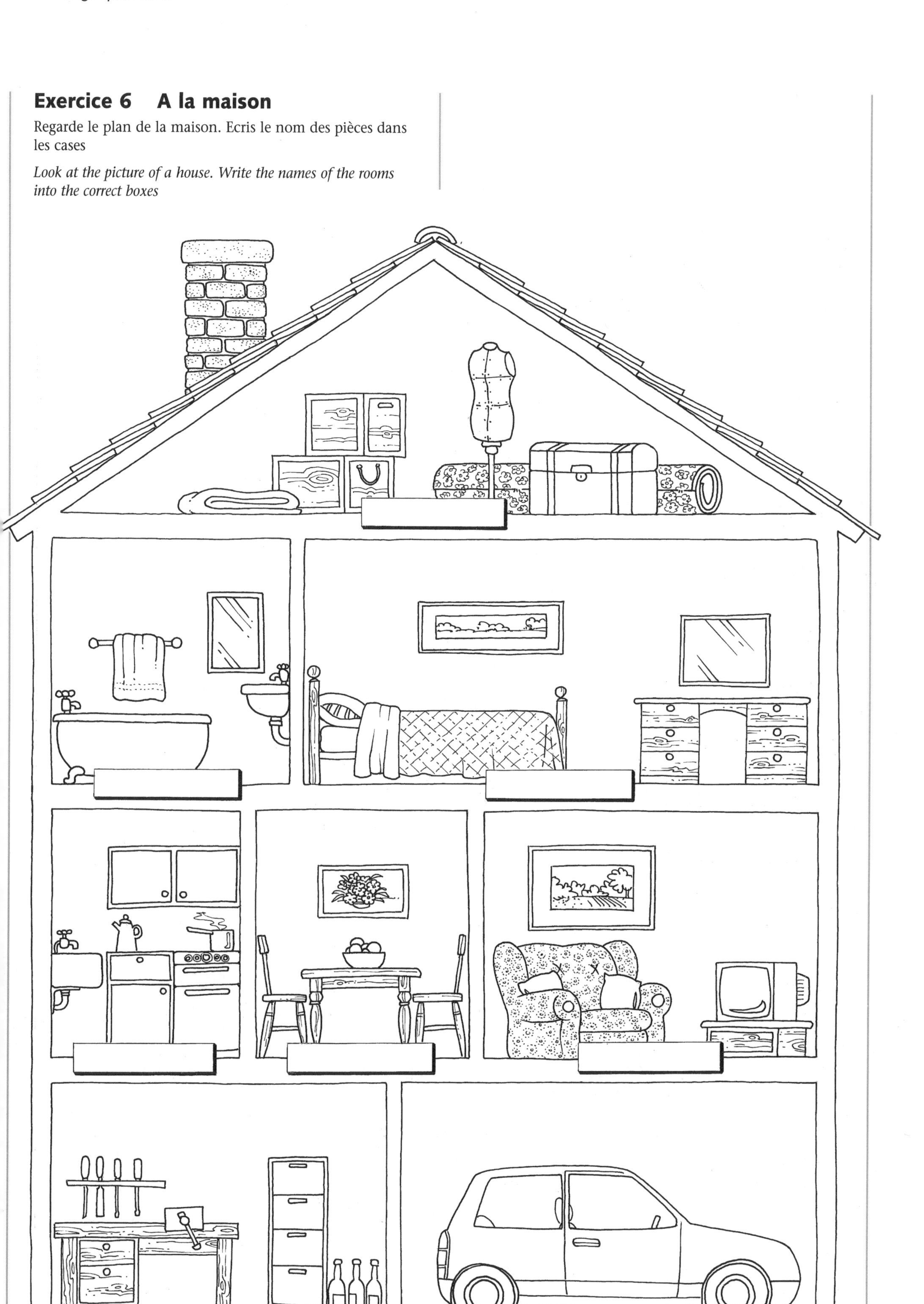

## Exercise 7 Ma chambre

Comment s'appellent les meubles?

*What are the items of furniture called?*

## Exercice 8 Les passetemps

Fais une copie de la lettre. Remplace les images par des mots

*Copy out the letter by replacing the pictures with the correct words:*

Cher Marie,

Merci de ta lettre. Moi aussi, j'aime écouter de la musique

Je joue depuis trois ans du  . J'aime faire de la  .
Le vendredi je vais à la 

. Mon frère collectionne des  .
Il aime aussi faire du 

Ecris-moi bientôt

Amy

## Exercice 9 Qu'est-ce que tu aimes faire?

Complète les phrases

*Complete the sentences*

**Exemple:**

J'aime

*J'aime **nager***

1 ____________________

2 ____________________

3 ____________________

4 ____________________

5 ____________________

6 ____________________

7 ____________________

8 ____________________

9 ____________________

CINEMA

**danser** **jouer au foot** **jouer de la guitare** **lire** **faire du jardinage**

**voir mes amis** **faire de la cuisine** **aller au cinéma**

**faire de l'équitation**

## Exercice 10 Le plan de la ville

Ecris le nom des bâtiments sous les symboles pour aider ton correspondant/ta correspondante. (En français, naturellement!)

*Write the names of the buildings under the symbols in the town plan to help your penfriend. (In French, of course)*

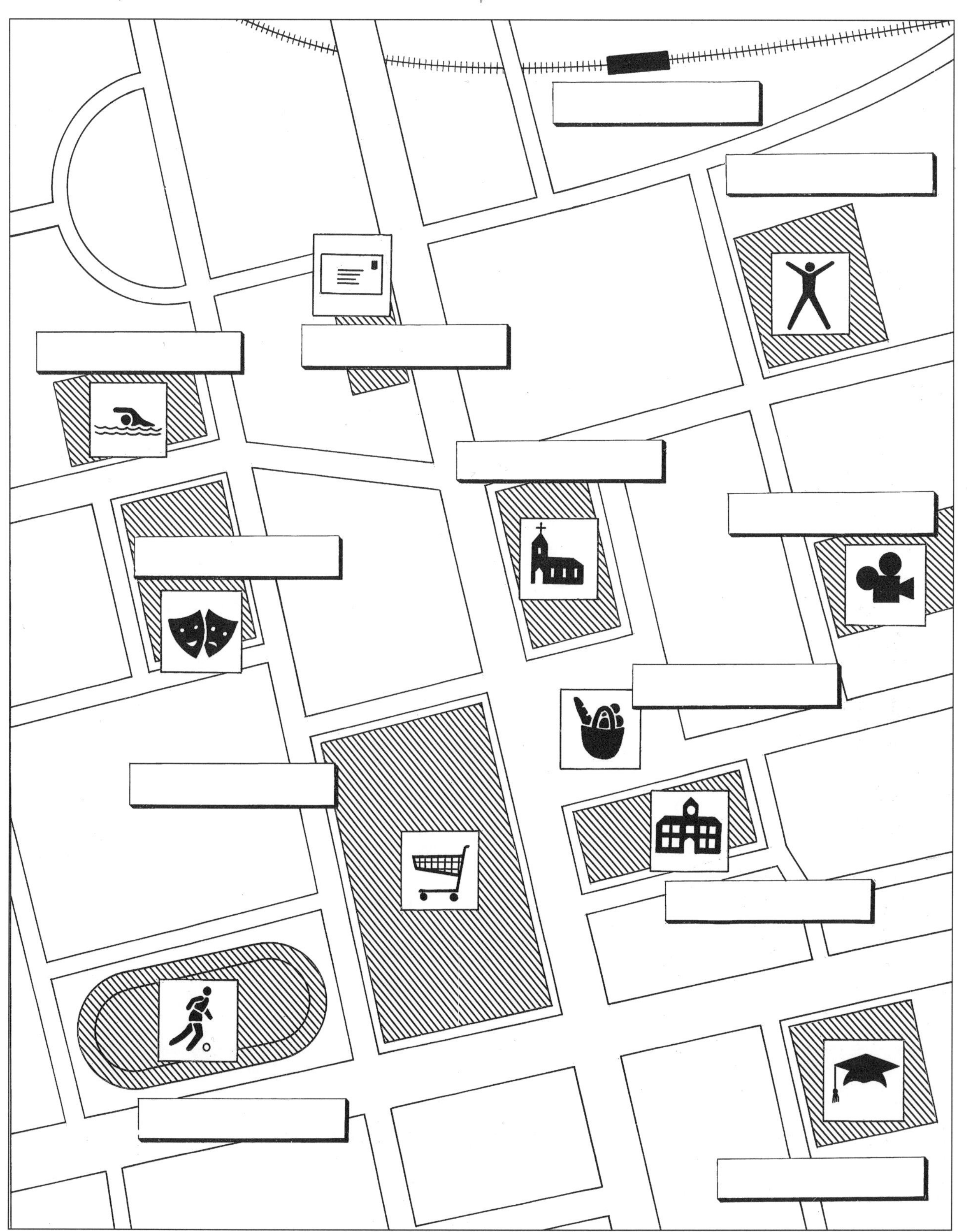

**piscine** **école** **gare SNCF** **poste** **centre commercial** **centre sportif**

**marché** **église** **cinéma** **théâtre** **stade** **hôtel de ville**

## Exercice 11 Quel temps fait-il?

Quel temps fait-il? Ecris une phrase pour chaque symbole

*What's the weather like? Write a sentence for each symbol*

1 ______________________________

2 ______________________________

3 ______________________________

4 ______________________________

5 ______________________________

## Exercice 12 Mon emploi du temps

Ecris ton emploi du temps personnel ici:

*Write your personal timetable in French here*

### EMPLOI DU TEMPS

| heure | lundi | mardi | mercredi | jeudi | vendredi | samedi |
|---|---|---|---|---|---|---|
| 1 | | | | | | |
| 2 | | | | | | |
| 3 | | | | | | |
| 4 | | | | | | |
| 5 | | | | | | |
| 6 | | | | | | |
| 7 | | | | | | |
| 8 | | | | | | |
| 9 | | | | | | |

## DEVOIRS

| | lundi | mardi | mercredi | jeudi | vendredi | samedi |
|---|---|---|---|---|---|---|
| 1 | | | | | | |
| 2 | | | | | | |
| 3 | | | | | | |

## Exercice 13 Les courses

**A** Tu vas faire des courses au marché. Ecris une liste de 5 fruits et 5 légumes que tu vas acheter

*You are going shopping in the market. Write a list with five fruits and five vegetables which you want to buy*

**B** Ecris une liste de 10 produits que ton correspondant/ta correspondante va acheter pour toi au supermarché

*Now write a shopping list for ten items of food which your French penfriend is to buy for you in a supermarket*

**C** Ton correspondant/ta correspondante va faire des courses pour toi
Ecris une liste avec cinq choses à acheter et cinq magasins différents

*Your penfriend wants to go shopping for you. You write a list with five shops and five items which she is to buy*

## Exercice 14 On part en voyage

Ton correspondant/ta correspondante va partir en vacances avec toi. Ecris une liste de dix choses à mettre dans son sac à dos

*Your penfriend is coming on holiday with you. Write a list for him/her with ten items which he/she needs to pack in his/her rucksack*

## Exercice 15 Les cartes postales

Regarde ces cartes postales. Puis remplis les blancs des cartes postales

*Look at these postcards, then fill in the blanks in the ones on the next page.*

Chère Maman,
Bonjour. Je suis au Pays de GALLES
Ici, on mange bien. On mange
beaucoup d'agneau et de légumes.
Est-ce que tu as passé de bonnes
vacances en Bretagne? Nous
rentrons la semaine prochaine
Grosses bises
Céline

Salut!
Je suis en Ecosse. Il ne fait pas beau.
Il pleut. Hier nous sommes allés à Edimbourg.
Demain nous faisons une randonnée en
montagne.
A bientôt.
Patrick

Remplis les blancs des cartes postales

*Fill in the gaps in these postcards*

**A**

**Cher ________________,**

**Je suis ________________ . Il ne fait pas ________________ . Il ________________ . Hier, nous sommes allés ________________ . Demain, nous ________________ .**

**A ________________**

**________________**

**B**

**Chère ________________,**

**Bonjour! Je suis ________________ . Ici, on mage bien. Il y a beaucoup de ________________ et beaucoup de ________________ . Est-ce que tu as ________________ de bonnes vacances ________________ ? Nous rentrons ________________**

**________________**

**Amitiés,**

**________________**

## Exercice 16 On fait une réservation au camping

Regarde cette lettre addressée à un camping

*Look at the following letter to a camp site*

12 North Road
Harlow
GB - CM20 2PP
le 10 juin

Camping Municpal de Bayeux
11 avenue de la Libération
14400 Bayeux
France

Messieurs

J'ai l'intention de venir en France à Bayeux du 13 au 15 juillet. Veuillez me réserver un emplacement pour deux tentes et cinq personnes. Veuillez confirmer cette réservation. Veuillez trouver ci-joint un coupon-réponse international.

Je vous prie d'agréer, Messieurs, l'expression de mes sentiments distingués.

***John McKeane***

Remplis la lettre ci-dessus en suivant les indications données

*Fill in the gaps in the following letter with suitable words*

Glasgow, le 5 AVRIL

M______________________,

J'ai l'intention de venir en France à La Baule du 

Veuillez me réserver des emplacements pour

 et  personnes. Veuillez confirmer cette

réservation. Ci-joint trouvez-vous  Je vous prie

d'agréer, Messieurs, l'expression de mes sentiments distingués.

____________________

## Exercice 17
## Une réservation d'hôtel

Regarde cette lettre de réservation d'hôtel. Remplis les blancs de la seconde lettre. La première lettre de chaque mot est indiquée.

*Look at the letter to a hotel. Then fill in the gaps in the second letter. The first letter of each word is given:*

20 Pont Severn Road
Whitchurch
Cardiff
GB - CF4 1YZ
le 20 mars

Hôtel de la Paix
3, place de la république,
44700 St Michel-Chef-Chef

Messieurs,

Je voudrais réserver une chambre pour deux personnes avec douche et une chambre pour une personne avec salle de bain. C'est pour la période entre le 20 et le 23 avril.

Est-ce que vos chambres ont le téléphone et la télevision? Y a-t-il un restaurant dans votre hôtel?
Veuillez confirmer cette réservation, et m'envoyer vos tarifs.
Je vous prie d'agréer, Messieurs, l'expression de mes sentiments distingués.

***Iolo Jones***

______, le ______ ______

Hôtel de la Paix

3, place de la république,

44700 St Michel-Chef-Chef

Messieurs,

Je voudrais réserver une **c**__________ pour deux **p**__________ avec **s**__________ de **b**__________ et une chambre pour **u**__________ personne avec **d**__________ . C'est pour la période entre **le** __________ et **le** __________ **m**__________ .

Est-ce que vos chambres ont le **t**__________ et la télevision? Y a-t-il un **r**__________ dans votre hôtel?
**V**__________ confirmer cette **r**__________ , et envoyez vos **t**__________ . Je vous prie d'__________ , Messieurs, l'expression de **m**__________ **s**__________ distingués.

__________________

# Writing: *answers*

## Exercice 1 Mon arbre généalogique

Answers for this will vary according to your circumstances.

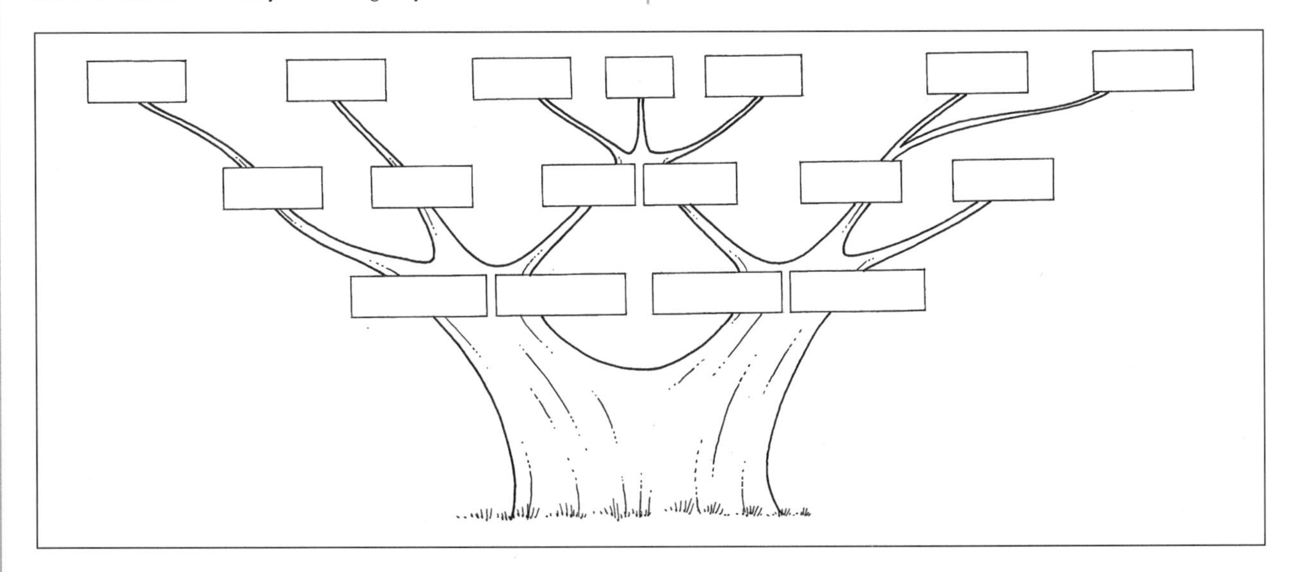

## Exercice 2 Mon identité

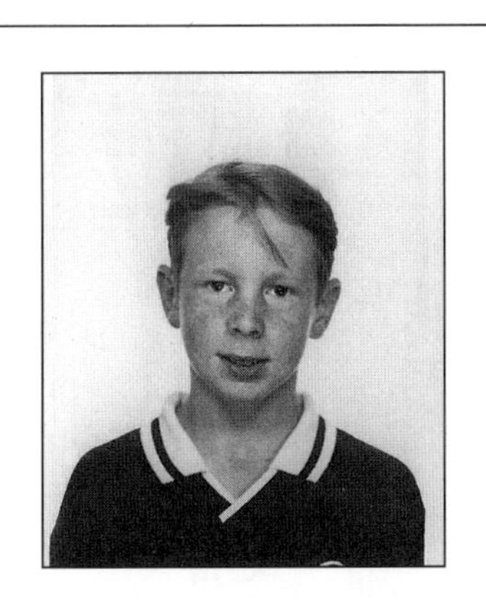

| | |
|---|---|
| Je m'appelle | **Alasdair McKeane** |
| Nom | **McKeane** |
| Prénom | **Alasdair** |
| Adresse | **3 Lower Close** |
| Ville | **Banbury** |
| Code Postal | **OX15 6NA** |
| Téléphone | **01684 893756** |

## Exercice 3 Dans la salle de classe

Ecris le nom des articles dans la salle de classe

*Write the names of the classroom objects (illustration below)*

| | | |
|---|---|---|
| le | bureau | *desk* |
| le | cahier | *exercise book* |
| la | chaise | *chair* |
| un | élève | *pupil (male)* |
| une | élève | *pupil (female)* |
| une | étagère | *shelf* |
| la | fenêtre | *window* |
| une | image | *picture* |
| le | magnétophone | *cassette recorder* |
| le | manuel | *text book* |
| le | mur | *wall* |
| un | ordinateur | *computer* |
| le | placard | *cupboard* |
| le | plafond | *ceiling* |
| le | plancher | *floor* |
| la | porte | *door* |
| le | poster | *poster* |
| le | rétro-projecteur | *overhead projector* |
| la | table | *table* |
| le | tableau | *board* |

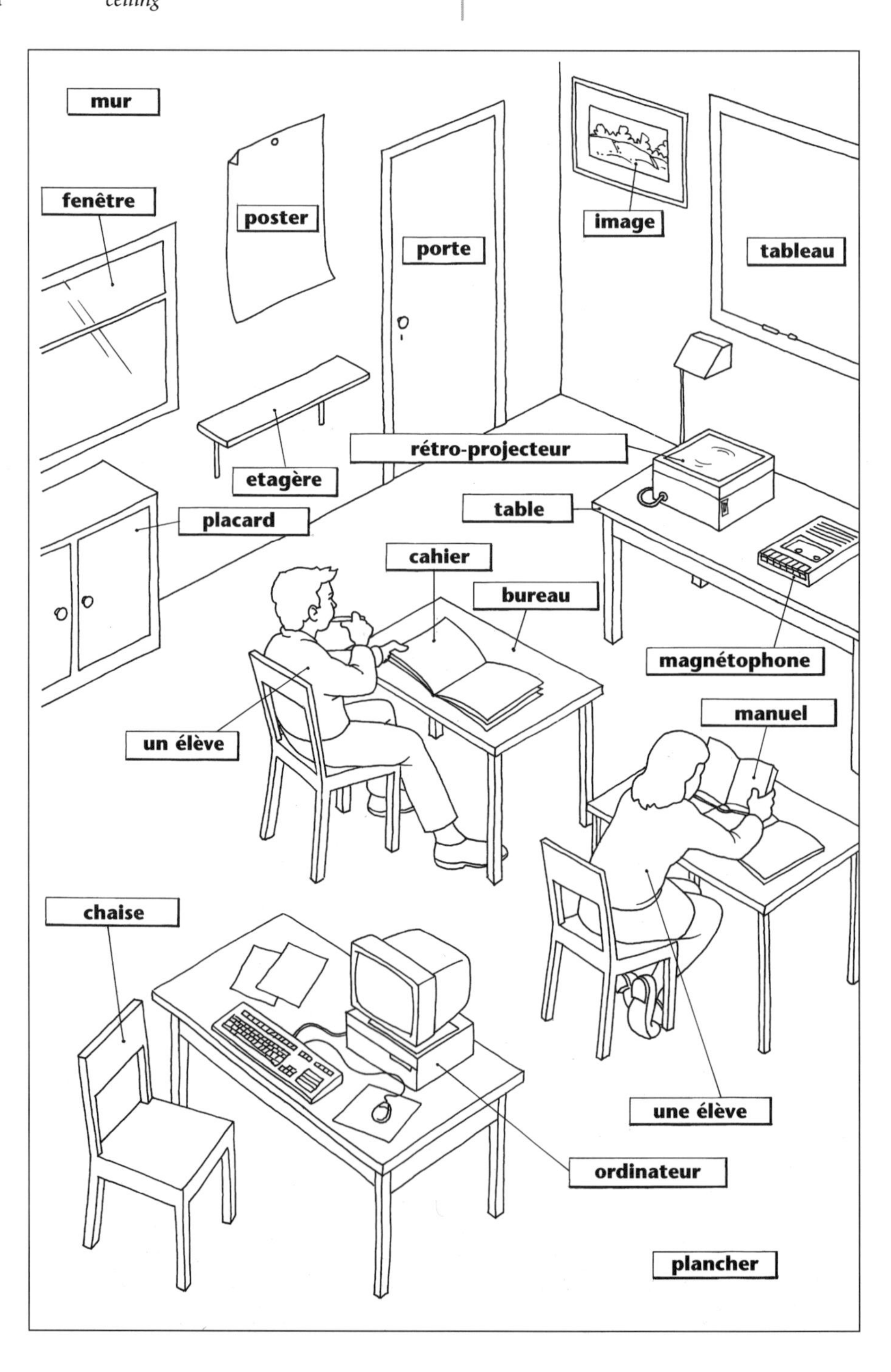

## Exercice 4 Mots croisés: mon matériel scolaire

Qu'est-ce que c'est en français?

*What are these in French?*

| | | | | | | | | | 1 M |
|---|---|---|---|---|---|---|---|---|---|
| | 2 C | A | H | I | E | R | | | A |
| | R | | | | | | | | N |
| | A | | | | | | | | U |
| | Y | | 3 T | 4 R | O | U | 5 S | S | E |
| 6 G | O | M | M | E | | | T | | L |
| | N | | | G | | | Y | | |
| | | | | L | | | L | | |
| 7 P | A | P | I | E | R | | O | | |

## Exercice 5 Une lettre de Sophie

**A**

Basingstoke, le 10 octobre

Chère Gisèle

Je suis ta nouvelle correspondante anglaise. Je m'appelle Sophie Clarke et j'ai douze ans. J'habite Basingstoke. Basingstoke, c'est au **sud** de l'Angleterre. Nous habitons une **maison**. J'ai deux **frères** et une **sœur**. Nous avons un **chien** et une **perruche**.

J'aime **lire** et j'ai mon **vélo**. Comme mon père, j'aime regarder l'équipe de foot de Liverpool. Je vais au **stade** tous les samedis
A bientôt
Sophie

**B** Answers to this will vary according to individual circumstances.

## Exercice 6 A la maison

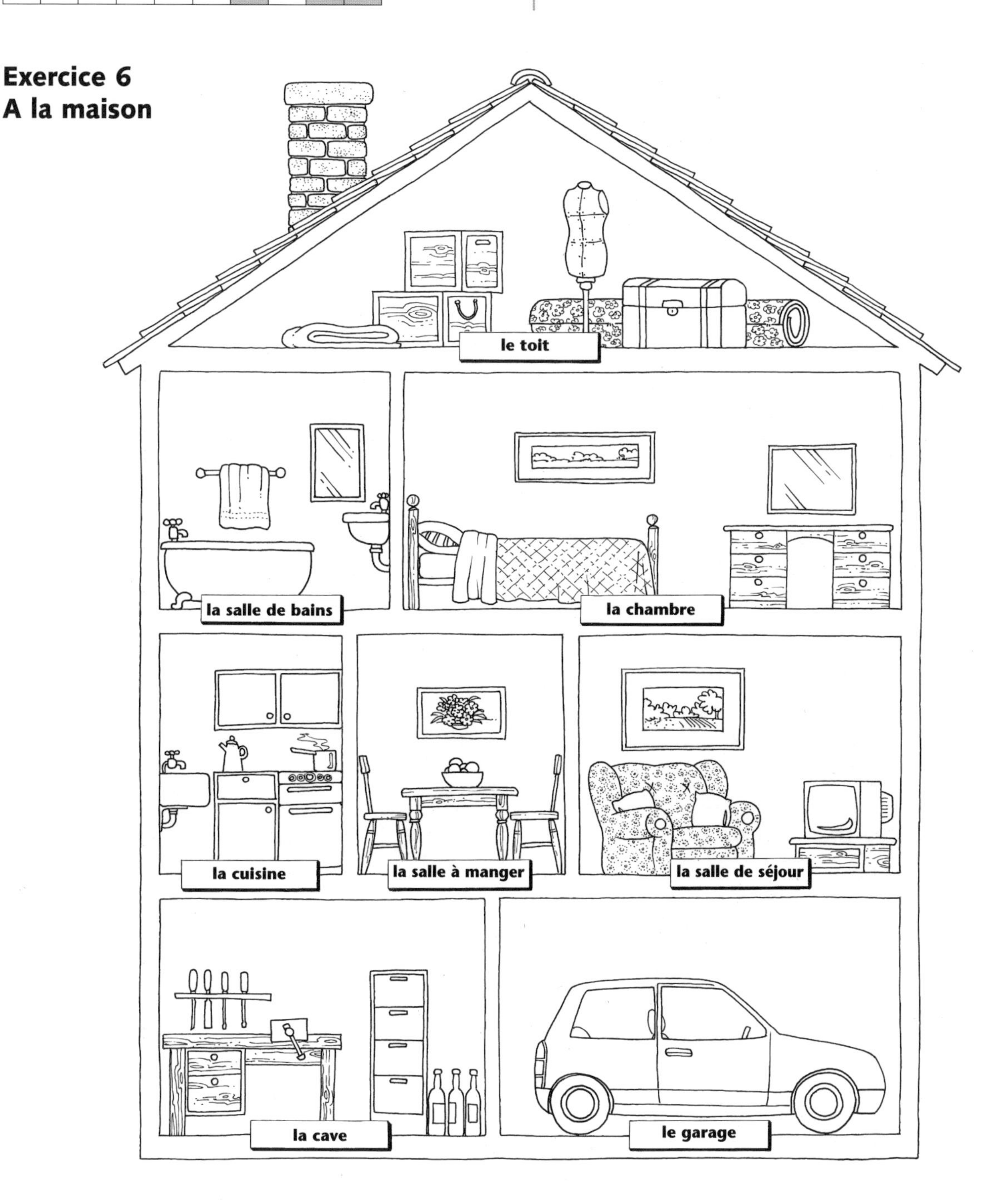

## Exercice 7 Ma chambre

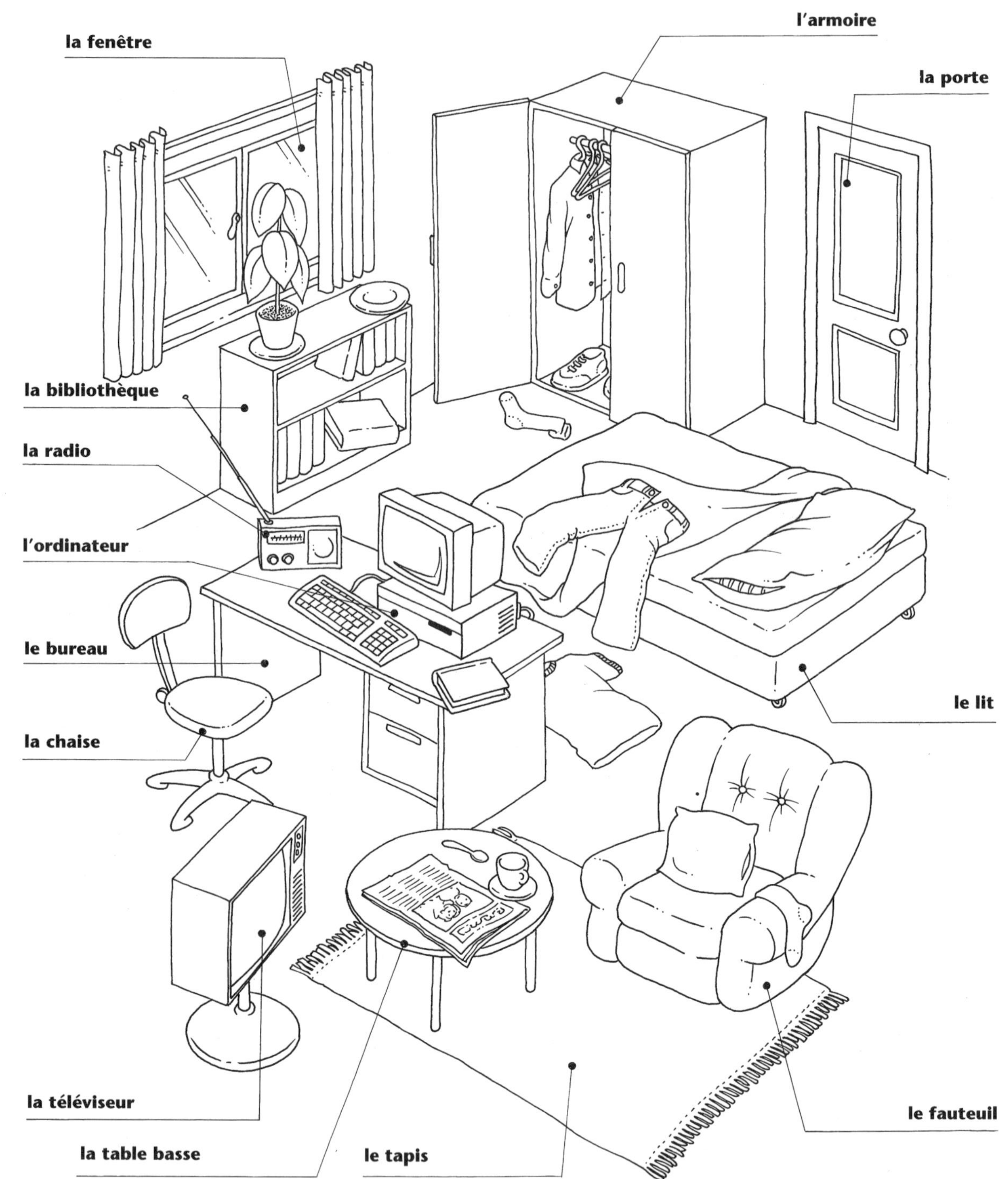


## Exercice 8 Les passetemps

Cher Daniel,

Merci de ta lettre. Moi aussi, j'aime écouter de la musique Je joue depuis trois ans du **piano**. J'aime faire de la **gymnastique**. Le vendredi je vais à la **discothèque**. Mon frère collectionne des **timbres** Il aime aussi faire du **vélo**

Ecris-moi bientôt

John

## Exercice 9 Qu'est-ce que tu aimes faire?

1 J'aime jouer au foot
2 J'aime danser
3 J'aime aller au cinéma
4 J'aime jouer de la guitare
5 J'aime lire
6 J'aime faire du jardinage
7 J'aime voir mes amis
8 J'aime faire de la cuisine
9 J'aime faire de l'équitation

## Exercice 10 Le plan de la ville

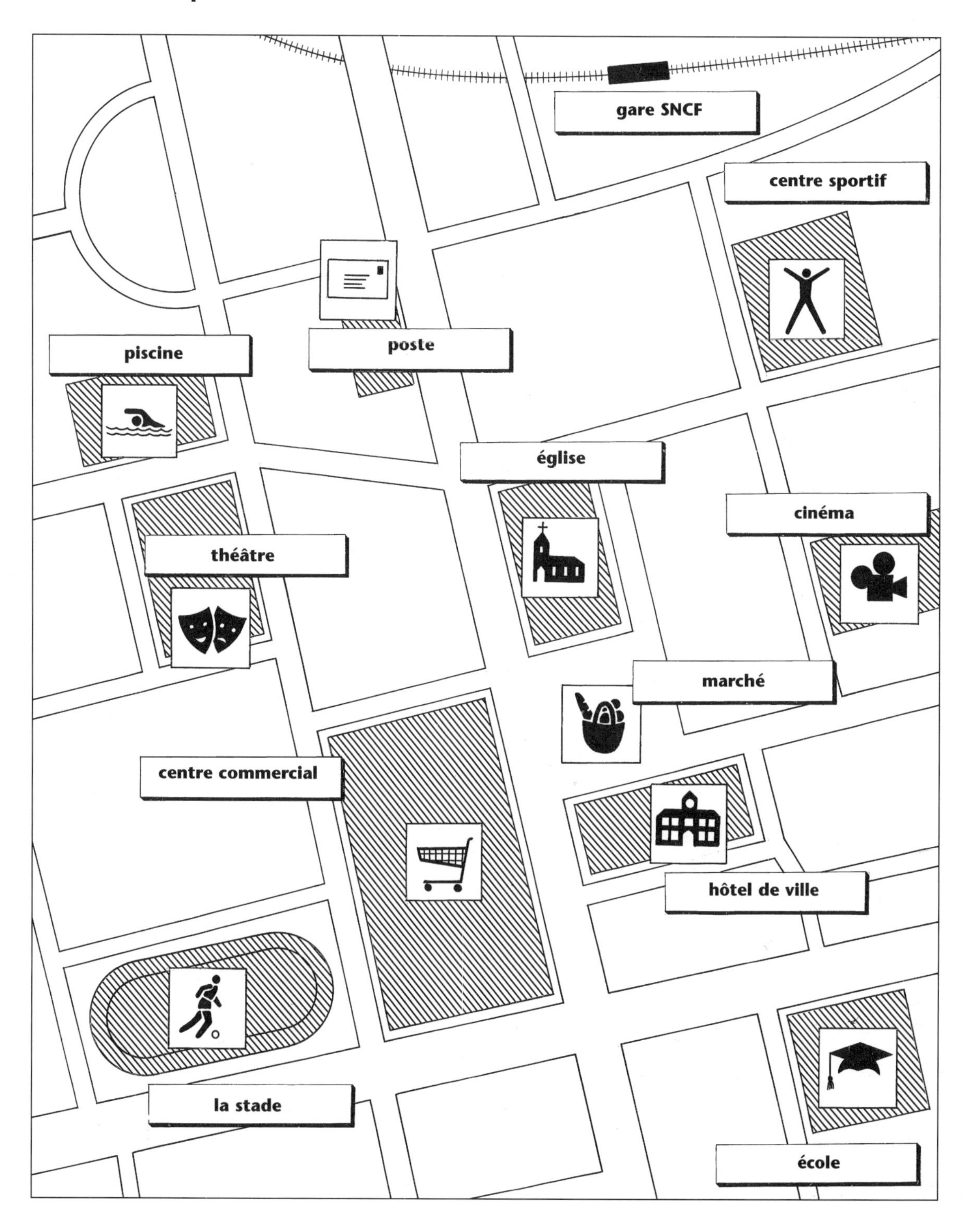


## Exercice 11 Quel temps fait-il?

**1** Il pleut
**2** Il fait beau/Il fait du soleil
**3** Il fait du vent
**4** Il fait du brouillard
**5** Il y a un orage

## Exercice 12 Mon emploi du temps

Answers for this will vary according to individual circumstances

## Exercice 13 Les courses

**A**

Possible answers include:

| ***Fruits*** | ***Légumes*** |
|---|---|
| *oranges* | *pommes de terre* |
| *pommes* | *carottes* |
| *fraises* | *petits pois* |
| *citrons* | *haricots verts* |
| *melons* | *laitue* |

**B**

Possible answers include:

*beurre*
*biscuits*
*fromage*
*sucre*
*lait*
*yaourt*
*moutarde*
*sel*
*poivre*
*margarine*

**C**

Possible answers include:

| **Objet** | **magasin** |
|---|---|
| *gâteau* | *pâtisserie* |
| *poisson* | *poissonnerie* |
| *pain* | *boulangerie* |
| *viande* | *boucherie* |
| *pizza* | *charcuterie* |

## Exercice 14 On part en voyage

Possible answers:

*sac de couchage*
*pull*
*livre*
*lampe*
*slips*
*chaussures de sport*
*maillot de bain*
*appareil-photo*
*serviette*
*savon*

## Exercice 15 Les cartes postales

**A**

Cher Jean

Je suis **en Angleterre**. Il ne fait pas **chaud**. Il **neige**. Hier, nous sommes allés à **Oxford**. Demain, nous **allons à Birmingham faire des courses**.

A **bientôt**

Peter

**B**

Chère Gisèle,

Bonjour! Je suis **en France**. Ici, on mange bien. Il y a beaucoup de **bœuf** et beaucoup de **fromage**. Est-ce que tu as **passé** de bonnes vacances **en Espagne**? Nous rentrons **demain**.

Amitiés,

**Catharine**

## Exercice 16 On fait une réservation au camping

**A**

Glasgow, le **5 avril**

**Messieurs**

J'ai l'intention de venir en France à La Baule du **22 au 25 mai**. Veuillez me réserver des emplacements pour **une caravane** et **quatre personnes**. Veuillez confirmer cette réservation. Veuillez trouver ci-joint **un coupon-réponse international**.

Je vous prie d'agréer, Messieurs, l'expression de mes sentiments distingués.

**James McKeane**

## Exercice 17 Une réservation d'hôtel

Belfast, le 5 mai

Hôtel de la Paix
3, place de la république,
44700 St Michel-Chef-Chef

Messieurs,

Je voudrais réserver une **chambre** pour deux **personnes** avec **salle** de **bain** et une chambre pour une personne avec **douche**. C'est pour la période entre le **4** et **le** 7 **mai**. Est-ce que vos chambres ont le **téléphone** et la télevision? Y a-t-il un **restaurant** dans votre hôtel?

**Veuillez** confirmer cette **réservation**, et envoyez vos **tarifs**.

Je vous prie d'**agréer**, Messieurs, l'expression de **mes sentiments** distingués.

**Seamus Reilly**

# Section four

## Vocabulary

The **topics** to be covered are arranged in three **Areas of Experience**, **A**, **B** and **C** respectively. Each of these can in turn be broken down into three headings.

- **Area of Experience A** is called **Everyday activities**, and includes:
  - classroom language
  - home and school life
  - food, health, and fitness
- **Area of Experience B** is called **Personal and social life**, and includes:
  - yourself, your family, and your personal relationships
  - your free time and social activities
  - holidays and special occasions
- **Area of Experience C** is called **The world around us** and includes:
  - your home town and local area
  - the natural and man-made environment
  - people, places and customs

The vocabulary in this book has not been arranged in the same order as the Areas of Experience listed above. Instead, we have used our teaching experience to put vocabulary in the order in which you might expect to come across it in Key Stage 3 by the end of Year 9. If you are learning French as a second language, it is possible you might not cover all the ground by the end of year 9, depending on when you started learning French.

The chart overleaf will tell you, at a glance, the order in which the vocabulary topics are arranged in this book and where you can find them.

| *topic* | | *AoE* |
|---|---|---|
| **Généralités (pp. 101–102)** | Salutations (p. 101)<br>Expressions générales (101)<br>Des vœux (p. 101)<br>Les opinions (p. 101)<br>Des questions (p. 101)<br>Des prépositions (p. 101)<br>Les couleurs (p. 102) | |
| **Moi, ma famille, mes amis (pp. 102–105)** | Détails personnels (p. 102)<br>L'adresse (p. 103)<br>Les animaux (p. 104)<br>Les membres de la famille (p. 104)<br>Les professions (p. 105) | B |
| **En Classe (pp. 105–107)** | Dans la salle de classe (p. 105)<br>Le profeseur dit: (p. 106)<br>Le professeur corrige (p. 106)<br>L'élève dit (p. 106)<br>L'alphabet (p. 107)<br>La ponctuation (p. 107) | A |
| **Le Temps libre (pp. 107–109)** | Les passetemps (p. 107)<br>Les sports (p. 107)<br>La musique (p. 108)<br>L'informatique (p. 109)<br>D'autres passetemps (p. 109) | B |
| **La ville (pp. 109–110)** | En ville (p. 109) | C |
| **Pour aller à... (pp. 110–111)** | Les directions (p. 110) | C |
| **A la campagne (p. 111)** | | C |
| **Le temps (pp. 111–112)** | | C |
| **A l'école (pp. 112–114)** | A l'école (p. 112)<br>Le personnel (p. 112)<br>Les matières (p. 112)<br>Les bâtiments (p. 112)<br>Des verbes scolaires (p. 113) | A |
| **La santé et la forme (pp. 114–115)** | Les parties du corps (p. 114)<br>Chez le médecin, chez le dentiste (p. 114)<br>A la pharmacie (p. 114) | A |
| **La vie familiale (pp. 115–117)** | Le logement (p. 115)<br>Les pièces (p. 115)<br>Les élélments du bâtiment (p. 115)<br>Dans la salle de bains (p. 115)<br>Dans la chambre à coucher (p. 115)<br>Dans la salle de séjour (p. 115)<br>Dans la salle à manger (p. 116)<br>A la cuisine (p. 116)<br>Au jardin (p. 116) | A |

| *topic* | | *AoE* |
|---|---|---|
| **La routine journalière (p. 117)** | | A |
| **L'argent de poche (p. 117)** | | B |
| **Au café (p. 118)** | Les boissons (p. 118)<br>Les casse-croûte (p. 118)<br>Au café (p. 118) | A |
| **Au restaurant (pp. 118–119)** | Le menu (p. 118) | A |
| **Les commissions (pp. 119–121)** | On achète des vêtements (p. 119)<br>On achète à manger (p. 120)<br>La viande (p. 120)<br>Les légumes (p. 120)<br>Les fruits (p. 120)<br>Les boissons (p. 121)<br>L'alimentations générale (p. 121)<br>Les souvenirs (p. 121) | C |
| **La banque et la poste (pp. 121–122)** | A la banque (p. 121)<br>A la poste (p. 121) | C |
| **En voyage (pp. 122–123)** | Les moyens de transport (p. 122)<br>En train (p. 122)<br>En autobus (p. 122)<br>Par avion (p. 123)<br>La traversée de la Manche (p. 123) | C |
| **Les excursions (p. 122)** | On sort (p. 123) | B |
| **Les jours de fête (p. 124)** | | B |
| **Les vacances (pp. 124–126)** | Au camping (p. 125)<br>A l'auberge de jeunesse (p. 125)<br>A l'hôtel (p. 126)<br>A la plage (p. 126)<br>A la campagne (p. 126) | B |
| **Les médias (p. 127–128)** | Les différents médias (p. 127)<br>Les appareils (p. 127)<br>Au cinéma (p. 127)<br>La télé, la radio (p. 127)<br>Les émissions (p. 127)<br>La lecture (p. 128) | A |

# Checklist of language tasks:

This list follows the order of topics in the Vocabulary topic section (see page 101).

Tick off each thing you learn how to do as you go through your course.

There is a second box provided to help you with your revision.

| | | Learnt | Revised |
|---|---|---|---|
| **Généralités** | | | |
| I can | greet people | | |
| | make sociable noises | | |
| | give good wishes | | |
| | give my opinion | | |
| I know | the question words | | |
| | my French prepositions | | |
| | the colours | | |
| **Moi, ma famille, mes amis** | | | |
| I can give my | age | | |
| | name | | |
| | date of birth | | |
| | address | | |
| | phone number | | |
| I can say | where I come from | | |
| I can talk about | my pets | | |
| | my family | | |
| I know | the names of jobs and professions | | |
| **En classe** | | | |
| I know | classroom objects | | |
| I understand | classroom commands | | |
| I can | make classroom requests in French | | |
| | spell out loud using the French alphabet | | |
| | use the French words for punctuation | | |
| **Le temps libre** | | | |
| I can talk about | hobbies | | |
| | sport | | |
| | music | | |
| | information technology | | |
| | other hobbies | | |
| **La ville** | | | |
| I know | the names of places in town | | |
| I can | describe the town/village I live in | | |

| | | Learnt | Revised |
|---|---|---|---|
| **Pour aller á... ?** | | | |
| I can | ask for directions | | |
| | understand directions | | |
| | give directions | | |
| **A la campagne** | | | |
| I know | the names of features of the countryside | | |
| I can | give my opinion of living in the country | | |
| **Le temps** | | | |
| I can | understand simple weather forecasts | | |
| | discuss the weather | | |
| **A l'école** | | | |
| I know | the names of different types of school | | |
| I can discuss | holidays, terms, timetable and staff | | |
| I know | the names of school subjects | | |
| I can | describe the building | | |
| I know | useful 'school' verbs | | |
| I can discuss | school routine | | |
| **La santé et la forme** | | | |
| I know | parts of the body | | |
| I can survive | at the doctor's | | |
| | at the dentist's | | |
| | at the chemist's | | |
| **La vie familiale** | | | |
| I can describe | housing | | |
| | rooms | | |
| | parts of buildings | | |
| | the contents of the bathroom | | |
| | the contents of the bedroom | | |
| | the contents of the living-room | | |
| | the contents of the dining-room | | |
| | the contents of the kitchen | | |
| | the garden | | |
| I can | describe family activities | | |
| | offer to help | | |
| **La routine journalière** | | | |
| I can | describe morning and evening routines | | |

| | | Learnt | Revised |
|---|---|---|---|
| **L'argent de poche** | | | |
| I can | talk about coins and notes | | |
| | say how much pocket money I get | | |
| | say what I spend it on | | |
| | say what I am saving up for | | |
| **Au café** | | | |
| I know | the names of drinks | | |
| | the names of foods | | |
| I can | order what I want | | |
| **Au restaurant** | | | |
| I know | the names of drinks | | |
| | the names of foods | | |
| I can | order what I want | | |
| **Les commissions** | | | |
| I know | the names of shops and departments in shops | | |
| I know | the names of clothing items | | |
| | the names of materials | | |
| I can | buy clothes | | |
| I know | the names of meats | | |
| | the names of vegetables | | |
| | the names of fruits | | |
| I can | buy meat, fruit and vegetables | | |
| I know | the names of drinks and snacks | | |
| | the names of souvenirs | | |
| I can | buy drinks, snacks and souvenirs | | |
| **La banque et la poste** | | | |
| I know | money vocabulary | | |
| I can | change money | | |
| I know | post office vocabulary | | |
| I can survive | in the post office | | |
| **En voyage** | | | |
| I know | the names of means of transport | | |
| | railway vocabulary | | |
| I can | buy tickets | | |
| | enquire about trains | | |
| I know | bus vocabulary | | |
| I can | enquire about buses | | |
| I know | plane vocabulary | | |
| I can | buy tickets | | |

| | | Learnt | Revised |
|---|---|---|---|
| I can | enquire about planes | | |
| | discuss Channel crossings | | |
| **Les excursions** | | | |
| I can | talk about going out for the evening | | |
| | discuss sport, cinema, theatre, youth club | | |
| | invite someone out | | |
| | make excuses | | |
| | agree | | |
| | make arrangements | | |
| | ask about price and times | | |
| | buy tickets | | |
| | say what I did yesterday evening | | |
| **Les jours de fête** | | | |
| I know | the names of holidays and festivals | | |
| I can | discuss how they are celebrated | | |
| **Les vacances** | | | |
| I can | discuss holiday plans | | |
| | obtain tourist information | | |
| I know | camping vocabulary | | |
| | youth hostel vocabulary | | |
| I can | survive in a youth hostel | | |
| I know | hotel vocabulary | | |
| I can | survive in a hotel | | |
| I know | seaside vocabulary | | |
| | country holiday vocabulary | | |
| I can | discuss what I did on holiday | | |
| | give my opinion | | |
| **Les médias** | | | |
| I know | the names of the media | | |
| | the names of media equipment | | |
| | the types of film | | |
| I can | discuss a cinema visit | | |
| I know | the types of TV programme | | |
| I can | discuss viewing habits | | |
| | give my opinion | | |
| | ask permission to watch TV | | |
| | ask permission to listen to the radio | | |
| I know | the types of books and magazines | | |
| I can | discuss reading habits | | |

# Vocabulary topics

## Key:

| | |
|---|---|
| (e) | feminine form |
| (s) | plural form |
| (m) | masculine |
| (f) | feminine |
| (m pl) | masculine plural |
| (f pl) | feminine plural |
| (sing) | singular |
| * | verb takes *être* in the perfect tense |

# Généralités / General

## Salutations / Greetings

| | |
|---|---|
| bonjour | Good morning, Good day, Good afternoon! |
| bonsoir | Good evening! |
| bonne nuit | Good night! |
| au revoir | Goodbye! |
| salut! | Hi! |
| à tout à l'heure | See you later! |
| à demain | See you tomorrow! |
| Ça va? | How are you? |
| Ça va bien, merci | Fine, thanks! |
| Je te présente mon ami Michel | May I introduce my friend Michel? |
| enchanté(e) | Pleased to meet you. |
| s'il te plaît/s'il vous plaît | please |
| merci | thank you |
| excusez-moi | excuse me, sorry |
| pardon | pardon |
| oui | yes |
| non | no |
| pas du tout | not at all |

## Expressions générales / Fillers

| | |
|---|---|
| Oui, bien sûr | Yes, of course |
| D'accord | Agreed |
| C'est gentil | That is very kind |
| Je crois que oui | I think so |
| peut-être | perhaps |
| probablement | I suppose so |
| Ça ne fait rien | It doesn't matter |
| Cela m'est égal | I don't mind |
| Quel dommage | What a pity |
| Amuse-toi bien | Enjoy yourself |

## Des vœux / Best wishes

| | |
|---|---|
| Meilleurs vœux | Best wishes |
| Bon anniversaire! | Happy Birthday! |
| Bonne année! | Happy New Year! |
| Bonne chance! | Good luck! |
| Bonne journée! | Have a nice day! |
| Bon voyage! | Have a good journey! |
| Joyeux Noël | Happy Christmas |
| Joyeuses Pâques | Happy Easter |

## Les opinions / Opinions

| | |
|---|---|
| J'aime... | I like... |
| J'adore... | I love... |
| Je n'aime pas... | I don't like... |
| Je déteste... | I hate... |
| C'est intéressant | It's interesting |
| C'est ennuyeux | It's boring |
| Je trouve... | I think |

## Des questions / Question words

| | |
|---|---|
| A quelle heure...? | At what time...? |
| Combien (de)...? | How many...? |
| Comment? | How? |
| Comment est...? | What is ... like? |
| Où? | Where? |
| Pourquoi? | Why? |
| Peut-on...? | Can you...? |
| Puis-je...? | May I...? Can I...? |
| Quand? | When? |
| Quel, Quels? (m) | Which? |
| Quelle, Quelles? (f) | Which? |
| Qu'est-ce qui...? | What? |
| Qu'est-ce que...? | What? |
| Qui? | Who? |
| Y a-t-il...? | Is there..?/Are there..? |

## Des prépositions / Prepositions

These have been given with their most common meanings. Check them also in the grammar section.

| | |
|---|---|
| à | to, at, in |
| à côté de | next to, beside |
| après | after |
| avant | before |
| avec | with |
| chez | at the house of |
| dans | in |
| de | from, of |
| derrière | behind |
| devant | in front of |
| en | by, in, with |
| en face de | opposite |
| entre | between |
| pour | for, in order to |
| près de | near |
| sous | under |
| sur | on |
| sans | without |
| vers | towards (place), at about (time) |

## Les couleurs — Colours

| Masculine Singular | Feminine Singular | Masculine Plural | Feminine Plural | Meaning |
|---|---|---|---|---|
| bleu | bleue | bleus | bleues | *blue* |
| bleu **marine** | bleu **marine** | bleu **marine** | bleu **marine** | ***navy** blue* |
| blanc | blanche | blancs | blanches | *white* |
| brun | brune | bruns | brunes | *brown* |
| gris | grise | gris | grises | *grey* |
| gris **clair** | gris **clair** | gris **clair** | gris **clair** | ***light** grey* |
| gris **foncé** | gris **foncé** | gris **foncé** | gris **foncé** | ***dark** grey* |
| jaune | jaune | jaunes | jaunes | *yellow* |
| marron | marron | marron | marron | *chestnut brown* |
| noir | noire | noirs | noires | *black* |
| rose | rose | roses | roses | *pink* |
| rouge | rouge | rouges | rouges | *red* |
| vert | verte | verts | vertes | *green* |

# Moi, mes amis, ma famille — Myself, family, friends

### Détails personnels — Personal details

| | | |
|---|---|---|
| l' | âge (m) | age |
| un | anniversaire | birthday |
| la | carte d'identité | identity card |
| la | dame | lady |
| le | lieu de naissance | place of birth |
| | Madame | Mrs, Ms |
| | Mademoiselle | Miss |
| le | mois | month |
| | Monsieur | Mr, Sir, gentleman |
| le | nom | name |
| le | nom de famille | surname |
| le | parent | parent |
| le | passeport | passport |
| la | pièce d'identité | identification |
| le | prénom | first name, Christian name |
| la | signature | signature |
| le | signe du zodiaque | star sign |
| | Verseau | Aquarius |
| | Poissons | Pisces |
| | Bélier | Aries |
| | Taureau | Taurus |
| | Gémeaux | Gemini |
| | Cancer | Cancer |
| | Lion | Leo |
| | Vierge | Virgo |
| | Balance | Libra |
| | Scorpion | Scorpio |
| | Sagittaire | Sagittarius |
| | Capricorne | Capricorn |
| s' | appeler | to be called |
| | écrire | to write |
| | habiter | to live |
| | signer | to sign |

### Phrases

#### Questions — Questions

| | |
|---|---|
| Comment t'appelles-tu? | What's your name? |
| Quel âge as-tu? | How old are you? |
| Où habites-tu? | Where do you live? |
| Quelle est la date de ton anniversaire? | When is your birthday? |
| En quelle année es-tu né(e)? | In which year were you born? |
| Tu es de quelle nationalité? | Which nationality are you? |
| D'où viens-tu? | Where do you come from? |

#### Réponses — Answers

| | |
|---|---|
| Je m'appelle Michelle Janneau | My name is Michelle Janneau |
| Mon prénom, c'est Michelle | My first name is Michelle |
| Mon nom de famille, c'est Janneau | My surname is Janneau |
| J'ai douze ans | I am twelve years old |
| J'habite Nantes | I live in Nantes |
| Mon anniversaire, c'est le sept novembre | My birthday is on 7th November |
| Je suis né(e) en 1983. | I was born in 1983 |

| | |
|---|---|
| Je suis anglais(e) | I am English |
| écossais(e) | Scottish |
| gallois(e) | Welsh |
| irlandais(e) | Irish |
| britannique | British |
| Je viens de Liverpool dans le nord de l'Angleterre | I come from Liverpool in the North of England |

## L'adresse — Address

| | | |
|---|---|---|
| une | adresse | address |
| une | allée | avenue |
| | CEDEX | PO box |
| le | code postal | postcode |
| une | impasse | cul-de-sac |
| le | numéro de téléphone | telephone number |
| le | pays | country |
| la | place | square, place |
| le | quartier | district, part of a town |
| la | région | region |
| la | route | road (main) |
| la | rue | street |
| le | village | village |
| la | ville | town |

## Exemples d'adresses françaises

**Monsieur et Madame DURAND Jean**
**31 rue de la République**
**75001 PARIS**
**France**

**Mademoiselle MARTINEAU Odile**
**133 avenue du Général de Gaulle**
**69200 VENISSIEUX**
**France**

## Les animaux — Pets

| | | |
|---|---|---|
| le | canari | canary |
| le | chat | cat |
| le | cheval | horse |
| le | chien | dog |
| le | cobaye/cochon d'Inde | guinea pig |
| la | gerbille | gerbil |
| un | hamster | hamster |
| le | lapin | rabbit |
| un | oiseau | bird |
| la | perruche | budgie |
| le | poisson | fish |
| le | poisson rouge | goldfish |
| le | poney | pony |
| le | rat | rat |
| le | serpent | snake |
| la | souris | mouse |
| la | tortue | tortoise |
| | aimable | likeable |
| | amusant | funny |
| | délicat | dainty, delicate |
| | gentil | affectionate |
| | grand | big |
| | méchant | vicious |
| | mignon | cute, sweet |
| | petit | small |
| | brosser | to brush |
| | donner à manger | to feed |
| | promener | to take for a walk |
| | nettoyer | to clean |

### Phrases

| | |
|---|---|
| J'ai un chien | I have a dog |
| Il est assez grand et brun | He is fairly big and brown |
| C'est un colley | He's a collie |
| Je promène mon chien tous les jours | I take my dog for a walk every day |
| Mon chat est très gentil | My cat is very affectionate |
| Ma soeur a des poissons | My sister has fish |
| Elle leur donne à manger tous les jours | She feeds them every day |
| Une fois par semaine elle nettoie l'aquarium | Once a week she cleans out the aquarium |
| Je n'ai pas d'animal à la maison | I haven't got any pets |
| J'ai une allergie contre les chiens et les chats | I am allergic to dogs and cats |

## Les membres de la famille — Family members

| | | |
|---|---|---|
| la | belle-mère | stepmother, mother-in-law |
| la | demi-sœur | half-sister |
| le | beau-père | stepfather, father-in-law |
| le | demi-frère | half-brother |
| un/une | adolescent(e) | adolescent |
| un | adulte | adult |
| un | ami | friend (male) |
| une | amie | friend (female) |
| le | bébé | baby |
| le | correspondant | penfriend (male) |
| la | correspondante | penfriend (female) |
| le | cousin | cousin (male) |
| la | cousine | cousin (female) |
| un | enfant | child |
| la | famille | family |
| la | femme | woman/wife |
| le/la | fiancé(e) | fiancé(e) |
| la | fille | girl, daughter |
| le | fils | son |
| le | frère | brother |
| le | garçon | boy |
| la | grand-mère | grandmother |
| les | grand-parents (pl) | grandparents |
| le | grand-père | grandfather |
| un | homme | man |
| la | maman | mummy |
| la | mami | grandma |
| le | mari | husband |
| la | mère | mother |
| un | oncle | uncle |
| le | papa | daddy |
| le | papi | grandpa |
| le | parent | parent |
| le/la | parent(e) | relative of any kind |
| le | père | father |
| le | petit-fils | grandson |
| la | petite-fille | granddaughter |
| la | sœur | sister |
| la | tante | aunt |
| | divorcé(e) | divorced |
| | fiancé(e) | engaged |
| | marié(e) | married |
| | mort(e) | dead |
| | veuf/veuve | widowed |
| | aimer | to like |
| se | disputer | to argue |
| s' | entendre bien/mal avec | to get on well/badly with |
| s' | expliquer avec | to have an argument with |

### Phrases

| | |
|---|---|
| As-tu des frères et des sœurs? | Have you got any brothers or sisters? |
| Oui, j'ai un frère/une sœur | Yes, I have got a brother/sister |
| Oui, j'ai deux frères/deux sœurs | Yes, I have got two brothers/sister |
| Non, je suis enfant unique | No, I am an only child |

| | |
|---|---|
| As-tu une grande famille? | Have you got lots of relatives? |
| Oui, j'ai une tante, Jenny, et deux oncles, Keith et Nigel | Yes, I have one aunt, Jenny, and two uncles, Keith and Nigel |
| Est-ce que tu t'entends bien avec tes parents | Do you get on with your relatives? |
| Je m'entends bien avec mes cousins, mais je n'aime pas mon oncle Nigel | I get on well with my cousins, but I don't like my uncle Nigel |

## Les professions — Jobs

| | | |
|---|---|---|
| un | agent de police | police officer |
| un | chauffeur | driver |
| un | coiffeur | hairdresser (male) |
| une | coiffeuse | hairdresser (female) |
| le/la | commerçant(e) | shopkeeper |
| un | électricien | electrician |
| un | employé de bureau | office worker (male) |
| une | employée de bureau | office worker (female) |
| le | facteur | postman |
| la | factrice | postwoman |
| la | femme de ménage | cleaner |
| le/la | fonctionnaire | public service worker |
| le/la | gérant(e) | manager |
| un | infirmier | nurse (male) |
| une | infirmière | nurse (female) |
| un | ingénieur | engineer |
| un | instituteur | primary school teacher (male) |
| une | institutrice | primary school teacher (female) |
| le | maçon | bricklayer/builder |
| le | mécanicien | mechanic |
| la | mécanicienne | mechanic (female) |
| le | médecin | doctor |
| un | ouvrier | worker (unskilled) |
| une | ouvrière | worker (female, unskilled) |
| le | professeur | teacher (secondary school) |
| le | routier | lorry driver |
| la | secrétaire | secretary |
| le | vendeur | sales assistant (male) |
| la | vendeuse | sales assistant (female) |
| au | chômage | unemployed |
| | employé | employed |
| à | l'heure | hourly |
| à | temps partiel | part-time |
| | travailler | to work |

### Phrases

| | |
|---|---|
| Mon frère travaille chez Renault | My brother works for Renault |
| Ma mère travaille à l'heure chez un pharmacien | My mother works on an hourly basis for a chemist |
| Mon père est au chômage depuis deux ans | My father has been unemployed for two years |

# En Classe — In class

## Dans la salle de classe — In the classroom

| | | |
|---|---|---|
| le | bulletin scolaire | school report |
| le | bureau | desk |
| le | cahier | exercise book |
| la | cassette | cassette |
| la | chaise | chair |
| le | cours | lesson |
| la | craie | chalk |
| le | crayon | pencil |
| le | crayon de couleur | coloured pencil |
| les | devoirs (m pl) | homework |
| un | élève | pupil (male) |
| une | élève | pupil (female) |
| un | emploi du temps | timetable |
| une | erreur | mistake |
| une | étagère | shelf |
| un | exemple | example |
| la | faute | mistake |
| la | fenêtre | window |
| le | feutre | felt-tip |
| la | gomme | rubber |
| une | image | picture |
| le | lavabo | sink |
| la | leçon | lesson |
| le | magnétophone | cassette recorder |
| le | manuel | textbook |
| le | mur | wall |
| la | note | mark, grade |
| un | ordinateur | computer |
| le | papier | paper |
| la | phrase | sentence |
| le | placard | cupboard |
| le | plafond | ceiling |
| le | plancher | floor |
| la | porte | door |
| le | poster | poster |
| le | problème | problem |
| la | question | question |
| la | règle | ruler/rule |
| la | réponse | answer |
| le | rétro-projecteur | overhead projector |
| le | stylo | ink pen |
| le | stylo à bille | biro |
| la | table | table |
| le | tableau | board |
| la | trousse | pencil case |
| un | uniforme | uniform |
| | apprendre | to learn |
| | apprendre par cœur | to learn by heart |
| | copier | to copy |
| | corriger | to correct |

| | |
|---|---|
| écouter | to listen |
| écrire | to write |
| répéter | to practise/to repeat |

## Phrases

| **Le professeur dit:** | **The teacher says:** |
|---|---|
| Entrez! | Come in! |
| Asseyez-vous! | Sit down! |
| Taisez-vous! | Be quiet! |
| Silence! | Silence! |
| Ferme la porte/la fenêtre | Close the door/the window |
| Je fais l'appel | I'm going to call the register |
| Qui est absent? | Who is absent? |
| Sortez vos cahiers! | Take out your excercise books! |
| Sortez votre manuel de français! | Get out your French textbook! |
| Ouvrez à la page 43 | Turn to page 43 |
| Lisez le texte | Read the text |
| Cherchez le mot dans le dictionnaire | Look the word up in the dictionary |
| Cherchez le mot dans le vocabulaire | Look the word up in the vocabulary |
| Ecoutez (la cassette)! | Listen (to the cassette)! |
| Répétez! | Repeat! |
| Encore une fois, tout le monde! | Once more, everybody! |
| Répondez aux questions | Answer the questions |
| Ecrivez les réponses | Write the answers down |
| Prenez des notes | Take notes |
| Depuis combien d'années apprends-tu le français? | How long have you been learning French? |
| Regardez le tableau! | Look at the board! |
| Ecrivez la date (à droite) | Write the date (on the right) |
| Ecrivez le titre | Write the title |
| Soulignez le titre | Underline the title |
| Numérotez les réponses de un à cinq | Number the answers from 1 to 5 |
| Corrigez votre travail | Correct your work |
| Epelle le mot 'banane' | Spell 'banane' |
| Cochez la bonne case | Tick the correct box |
| Vrai ou faux? | True or false? |
| Choisissez la bonne réponse | Choose the correct answer |
| C'est correct | That's correct |
| Fermez vos livres! | Close your books! |
| Passez vos cahiers à Laura! | Pass your exercise books to Laura! |
| Laura, apporte-moi les cahiers à la salle des professeurs, s'il te plaît | Laura bring the books to me in the staffroom, please |
| Choisis une carte, Sam! | Sam, choose a card! |
| Choisissez un partenaire! | Choose a partner! |
| Travaillez par groupe de trois | Work in groups of three |
| Travaillez avec votre partenaire | Work with your partner |
| Préparez un dialogue | Prepare a dialogue |
| Répétez le dialogue | Practise the dialogue |
| Notez le devoir | Write down the homework |
| C'est pour vendredi | It is for Friday |
| Apprenez le vocabulaire | Learn the vocabulary |
| Faites ça pour demain | Do this for tomorrow |
| C'est pour un test, lundi | It is for a test on Monday |
| Vous avez compris? | Do you understand this? |
| Dépêchez-vous! | Hurry up! |
| Rangez vos affaires! | Pack your things away! |
| Levez-vous! | Stand up! |
| Mettez les chaises sur/sous les tables | Put the chairs on/under the tables |
| Viens me voir demain matin à neuf heures à la salle des professeurs | Come and see me tomorrow at 9 a.m. in the staffroom |

| **Le professeur corrige** | **The teacher marks** |
|---|---|
| Tu as dix-huit sur vingt | You've got 18 out of 20 |
| Tu n'as que quatre sur vingt | You've only got 4 out of 20 |
| excellent | excellent |
| très bien | very good |
| bien | good |
| assez bien | quite good |
| faible | poor |
| mauvais | terrible |
| bon essai | good attempt |
| bon travail | good work |

| **L'élève dit:** | **The pupil says:** |
|---|---|
| J'apprends le français depuis deux ans | I have been learning French for two years |
| Je comprends | I understand |
| Je ne comprends pas | I don't understand |
| Je ne sais pas | I don't know |
| J'ai une bonne/ mauvaise note | I got a good/bad mark |
| Parles-tu/Parlez-vous français? | Do you speak French? |
| J'ai oublié mon manuel | I've forgotten my textbook |
| J'ai oublié mon cahier | I've forgotten my exercise book |
| J'ai oublié ma trousse | I've forgotten my pencil case |
| J'ai besoin d'un nouveau cahier | I need a new exercise book |
| Mon cahier est fini | My exercise book is full up |
| Excusez-moi, madame | Please Miss |
| Excusez-moi, monsieur | Please Sir |
| A quelle page sommes-nous? | Which page are we on? |
| Comment dit-on 'felt-tip' en français? | How do you say 'felt-tip' in French? |
| Comment écrit-on 'banane'? | How do you spell 'banane'? |
| Comment est-ce que ça se prononce? | How do you pronounce it? |
| Nous le faisons dans quel cahier? | Which exercise book shall we do this in? |

| | |
|---|---|
| Puis-je ouvrir la fenêtre? | May I open the window? |
| Puis-je sortir? | May I leave the room? |
| Puis-je tailler mon crayon? | May I sharpen my pencil? |
| Je suis en sixième/ cinquième/quatrième | I am in year 7/8/9 |

## L'alphabet — Alphabet

Approximate English sound equivalents are given here. In italics are the correct French spellings where these are relevant.

| | | |
|---|---|---|
| a | a | |
| b | bay | |
| c | say | |
| d | day | |
| e | uh? | |
| f | eff | |
| g | shay | |
| h | ash | |
| i | ee | |
| j | gee | |
| k | ca (as in cat) | |
| l | ell | |
| m | emm | |
| n | enn | |
| o | oh! | |
| p | pay | |
| q | coo | |
| r | air | |
| s | ess | |
| t | tay | |
| u | ooo! | |
| v | vay | |
| w | dooble vay | *double v* |
| x | ekks | |
| y | ee greck | *i grec* |
| z | zed | |
| ´ | accen aygoo | *accent aigu* |
| ` | accen graahv | *accent grave* |
| ^ | sirkonflex | *accent circonflex* |
| ç | say sedee | *c cédille* |

## La ponctuation — Punctuation

| | | |
|---|---|---|
| | deux points (m) | colon |
| les | guillemets | speech marks |
| la | majuscule | written with a capital letter |
| la | minuscule | written with a lower-case (small) letter |
| le | paragraphe | paragraph |
| la | parenthèse | bracket |
| la | phrase | sentence |
| le | point | full stop |
| le | point d'exclamation | exclamation mark |
| le | point d'interrogation | question mark |
| le | point virgule | semicolon |
| le | trait d'union | hyphen |
| la | virgule | comma |

### Phrases

| | |
|---|---|
| à la ligne | on a new line |
| ouvrez les guillemets | open speech marks |
| fermez les guillemets | close speech marks |
| ouvrez la parenthèse | open brackets |
| fermez la parenthèse | close brackets |
| entre parenthèses | in brackets |

# Le temps libre — Free time

## Les passetemps — Hobbies

| | | |
|---|---|---|
| l' | après-midi (m) | afternoon |
| le | club des jeunes | youth club |
| le | foyer de la jeunesse | youth centre |
| la | jeunesse | youth, young people |
| la | société | club |
| le | soir | evening |
| le | temps libre | free time, leisure time |
| les | vacances (f pl) | holidays |
| le | weekend | weekend |

## Les sports — sport (s)

| | | |
|---|---|---|
| l' | athlétisme (m) | athletics |
| le | court de tennis | tennis court |
| le | cricket | cricket |
| le | cyclisme | cycling |
| une | équipe | team |
| l' | équitation (f) | riding |
| le | foot/football | football |
| le | gymnase | gym |
| la | gymnastique | gymnastics |
| le | jeu | game |
| le | match | match |
| le | membre | member |
| la | natation | swimming |
| la | partie | match |
| la | piscine | swimming pool |
| la | salle de gym | gym |
| les | sports aquatiques (m pl) | watersports |
| les | sports d'hiver (m pl) | winter sports |
| le | stade | stadium |
| le | tennis | tennis |

| | | |
|---|---|---|
| s' | entraîner | to train |
| | faire de l'équitation | to ride |
| | faire de la planche à voile | to windsurf |
| | faire de la voile | to sail |
| | faire du cyclisme | to cycle |
| | faire du patin à roulettes | to roller-skate |
| | faire du ski | to ski |
| | faire du sport | to do sport |

| | | |
|---|---|---|
| | gagner | to win |
| | jouer | to play |
| | patiner | to ice-skate |
| | nager | to swim |
| | pêcher | to fish |
| | perdre | to lose |
| se | promener | to go for a walk |

## Phrases

| | |
|---|---|
| Qu'est-ce que tu fais dans ton temps libre? | What do you do in your free time? |
| Je suis membre d'un club de sports | I am a member of a sports club |
| Je joue au hockey dans l'équipe A | I play hockey in the A-team |
| Je vais tous les mardis à l'entraînement | I go to training every Tuesday |
| Nous avons un match samedi prochain | We have a match on Saturday |
| La semaine dernière nous avons gagné | Last week we won |
| Le score était trois à zéro | The score was 3–nil |
| Quels sports préfères-tu? | Which sports do you like? |
| En été, j'aime jouer au tennis | I like playing tennis in summer |
| En hiver je fais du ski | I go skiing in winter |
| Je n'aime pas faire du sport | I don't like doing sport |
| J'aime regarder l'athlétisme à la télé | I like watching athletics on TV |
| Es-tu membre d'un club? | Are you a member of a club? |
| Quand est-ce que tu joues au cricket? | When do you play cricket? |
| Je joue deux fois par semaine, le lundi et le jeudi | I play twice a week, on Mondays and Thursdays |
| J'aime nager à la piscine | I like swimming in the swimming pool |
| C'est combien, l'entrée pour les jeunes? | How much does it cost for a young person? |
| Quelles sont les heures d'ouverture de la piscine? | What are the opening times of the swimming pool? |
| Est-ce que la piscine est ouverte le dimanche? | Is the pool open on Sundays? |
| Je voudrais des billets pour un enfant et deux adultes | I'd like tickets for a child and two adults |

## La musique — Music

| | | |
|---|---|---|
| le | baladeur | Walkman® |
| la | batterie | drum kit |
| le | CD | CD |
| la | chanson | song |
| le | chanteur favori | favourite singer (male) |
| la | chanteuse favorite | favourite singer (female) |
| la | chorale | choir |
| la | clarinette | clarinet |
| le | concert | concert |
| la | flûte | flute |
| la | flûte à bec | recorder |
| le | groupe | group |
| le | groupe favori | favourite group |
| la | guitare | guitar |
| un | instrument | instrument |
| le | magnétophone | cassette player |
| la | musique classique | classical music |
| la | musique folklorique | folk music |
| la | musique pop | pop music |
| un | orchestre | orchestra |
| le | piano | piano |
| la | platine laser | CD player |
| la | radio | radio |
| la | trompette | trumpet |
| le | trombone | trombone |
| le | tube | hit song |
| le | violon | violin |
| le | violoncelle | cello |
| | chanter | to sing |
| | écouter | to listen to |
| | jouer | to play |
| | répéter | to practise |

## Phrases

| | |
|---|---|
| Joues-tu d'un instrument? | Do you play an instrument? |
| Oui, je joue du piano | Yes, I play the piano |
| Depuis quand joues-tu du piano? | How long have you been playing the piano? |
| Je joue depuis trois ans | I have been playing for three years? |
| Est-ce que tu joues souvent? | Do you play often |
| Je joue tous les jours pendant une heure | I play every day for an hour |
| Je ne joue aucun instrument | I don´t play an instrument |
| Je chante dans la chorale du collège | I sing in the school choir |
| Est-ce que la musique t'intéresse? | Are you interested in music? |
| Oui, la musique est très importante pour moi | Yes, music is very important to me |
| Quelle sorte de musique préfères-tu? | What is your favourite sort of music? |
| J'aime la musique pop | I like pop music |
| As-tu un chanteur favori/un groupe favori? | Do you have a favourite singer/group? |
| Mon chanteur favori, c'est XYZ | My favourite singer is XYZ |
| Mon groupe favori, c'est ABC | My favourite group is ABC |
| ABC est chouette | ABC are great |
| Non, je n'ai pas de groupe favori | No, I haven't got a favourite group |
| J'aime tous les groupes anglais | I like all English groups |
| J'ai horreur de DEF | I can't stand DEF |

| | |
|---|---|
| Vas-tu souvent au concert? | Do you often go to concerts? |
| Non, mais la semaine dernière je suis allé(e) à un concert de GHI | No, but last week I went to a concert by GHI |
| L'ambiance était super | The atmosphere was great |
| J'ai beaucoup de cassettes, mais pas beaucoup de CDs | I have lots of cassettes, but only a few CDs |
| Les CDs coûtent très cher | CDs are very expensive |

## L'informatique — IT

| | | |
|---|---|---|
| le | bug | bug |
| la | base de données | database |
| le | catalogue | disk manager |
| le | CD ROM | CD ROM |
| le | clavier | keyboard |
| le | disque dur | hard disk |
| la | disquette | disk |
| un | écran | screen |
| une | imprimante | printer |
| le | jeu électronique | computer game |
| le | lecteur de disquettes | disk drive |
| le | menu | menu |
| le | moniteur | monitor |
| un | ordinateur | computer |
| la | puce | chip |
| la | souris | mouse |
| le | traitement de texte | word processing |
| | charger | to load |
| | éditer | to edit |
| | effacer | to delete |
| | faxer/télécopier | to fax |
| | formater | to format |
| | sauvegarder | to save |

## D'autres passetemps — Other hobbies

| | | |
|---|---|---|
| un | appareil-photo | camera |
| le | caméscope | camrecorder |
| le | cheval | horse |
| la | collection | collection |
| le | film | film |
| l' | histoire (f) | history |
| le | jeu de société | board game |
| le | modellisme | making models |
| les | mots croisés (m pl) | crosswords |
| le | roman | novel |
| la | télé | TV |
| le | timbre | stamp |
| | aller* en ville | to go into town |
| | collectionner | to collect |
| | commencer | to begin |
| | coudre | to sew |
| | danser | to dance |
| | dessiner | to draw |
| | écouter | to listen to |
| | faire des commissions/des courses | to shop |
| | faire des photos | to take photos |
| | faire du bricolage | to do DIY |
| | faire du lèche-vitrines | to go window shopping |
| | jouer aux cartes | to play cards |
| | jouer aux échecs | to play chess |
| | lire | to read |
| | payer | to pay |
| | peindre | to paint |
| se | promener | to go for walks |
| | regarder la télé | to watch TV |
| | sortir* | to go out |
| | tricoter | to knit |
| | trouver | to find |
| | visiter un château | to visit a stately home |
| | voir des amis | to meet friends |
| | voyager | to travel |

### Phrases

| | |
|---|---|
| Fais-tu une collection? | Do you collect anything? |
| Je collectionne les pin's | I collect pin's |
| J'en ai déjà cent | I have already got a hundred |
| Qu'est-ce que tu lis? | What type of books do you read? |
| Je lis des romans d'aventure | I read adventure novels |
| Je joue aux dames | I play draughts |
| J'aime les jeux de société | I like playing board games |
| J'aime écouter la radio | I like listening to the radio |
| Quels sont les passetemps de ta famille? | What are your family's hobbies? |
| Mon frère chante dans la chorale du collège | My brother sings in the school choir |
| Ma sœur fait du théâtre d'amateur | My sister does amateur dramatics |
| Ma mère fait de la danse folklorique | My mother does folk dancing |
| Mon père aime la montagne | My father likes the hills |
| J'aime visiter les châteaux | I like visiting stately homes |

# La ville — Town

## En ville — In town

| | | |
|---|---|---|
| un | aéroport | airport |
| une | agence de voyages | travel agency |
| un | arrêt de bus | bus stop |
| la | banlieue | suburbs |
| la | bibliothèque | library |
| la | cathédrale | cathedral |
| le | centre commercial | shopping centre |
| le | cinéma | cinema |

| | | |
|---|---|---|
| une | église | church |
| la | gare routière | bus station |
| la | gare SNCF | railway station |
| le | grand magasin | department store |
| la | grande surface | hypermarket |
| un | hôpital | hospital |
| un | hôtel | hotel |
| un | hôtel de ville | town hall |
| la | mairie | town hall |
| le | marché | market |
| le | musée | museum |
| un | office de tourisme | tourist information office |
| le | parking | car park |
| la | poste | post office |
| le | quartier | part of town, quarter, area |
| le | stade | stadium |
| la | station service | filling station |
| le | syndicat d'initiative | tourist information office |
| le | théâtre | theatre |
| les | transports publics (m pl) | public transport |
| une | usine | factory |
| la | ville | town |
| la | ville industrielle | industrial town |
| la | zone piétonne | pedestrian precinct |

| | |
|---|---|
| bruyant | noisy, loud |
| calme | quiet |
| grand | big, large |
| historique | historic |
| moderne | modern |
| petit | small |
| pollué | polluted |
| propre | clean |
| sale | dirty |
| soigné | tidy |
| vieux | old |

| | | |
|---|---|---|
| | construire | to build |
| | faire des courses | to go shopping |
| | habiter | to live |
| se | promener | to go for walks |
| | rencontrer des amis | to meet friends |
| | renover | to renovate |
| | restaurer | to restore |

### Phrases

| | |
|---|---|
| Où habites-tu? | Where do you live? |
| J'habite Worcester, au centre de l'Angleterre | I live in Worcester, in the Midlands |
| C'est une grande/petite ville? | Is it a big/small town? |
| Combien d'habitants y a-t-il? | How many inhabitants are there? |
| Il y a cent mille habitants | There are 100,000 inhabitants |
| Qu'est-ce qu'il y a dans ton quartier? | What is there in your part of town? |
| Il y a une église, un cinéma et beaucoup de magasins | There is a church, a cinema and lots of shops |
| Qu'est-ce qu'il y a à voir en ville? | What is there to see in town? |
| Qu'est-ce qu'on peut faire à Worcester? | What is there to do in Worcester? |
| On peut visiter le musée et la cathédrale | You can visit the museum and the cathedral |
| Quelles possibilités sportives y a-t-il? | What sports facilities are there? |
| Il y a une piscine et un stade | There is a swimming pool and a stadium |
| Qu'est-ce que tu fais quand tu vas en ville? | What do you do when you go into town? |
| Je fais du lèche-vitrine | I go window shopping |
| Je retrouve mes amis à la maison des jeunes | I meet my friends at the youth club |

## Pour aller à...? / How do I get to...?

### Les directions / Directions

| | | |
|---|---|---|
| un | arrêt de bus | bus stop |
| la | cabine téléphonique | phone box |
| le | café | café |
| le | carrefour | crossroads |
| le | centre commercial | shopping centre |
| le | centre-ville | town centre |
| le | coin (de la rue) | corner |
| les | feux (m pl) | traffic lights |
| le | pont | bridge |
| le | rond-point | roundabout |
| le | sens unique | one-way street |
| la | zone industrielle | industrial estate |
| la | zone piétonnière | pedestrian precinct |

| | |
|---|---|
| aller* | to go |
| prendre | to take |
| tourner | to turn |
| traverser | to cross |

| | |
|---|---|
| à gauche | left |
| à droite | right |
| tout droit | straight on |

| | |
|---|---|
| à côté du théâtre | next to the theatre |
| après les feux | after the lights |
| au coin de la rue | on the corner of the street |
| derrière l'église | behind the church |
| devant le cinéma | in front of the cinema |
| en face de la mairie | opposite the townhall |
| entre la banque et la poste | between the bank and the post office |

## Phrases

| | |
|---|---|
| Pour aller à la gare, s'il vous plaît | What's the best way to the station, please? |
| Allez tout droit et prenez la deuxième rue à gauche | Go straight on here, and take the second road on the left |
| Passez le carrefour | Go across the junction |
| Prenez la première rue à droite | Take the first road on the right |
| Continuez tout droit | Keep going straight on |
| Est-ce qu'il y a un café près d'ici? | Is there a café near here? |
| Oui, en face de la banque | Yes, opposite the bank |
| C'est loin d'ici? | Is it far from here? |
| C'est cinq minutes à pied | It is only five minutes on foot |
| Vous êtes en voiture ou à pied? | Are you in a car or on foot? |
| Prenez le bus, ligne 7 | Take the bus, number 7 |
| Je cherche l'hôtel 'Les Biards' | I am looking for the Hotel Les Biards |
| Est-ce que vous le connaissez? | Do you know it? |

# La campagne The country

## A la campagne In the country

| | | |
|---|---|---|
| le | bois | wood |
| la | campagne | country (side) |
| le | champ | field |
| la | colline | hill |
| un | étang | pool |
| la | ferme | farm |
| la | forêt | forest, wood |
| une | île | island |
| le | lac | lake |
| la | mare | pond |
| la | montagne | mountain |
| la | prairie | meadow |
| la | région | region, area |
| la | rivière | river |
| la | route départementale | 'B' road |
| le | ruisseau | brook |
| la | vallée | valley |
| le | village | village |
| | à côté de | beside |
| | à dix kilomètres | 10 km away |
| | à droite de | to the right of |
| | à gauche de | to the left of |
| | au centre de | in the middle of |
| | devant | in front of |
| | isolé | out of the way |
| | loin de | far from |
| | situé | situated |
| | tout près | very near |
| | au nord | in the north |
| | au nord de | north of |
| | à l'est | in the east |
| | à l'est de | east of |
| | au sud | in the south |
| | au sud de | south of |
| | à l'ouest | in the west |
| | à l'ouest de | west of |
| | visiter | to visit (a monument) |
| | nager | to swim |
| | voir | to see |
| | jouer | to play |
| | faire une randonnée | to hike |
| se | promener (à la campagne) | to go for a walk (in the country) |

## Phrases

| | |
|---|---|
| J'habite Taddlecombe | I live in Taddlecombe |
| C'est un village près de Birmingham | It is a village near Birmingham |
| Dans le village il y a une vieille église, une poste et un pub | In the village there is an old church, a post office and a pub |
| La rivière est près du village | The river is near the village |
| J'aime habiter à la campagne, parce que c'est très calme | I like living in the country, because it is so quiet |
| L'air est moins pollué | The air is also less polluted |
| Je n'aime pas habiter à la campagne | I don't like living in the country |
| On s'ennuie, il n'y a pas assez de bus | It is boring, there aren't enough buses |
| Il n'y a rien pour les jeunes | There is nothing for young people |

# Le temps Weather

| | | |
|---|---|---|
| le | brouillard | fog |
| la | neige | snow |
| le | nuage | cloud |
| un | orage | thunderstorm |
| la | pluie | rain |
| le | soleil | sun |
| le | vent | wind |
| | chaud | hot |
| | froid | cold |
| | ensoleillé | sunny |
| | pleuvoir | to rain |
| | briller | to shine |
| | geler | to freeze |
| | faire du vent | to be windy |
| | faire chaud | to be hot |
| | faire froid | to be cold |
| | faire du brouillard | to be foggy |
| | neiger | to snow |

### Phrases

| | |
|---|---|
| Il pleut | It is raining |
| Le soleil brille | The sun is shining |
| Il neige | It is snowing |
| Il fait du vent | It is windy |
| Il y a un orage | There is a thunderstorm |
| Il fait trente degrés | The temperature is 30 degrees |
| Quel temps fait-il en Ecosse? | What is the weather like in Scotland? |
| Quel temps faisait-il pendant les vacances? | What was the weather like during the holidays? |
| Hier, il a plu toute la journée | Yesterday it rained all day long |
| L'après-midi, il faisait chaud | In the afternoon it was hot |
| Il a neigé au mois de décembre | It snowed in December |
| Demain le soleil va encore briller | Tomorrow it will be sunny again |

# L'école — School

## A l'école — At school

| | | |
|---|---|---|
| une | assemblée | assembly |
| le | collège/CES | comprehensive school (11–15) |
| le | congé de mi-trimestre | half-term holidays |
| le | cours | lesson |
| une | école maternelle | nursery school |
| une | école primaire | primary school |
| un | enseignement | teaching |
| les | grandes vacances (f pl) | summer holidays |
| la | leçon | lesson |
| le | lycée | secondary school |
| la | récréation | break |
| la | rentrée | start of school year |
| le | trimestre | term |
| les | vacances (f pl) | school holidays |
| les | vacances de Noël (f pl) | Christmas holidays |
| les | vacances de Pâques (f pl) | Easter holidays |

## Le personnel — Staff

| | | |
|---|---|---|
| le/la | concierge | caretaker |
| le | directeur | headmaster |
| la | directrice | headmistress |
| un | instituteur | teacher (male, primary) |
| une | institutrice | teacher (female, primary) |
| le/la | prof (professeur) | teacher (secondary) |
| le | proviseur | head of a lycée |
| la | secrétaire | secretary |

## Les matières — School subjects

| | | |
|---|---|---|
| l' | allemand (m) | German |
| l' | anglais (m) | English |
| les | arts ménagers (m) | home economics |
| la | biologie | biology |
| la | chimie | chemistry |
| le | dessin | art |
| l' | espagnol (m) | Spanish |
| le | français | French |
| la | géographie | geography |
| l' | histoire (f) | history |
| l' | histoire/géo | humanities |
| l' | informatique (f) | IT |
| l' | instruction civique (f) | citizenship/PSE |
| l' | italien (m) | Italian |
| le | latin | Latin |
| les | maths (f pl) | maths |
| la | physique | physics |
| la | poterie | pottery |
| la | religion | religious studies |
| les | sciences (f pl) | science |
| le | sport | sport |
| la | technologie | technology |

| | |
|---|---|
| amusant | fun |
| casse-pieds | boring |
| difficile | difficult |
| ennuyeux | boring |
| facile | easy |
| important | important |
| intéressant | interesting |
| inutile | useless |
| utile | useful |

## Les bâtiments — Buildings

| | | |
|---|---|---|
| la | bibliothèque | library |
| le | CDI | resource centre |
| la | cour | playground |
| le | gymnase | gymnasium |
| le | laboratoire | laboratory |
| le | préau | playground shelter |
| le | réfectoire | canteen |
| la | salle de classe | classroom |
| la | salle polyvalente | multipurpose room |
| la | salle des professeurs | staffroom |
| la | salle de gym | gym |
| les | toilettes (f pl) | toilets |
| le | vestiaire | changing room |

| | | |
|---|---|---|
| en | béton | of concrete |
| en | brique | of brick |
| pour | filles | for girls |
| pour | garçons | for boys |
| | mixte | mixed |
| | moderne | modern |
| | vieux | old |

| **Des verbes scolaires** | **School verbs** |
|---|---|
| apprendre | to learn |
| calculer | to calculate |
| chanter | to sing |
| choisir | to select/choose |
| commencer | to begin |
| compter | to count |
| copier | to copy |
| demander | to ask (for) |
| dessiner | to draw |
| durer | to last |
| écouter | to listen |
| écrire | to write |
| être collé(e) | to have a detention |
| être présent(e) | to be present |
| être reçu(e) | to pass (an exam) |
| expliquer | to explain |
| faire de la musique | to make music |
| faire des devoirs | to do homework |
| faire une expérience | to do an experiment |
| finir | to end |
| jouer | to play |
| oublier | to forget |
| parler | to talk |
| passer le bac | to take A Level/GNVQ |
| peindre | to paint |
| punir | to punish |
| redoubler une année | to repeat a year |
| répéter | to repeat |
| répondre (à) | to answer |

## Phrases

| | |
|---|---|
| A quelle heure est-ce que tu te lèves? | When do you get up? |
| Je me lève à sept heures | I get up at seven o'clock |
| A quelle heure est-ce que tu quittes la maison? | When do you leave your house? |
| Je quitte la maison à huit heures et demie | I leave home at half past eight |
| A quelle heure arrives-tu au collège? | When do you arrive at school? |
| J'arrive au collège à neuf heures moins le quart | I arrive at school at quarter to nine |
| Comment viens-tu au collège? | How do you get to school? |
| Je viens à pied | I walk |
| Je viens en train | I come by train |
| Je viens en car de ramassage scolaire | I come by school bus |
| Ma mère m'ammène en voiture | My mother brings me by car |
| Je viens à vélo/à bicyclette | I come by bike |
| A quelle heure commence le premier cours? | When does the first lesson start? |
| Les cours commencent à neuf heures | School starts at 9 o'clock |
| Combien de temps dure une leçon? | How long is a lesson? |
| Les leçons durent quarante-cinq minutes | Lessons last 45 minutes |
| Qu'est-ce que tu fais pendant la récréation? | What do you do during break? |
| Je joue au foot | I play football |
| Je bavarde avec mes amis | I chat with my friends |
| Où est-ce que tu manges à midi? | Where do you eat lunch? |
| Je mange à la cantine | I eat in the canteen |
| Qu'est-ce que tu manges à midi? | What do you eat for lunch? |
| Je mange des sandwichs | I eat sandwiches |
| A quelle heure finissent les cours? | When do lessons finish? |
| Les cours finissent à quatre heures | Lessons finish at 4 o'clock |
| Qu'est-ce que tu fais pour rentrer à la maison? | How do you get home? |
| Mon père vient me chercher | My dad picks me up from school |
| Combien d'élèves y a-t-il dans ta classe? | How many pupils are there in your class? |
| Il y a trente élèves dans ma classe | There are 30 pupils in my class |
| Quelles matières apprends-tu? | Which subjects do you study? |
| Je apprends le français, l'anglais, les maths, les sciences, l'histoire, la géographie, le sport, la religion et la technologie | I do French, English, maths, science, history, geography, sport, religious studies and technology |
| Quelle est ta matière préférée? | What is your favourite subject? |
| Ma matière préférée est le français | My favourite subject is French |
| Quelle matière est-ce que tu n'aimes pas? | Which subject don't you like? |
| Je n'aime pas la géographie | I don't like geography |
| Comment trouves-tu les maths? | What do you think of maths? |
| Je trouve les maths utiles | I think maths is useful |
| Combien de devoirs as-tu? | How much homework do you get? |
| J'en ai pour environ deux heures chaque jour | I have about two hours a night |
| Fais-tu partie d'une équipe du collège? | Are you member of a school team? |
| Je joue dans l'équipe de hockey | I play in the hockey team |
| Quelles sociétés y a-t-il dans ton collège? | What clubs are there in your school? |
| Il y a un club de joueurs d'échecs | There is a chess-club |
| Il y a un groupe théâtral | There is a theatre group |
| Je chante dans la chorale du collège | I sing in the school choir |

| | |
|---|---|
| Combien de vacances as-tu? | How much holiday do you get? |
| J'ai deux semaines à Noël et à Pâques | I get two weeks at Christmas and Easter |
| On a six semaines en été | We have six weeks in the summer |

## La santé et la forme / Health and fitness

### Les parties du corps / Parts of the body

| | | |
|---|---|---|
| la | bouche | mouth |
| le | bras | arm |
| la | cheville | ankle |
| la | dent | tooth |
| le | doigt | finger |
| le | dos | back |
| un | estomac | stomach |
| le | genou | knee |
| la | gorge | throat |
| la | jambe | leg |
| la | main | hand |
| le | nez | nose |
| un | œil (pl: les yeux) | eye |
| une | oreille | ear |
| le | pied | foot |
| le | sang | blood |
| la | tête | head |
| le | ventre | abdomen |

### Chez le médecin/ Chez le dentiste / At the doctor's/ At the dentist's

| | | |
|---|---|---|
| le | cabinet | surgery |
| le | dentiste | dentist |
| la | douleur | pain |
| un | infirmier | nurse (male) |
| une | infirmière | nurse (female) |
| la | maladie | illness |
| le | médecin | doctor |
| le | médicament | medicine |
| une | ordonnance | prescription |
| le | pansement | bandage |
| la | piqûre | injection |
| le | plombage | filling |
| la | réceptionniste | receptionist |
| le | rendez-vous | appointment |
| la | salle d'attente | waiting room |
| le | sparadrap | sticking plaster |

### Phrases

| | |
|---|---|
| Je voudrais un rendez-vous, s'il vous plaît | I would like an appointment, please |
| Peux-tu venir lundi à trois heures? | Can you come at three o'clock on Monday? |
| Je ne me sens pas bien | I don't feel well |
| Où as-tu mal? | Where does it hurt? |
| J'ai mal à l'oreille | I've got earache |
| J'ai mal aux dents | I've got toothache |
| J'ai mal à la gorge | I've got a sore throat |
| J'ai mal à la tête | I've got a headache |
| J'ai mal au pied | My foot hurts |
| J'ai mal au bras | My arms hurt |
| J'ai mal à l'estomac | I've got stomach ache |
| J'ai mal au ventre/J'ai mal au cœur | I feel sick |
| J'ai vomi | I have been sick |
| J'ai chaud | I am hot |
| J'ai froid | I am cold |
| J'ai de la fièvre | I have a temperature |
| Je me suis foulé la cheville | I have twisted my ankle |
| J'ai la diarrhée | I've got diarrhoea |
| Je suis constipé(e) | I am constipated |
| J'ai mes règles | I've got my period |
| Donnez cette ordonnance au pharmacien | Take this prescription to the chemist |
| Prenez les comprimés trois fois par jour | Take the tablets three times a day |

### A la pharmacie / At the chemist's

| | | |
|---|---|---|
| le | comprimé | tablet |
| le | coton hydrophile | cotton wool |
| le | coup de soleil | sun burn |
| la | crème | cream |
| le | dentifrice | toothpaste |
| la | diarrhée | diarrhoea |
| la | fièvre | high temperature |
| la | grippe | flu |
| une | insolation | sunstroke |
| le | mal de mer | seasickness |
| le | pansement | bandage, dressing |
| la | pastille | cough sweet |
| la | piqûre | insect bite |
| le | rhume | cold |
| le | savon | soap |
| la | serviette hygiénique | sanitary towel |
| le | sirop | cough mixture |
| le | sparadrap | sticking plaster |
| le | tube | tube |

### Phrases

| | |
|---|---|
| Avez-vous quelque chose contre un rhume? | Have you got anything for a cold? |
| Avez-vous quelque chose pour un mal de tête? | Have you got something for a headache? |
| Je suis allergique à l'aspirine | I am allergic to aspirin |
| Est-ce que je dois payer l'ordonnance? | Do I have to pay for the prescription? |
| Avez-vous de la crème solaire? | Do you sell suntan lotion? |
| Pouvez-vous me donner quelque chose contre le rhume des foins? | Can you give me something for hay fever? |

# La vie familiale — Family life

## Le logement — Housing

| | | |
|---|---|---|
| un | appartement | flat |
| le | bungalow | bungalow |
| une | HLM | council flat |
| un | immeuble | block of flats |
| la | maison | house |
| la | maison jumelée | semi-detached house |
| le | pavillon | detached house |

## Les pièces — Rooms

| | | |
|---|---|---|
| un | ascenseur | lift |
| le | bureau | study |
| la | cave | cellar |
| la | chambre (à coucher) | bedroom |
| la | chambre d'amis | guest room |
| le | couloir | corridor |
| la | cuisine | kitchen |
| un | escalier | staircase |
| le | grenier | loft |
| la | salle à manger | dining room |
| la | salle de bains | bathroom |
| la | salle de séjour/ le salon/le séjour | living-room |
| la | terrasse | patio |
| le | WC | toilet |

## Les éléments du bâtiment — Parts of the building

| | | |
|---|---|---|
| le | chauffage central | central heating |
| la | cheminée | open fireplace/chimney |
| la | clé | key |
| l' | électricité (f) | electricity |
| une | entrée | entrance |
| un | étage | floor, storey |
| le | gaz | gas |
| la | porte | door |
| le | radiateur | radiator |
| le | rez-de-chaussée | ground floor |
| le | toit | roof |
| le | volet | shutter |

## Dans la salle de bains — In the bathroom

| | | |
|---|---|---|
| la | baignoire | bathtub |
| le | bidet | bidet |
| le | bouchon | plug |
| la | brosse à dents | toothbrush |
| le | dentifrice | toothpaste |
| la | douche | shower |
| l' | eau (f) | water |
| une | éponge | sponge |
| le | gant de toilette | flannel |
| le | lavabo | basin |
| le | miroir | mirror |
| le | robinet | tap |
| le | savon | soap |
| la | serviette | towel |
| la | serviette de bain | bath towel |

## Dans la chambre à coucher — In the bedroom

| | | |
|---|---|---|
| une | armoire | wardrobe |
| la | chaise | chair |
| la | couette | duvet |
| une | étagère | shelf |
| la | housse | duvet cover |
| la | lampe | lamp |
| le | lit | bed |
| la | moquette | fitted carpet |
| un | oreiller | pillow |
| le | réveil | alarm clock |
| le | rideau | curtain |
| la | table | desk |
| la | table de chevet | bedside table |
| le | tapis | rug |

## Dans la salle de séjour — In the living-room

| | | |
|---|---|---|
| la | bibliothèque | bookcase |
| le | bouquet de fleurs | bunch of flowers |
| le | canapé | sofa |
| la | chaîne stéréo | stereo |
| le | fauteuil | armchair |
| le | magnétoscope | video recorder |
| la | photo familiale | family photo |
| la | platine laser | CD player |
| le | radiateur | radiator |
| la | table basse | coffee-table |
| le | tableau | picture |
| le | téléviseur | TV set |
| le | vase | vase |

## Dans la salle à manger — In the dining-room

| | |
|---|---|
| une assiette | plate |
| la chaise | chair |
| la nappe | tablecloth |
| la pendule | clock |
| la table | table |
| le verre | glass |

## A la cuisine — In the kitchen

| | |
|---|---|
| un aspirateur | vacuum cleaner |
| le balai | broom |
| la casserole | saucepan |
| le congélateur | freezer |
| la cuisinière | cooker |
| un évier | sink |
| le four | oven |
| le four à micro-ondes | microwave oven |
| le frigo | fridge |
| le lave-linge | washing-machine |
| le lave-vaisselle | dishwasher |
| le placard | cupboard |
| la poêle | frying pan |
| la poubelle | rubbish bin |

## Au jardin — In the garden

| | |
|---|---|
| un abri | shed |
| un arbre | tree |
| un arbuste | bush |
| le banc | bench |
| la fleur | flower |
| le gazon | lawn |
| le jardin potager | vegetable garden |
| la jonquille | daffodil |
| le légume | vegetable |
| la plate-bande | flower bed |
| le pommier | apple tree |
| la rose | rose |
| le sapin | fir tree |
| la serre | greenhouse |

## Des verbes domestiques — Domestic verbs

| | |
|---|---|
| aider | to help |
| arroser | to water |
| débarrasser la table | to clear the table |
| déménager | to move house |
| essuyer la vaisselle | to dry up |
| faire la cuisine | to cook |
| faire la vaisselle | to wash up |
| habiter | to live |
| mettre la table | to lay the table |
| nettoyer | to clean |
| partager | to share |
| passer l'aspirateur | to hoover |
| ranger | to tidy up |
| sonner (à la porte) | to ring (door bell) |
| tapisser | to hang wallpaper |
| tondre le gazon | to mow the lawn |

## Phrases

| | |
|---|---|
| Habites-tu dans une maison ou dans un appartement? | Do you live in a house or a flat? |
| J'habite une maison de banlieue | I live in a house in the suburbs |
| J'habite un appartement au troisième étage | I live in a flat on the third floor |
| J'habite à deux kilomètres du collège | I live two kilometres from school |
| Ta maison, est-elle vieille ou moderne? | Is your house old or modern? |
| Comment est ta maison? | What is your house like? |
| Ma maison est assez moderne | My house is fairly modern |
| Elle est en brique | It is built of brick |
| Elle a deux étages | There are two storeys |
| Il y a un petit jardin autour de la maison | There is a small garden round the house |
| As-tu une chambre à toi? | Do you have your own room? |
| Non, je partage ma chambre avec mon frère | No, I share my room with my brother |
| Non, je partage ma chambre avec ma sœur | No, I share my room with my sister |
| Comment est ta chambre? | What is your room like? |
| Ma chambre est assez grande | My room is medium-sized |
| Il y a le chauffage central | It has central heating |
| Les murs sont jaunes | The walls are yellow |
| La moquette est grise | The fitted carpet is grey |
| Les rideaux sont gris aussi | The curtains are also grey |
| Quels meubles as-tu dans ta chambre? | What sort of furniture have you got in your room? |
| J'ai un lit, une table, une chaise et une armoire | I have a bed, a desk, a chair and a wardrobe |
| Sous la fenêtre il y a un petit canapé | Under the window is a small sofa |
| Ma stéréo est sur l'étagère | My stereo is on the shelf |
| Avez-vous un jardin? | Have you got a garden? |
| Oui, il y a un petit jardin devant la maison et un jardin plus grand derrrière la maison | Yes, there is a small garden in front of the house and a bigger one behind the house |
| Devant la maison il y a des plate-bandes et une pelouse | In the front garden there are flower beds and a lawn |
| Derrière la maison il y a un jardin potager et des arbres fruitiers | Behind the house there is a vegetable garden and some fruit trees |
| Où sont les toilettes, s'il vous plaît? | Where is the toilet, please? |

| | |
|---|---|
| Les toilettes sont ici, à côté de la porte d'entrée | The toilet is here, next to the front door |
| Est-ce que je peux prendre un bain? | May I have a bath? |
| Est-ce que je peux prendre une douche | May I have a shower? |
| As-tu tout ce qu'il te faut? | Have you got everything you need? |
| Non, j'ai oublié ma serviette | No, I have forgotten my towel |
| A quelle heure prends-tu le petit déjeuner? | When do you have breakfast? |
| Je prends le petit déjeuner à huit heures | I have breakfast at eight o'clock |
| A quelle heure est-ce que tu déjeunes? | When do you have lunch? |
| Je déjeune à une heure | I have lunch at one o'clock |
| A quelle heure est-ce que tu dînes? | When do you have your evening meal? |
| Je dîne à sept heures | I have my evening meal at seven o'clock |

| | |
|---|---|
| Est-ce que tu aides ton père/ta mère/tes parents pour le ménage? | Do you help your mother/ your father/your parents in the house |
| Je mets la table | I lay the table |
| Je travaille dans le jardin | I work in the garden |
| Je tonds le gazon | I mow the lawn |
| J'arrose les fleurs | I water the flowers |
| Je fais les courses quelquefois | I do the shopping sometimes |
| Je fais la vaisselle | I do the washing up |
| Je fais de la cuisine le mardi | I cook on Tuesdays |

## La routine journalière / Everyday routines

| | | |
|---|---|---|
| un | après-midi | afternoon |
| le | déjeuner | lunch |
| les | devoirs (m pl) | homework |
| le | dîner | evening meal |
| le | jour | day |
| la | journée | daytime |
| le | matin | morning |
| le | ménage | housework |
| le | petit déjeuner | breakfast |
| le | soir | evening, night |
| la | soirée | evening |
| le | travail | work |
| au | calme | calmly |
| à l' | heure | punctually |
| | lentement | slowly |
| | rapidement | fast, quickly |
| en | retard | late |
| à | temps | in time |
| | tôt | early |

| | | |
|---|---|---|
| se | brosser les dents | to brush one's teeth |
| se | changer | to get changed |
| se | coucher | to go to bed |
| se | déshabiller | to get undressed |
| | dormir | to sleep |
| s' | habiller | to get dressed |
| se | laver | to wash |
| se | lever | to get up |
| | manger | to eat |
| se | peigner | to comb one's hair |
| | prendre le petit déjeuner | to have breakfast |
| | prendre une douche | to shower |
| | prendre un bain | to have a bath |
| quitter la | maison | to leave the house |
| se | raser | to shave |
| | regarder la télé | to watch TV |
| | rentrer* (à la maison) | to come back (home) |
| se | réveiller | to wake up |

## L'argent de poche / Pocket money

| | | |
|---|---|---|
| l' | argent (m) | money |
| la | banque | bank |
| le | billet | bank-note |
| la | pièce | coin |
| la | tirelire | piggy bank/money-box |
| | beaucoup | a lot |
| | bon marché | cheap, good value for money |
| | cher | expensive |
| | économe | careful with money |
| | généreux | generous |
| par | mois | per month |
| | pauvre | poor |
| un | peu | a little |
| | riche | rich |
| par | semaine | per week |
| | acheter | to buy |
| | coûter | to cost |
| | dépenser (pour) | to spend (on) |
| | faire des économies | to save |

### Phrases

| | |
|---|---|
| Combien d'argent de poche as-tu? | How much pocket money do you get? |
| J'ai deux livres par semaine | I get £2 per week |
| Qu'est-ce que tu achètes avec ton argent? | What do you buy with your pocket money? |
| J'achète des bandes dessinées et du chocolat | I spend it on comics and chocolate |

| | |
|---|---|
| Je fais des économies pour un vélo | I am saving up for a bike |
| J'achète des livres et des vêtements | I buy books and clothes |

# Au café / In the cafe

## Les boissons / Drinks

| | | |
|---|---|---|
| la | bière | beer |
| le | café | coffee (black) |
| le | café crème | white coffee |
| le | chocolat chaud | hot chocolate |
| le | chocolat froid | cold chocolate |
| le | cidre | cider |
| le | citron pressé | freshly squeezed lemon juice |
| le | coca | cola |
| l' | eau minérale (f) | mineral water |
| le | jus de fruit | fruit juice |
| la | limonade | lemonade |
| un | orangina | Orangina® |
| le | thé au citron | tea with lemon |
| le | thé au lait | tea with milk |
| le | vin blanc | white wine |
| le | vin rouge | red wine |

## Les casse-croûte / Snacks

| | | |
|---|---|---|
| les | chips (m) | crisps |
| la | crêpe | pancake |
| le | croque-monsieur | toasted ham and cheese sandwich |
| la | glace | ice cream |
| le | sandwich au fromage | cheese sandwich |
| le | sandwich au jambon | ham sandwich |

## Au café / In the café

| | | |
|---|---|---|
| une | assiette | plate |
| le | bar | bar |
| le | serveur | waiter |
| la | serveuse | waitress |
| la | tasse | cup |
| le | verre | glass |

## Phrases

| | |
|---|---|
| Vous désirez? | What would you like? |
| Combien je vous dois? | How much do I owe you?. |

# Au restaurant / In the restaurant

**Menu à 85 francs**

| | |
|---|---|
| **Hors d'œuvre variés** | **Starters** |
| Crudités | Fresh raw vegetables |
| Melon | Melon |
| Pâté de campagne | Country pâté |
| Salade de tomates | Tomato salad |
| Sardines beurre | Sardines in butter |
| * * * * * * * * * * * * * | * * * * * * * * * * * * * |
| **Plats chauds** | **Cooked dishes** |
| Escalope de dinde | Turkey escalope |
| Omelette aux champignons | Mushroom omelette |
| Poulet rôti | Roast chicken |
| Steak grillé | Grilled steak |
| Truite meunière | Trout baked in flour |
| * * * * * * * * * * * * * | * * * * * * * * * * * * * |
| **Légumes** | **Vegetables** |
| Carottes | Carrots |
| Frites | Chips |
| Haricots verts | French beans |
| Petits pois | Peas |
| Pommes de terre sautées | Sauté potatoes |
| Pommes vapeur | Boiled potatoes |
| Salade composée | Mixed salad |
| * * * * * * * * * * * * * | * * * * * * * * * * * * * |
| **Fromage ou Yaourt** | **Cheese or Yoghurt** |
| * * * * * * * * * * * * * | * * * * * * * * * * * * * |
| **Desserts** | **Desserts** |
| Fruits | Fruit |
| Gâteau au chocolat | Chocolate gateau |
| Glaces | Ice cream |
| Tarte aux pommes | Apple tart |
| * * * * * * * * * * * * * | * * * * * * * * * * * * * |
| **Café express** | **Espresso Coffee** |
| * * * * * * * * * * * * * | * * * * * * * * * * * * * |
| *Boisson en supplément* | *Drinks extra* |
| *Service et TVA compris* | *Service and VAT included* |

## Phrases

| | |
|---|---|
| Je voudrais une table sur la terrasse, s'il vous plaît | I'd like a table on the terrace, please |
| Avez-vous une table pour quatre près de la fenêtre, s'il vous plaît? | A table for four near the window, please |
| Je voudrais voir la carte, s'il vous plaît | I'd like to see the menu, please |
| Je voudrais commander maintenant, s'il vous plaît? | I'd like to order now, please |
| Quel est le plat du jour? | What's the dish of the day? |
| Le plat du jour est... | The dish of the day is... |
| Je prendrai le menu à 85 francs, s'il vous plaît | I'll have the 85 franc menu, please |
| Qu'est-ce que vous prenez comme hors d'œuvre? | What starter would you like? |
| Comme hors d'œuvre, je prendrai du pâté | As a starter, I'll have pâté |
| Qu'est-ce que vous prenez comme plat principal? | What main course would you like? |
| Qu'est-ce que c'est, 'truite meunière'? | What is 'truite meunière'? |
| Comme plat principal, je prendrai la truite | For main course, I'll have trout |
| Qu'est-ce que vous prenez comme légumes? | Which vegetables would you like? |
| Je prendrai des petits pois, s'il vous plaît | I'll have peas, please |
| Qu'est-ce que vous prenez comme dessert? | What would you like for dessert? |
| Comme dessert je prendrai des fruits, s'il vous plaît | I'll have fruit for dessert, please |
| Qu'est-ce que vous prenez comme boisson? | What would you like to drink? |
| Comme boisson je prendrai de l'eau minérale | I'll have mineral water to drink |
| Pardon, monsieur, mais le steak n'est pas assez cuit | Excuse me, my steak is not well enough cooked |
| Encore du pain, s'il vous plaît | Some more bread, please |
| L'addition, s'il vous plaît | May I have the bill, please? |

# Les commissions — Shopping

| | | |
|---|---|---|
| un | ascenseur | lift |
| la | bibliothèque | library |
| la | boucherie | butcher's shop |
| la | boulangerie | baker's shop |
| la | boulangerie | bread shop |
| la | boutique | shop |
| la | caisse | cash register, till |
| la | charcuterie | delicatessen |
| le | chariot | shopping trolley |
| le/la | client(e) | customer |
| le | coiffeur/la coiffeuse | hairdresser's |
| le/la | commerçant(e) | trader |
| la | crémerie | cheese shop |
| une | entrée | entrance |
| une | épicerie | grocer's |
| un | escalator | escalator |
| le | grand magasin | department store |
| la | grande surface | hypermarket |
| les | heures d'ouverture (f pl) | opening times |
| le | libre-service | self-service |
| le | magasin | shop |
| le | magasin d'alimentation générale | general food shop |
| le | magasin de vêtements | clothes shop |
| les | marchandises (f pl) | goods |
| le | marché | market |
| le | panier | shopping basket |
| la | pâtisserie | cake shop |
| la | pharmacie | chemist's |
| la | poissonnerie | fish shop |
| le | prix | price |
| en | promotion | on special offer |
| la | quincaillerie | ironmonger's shop |
| le | rayon | department |
| la | sortie de secours | emergency exit |
| le | tabac | tobaconist's shop |
| le | vendeur | shop assistant (male) |
| la | vendeuse | shop assistant (female) |
| la | vitrine | shop window |
| | Veuillez payer à la caisse | Please pay at the till |
| | fermé | closed |
| | ouvert | open |
| | poussez | push |
| | tirez | pull |
| à | vendre | for sale |

## On achète des vêtements — Buying clothes

| | | |
|---|---|---|
| les | baskets (m pl) | trainers |
| le | blouson | blouson jacket |
| la | botte | boot |
| le | caleçon (sing) | leggings |
| la | casquette | cap |
| la | ceinture | belt |
| le | chapeau | hat |
| la | chaussette | sock |
| la | chaussure | shoe |
| la | chemise | shirt |
| le | chemisier | blouse |
| le | chou-chou | scrunchie |
| le | collant (sing) | tights |
| une | écharpe | scarf |

| | | |
|---|---|---|
| le | gant | glove |
| un | imperméable | waterproof coat |
| le | jean (sing) | pair of jeans |
| le | jogging | tracksuit |
| la | jupe | skirt |
| le | manteau | coat |
| le | pantalon (sing) | trousers |
| le | pull | pullover |
| le | pyjama (sing) | pyjama |
| la | robe | dress |
| le | sac banane | bumbag |
| la | sandale | sandal |
| le | short (sing) | shorts |
| le | slip | pants |
| le | soutien-gorge | bra |
| le | survêtement | tracksuit |
| le | T-shirt | T-shirt |
| le | veston | jacket |

| | | |
|---|---|---|
| en | coton | made of cotton |
| en | cuir | made of leather |
| en | laine | made of wool |
| en | polycoton | made of polyester/cotton |
| en | soie | made of silk |

### Phrases

| | |
|---|---|
| Est-ce que je peux vous aider? | Can I help you? |
| Je regarde seulement | I'm just looking |
| Je cherche un pull | Yes, I'm looking for a jumper |
| Vous faites quelle taille? | What size do you take? |
| Je fais du 40 ou M | I need size 40 or M |
| Avez-vous la même chose en vert? | Do you have the same also in green? |
| Où est-ce je peux l'essayer? | Where can I try it on? |
| Les cabines sont par là there | The changing rooms are over |
| Ce pull est trop étroit | This jumper is too small |
| Est-ce que vous en avez un plus grand? | Do you have a slightly bigger one? |
| Gardez le ticket de caisse | Keep the till receipt |
| Comme ça vous pourrez l'échanger | Then you can change it |

## On achète à manger — Buying food

### La viande — Meat

| | | |
|---|---|---|
| l' | agneau (m) | lamb |
| le | bifteck | steak |
| le | bœuf | beef |
| le | canard | duck |
| la | charcuterie | processed meats |
| le | cheval | horse |
| la | dinde | turkey |
| le | jambon | ham |
| le | lapin | rabbit |
| le | porc | pork |
| le | poulet | chicken |
| le | rôti | roast |
| la | saucisse | sausage |
| le | saucisson | salami-type sausage |
| le | steak | steak |
| le | veau | veal |
| la | volaille | poultry |

### Les légumes — Vegetables

| | | |
|---|---|---|
| l' | ail (m) | garlic |
| la | carotte | carrot |
| le | champignon | mushroom |
| le | chou | cabbage |
| le | chou-fleur | cauliflower |
| les | choux de Bruxelles (m pl) | sprouts |
| le | concombre | cuçumber |
| les | épinards (m pl) | spinach |
| le | haricot | bean |
| le | haricot vert | green bean |
| la | laitue | lettuce |
| un | oignon | onion |
| les | petits pois (m pl) | peas |
| la | pomme de terre | potato |
| le | riz | rice |
| la | salade | salad |
| la | tomate | tomato |

### Les fruits — Fruit

| | | |
|---|---|---|
| un | abricot | apricot |
| un | ananas | pineapple |
| la | banane | banana |
| le | cassis | blackcurrant |
| la | cerise | cherry |
| le | citron | lemon |
| la | fraise | strawberry |
| la | framboise | raspberry |
| le | melon | melon |
| une | orange | orange |
| le | pamplemousse | grapefruit |
| la | pêche | peach |
| la | poire | pear |
| la | pomme | apple |
| la | prune | plum |
| le | raisin | grape |
| la | tomate | tomato |
| la | pastèque | water melon |

### Phrases

| | |
|---|---|
| Vous désirez? | What would you like? |
| C'est à qui maintenant? | Who is next, please? |
| Je voudrais... | I'd like... |
| cinq cent grammes de bananes | a pound of bananas |

| | |
|---|---|
| un kilo de pommes | a kilo of apples |
| deux cent grammes de fromage | 200 grammes of cheese |
| trois tranches de jambon | 3 slices of ham |
| un litre de lait | a litre of milk |
| une boîte de petits pois | a tin of peas |
| un paquet de biscuits | a packet of biscuits |
| une bouteille d'eau minérale | a bottle of mineral water |

| | |
|---|---|
| Ça vous fait un peu plus | It's a little over |
| Et avec cela? | Anything else? |
| Et ensuite? | Anything else? |
| C'est tout, merci | That's all, thank you |

## Les boissons — Drinks

| | | |
|---|---|---|
| de la | bière | beer |
| du | café | coffee |
| du | cidre | cider |
| de l' | eau minérale (f) | mineral water |
| du | jus de fruit | fruit juice |
| du | lait | milk |
| de la | limonade | lemonade |
| du | thé | tea |
| du | vin | wine |

## L'alimentation générale — Groceries

| | | |
|---|---|---|
| la | baguette | stick of French bread |
| le | biscuit | biscuit |
| les | chips (m pl) | crisps |
| le | chocolat | chocolate |
| le | fromage | cheese |
| le | gâteau | cake |
| la | glace | ice-cream |
| la | marmelade | jam |
| un | œuf | egg |
| le | pain | bread/French loaf |
| les | pâtes (f pl) | pasta |

## Les souvenirs — Souvenirs

| | | |
|---|---|---|
| la | carte postale | postcard |
| la | casquette | cap |
| la | cassette | cassette |
| une | écharpe | scarf |
| le | livre illustré | picture book |
| le | stylo | biro |
| le | T-shirt | T-shirt |
| le | timbre | stamp |

| | |
|---|---|
| acheter | to buy |
| aimer | to like |
| chercher | to look for |
| choisir | to choose |
| coûter | to cost |
| demander | to ask for |
| essayer | to try |
| fermer | to close |
| ouvrir | to open |
| payer | to pay |
| porter | to wear |
| prendre | to take |
| vendre | to sell |

### Phrases

| | |
|---|---|
| Je cherche un cadeau pour ma mère | I am looking for a present for my mum |
| C'est combien, ça, s'il vous plaît? | How much is that, please? |
| Je le prends | I'll take it |
| J'ai seulement un billet de deux cents francs | I've only got a 200 franc note |
| Avez-vous de la monnaie? | Have you got change? |
| Je voudrais une casquette, s'il vous plaît | I would like a cap, please? |
| Payez à la caisse | Pay at the till |

# La banque et la poste — Bank and post office

## A la banque — At the bank

| | | |
|---|---|---|
| l' | argent (m) | money |
| le | billet | note |
| la | caisse | cash till |
| le | centime | centime |
| le | change | currency exchange |
| le | chèque | cheque |
| le | chèque de voyage | traveller's cheque |
| le | distributeur de billets | cashpoint |
| le | franc | franc |
| la | livre sterling | pound sterling |
| la | pièce d'identité | ID |
| le | taux de change | exchange rate |
| les | travellers (m pl) | traveller's cheques |

| | |
|---|---|
| toucher un chèque | to cash a cheque |
| changer de l'argent | to change money |

### Phrases

| | |
|---|---|
| Je voudrais changer cent livres | I'd like to change £100 |
| Je voudrais changer un chèque de voyage | I'd like to cash a traveller's cheque |
| Combien vaut la livre aujourd'hui? | What is the rate for the pound today? |

## A la poste — At the post office

| | | |
|---|---|---|
| par | avion | by air mail |
| la | boîte aux lettres | letterbox |
| la | carte postale | postcard |
| le | colis | parcel |
| le | courrier | mail |
| le | facteur | postman |
| le | guichet | counter |
| la | lettre | letter |

| | | |
|---|---|---|
| le | paquet | package |
| la | poste | post office |
| le | timbre | stamp |
| | poster | to post |
| | envoyer | to send |

### Phrases

| | |
|---|---|
| C'est combien pour envoyer une lettre au Royaume-Uni? | How much is a letter to the UK? |
| Quand est-ce qu'elle arrivera? | When will it get there? |
| Est-ce que je peux téléphoner d'ici? | Can I phone from here? |
| Allez à la cabine numéro trois | Please go to booth three. |
| A quelle heure est la prochaine levée? | When is the next collection? |

# En voyage — Travelling

## Les moyens de transport — Transport

| | | |
|---|---|---|
| une | auto | car |
| la | bicyclette | bicycle |
| le | bus | bus |
| le | camion | lorry |
| la | camionnette | van |
| le | car | coach |
| le | métro | underground |
| la | moto | motorbike |
| le | moyen de transport | means of transport |
| le | train | train |
| le | tramway | tram |
| le | vélo | bicycle |
| le | vélomoteur | moped |
| la | voiture | car |
| | voyager | travel |
| | conduire | drive |

## En train — By train

| | | |
|---|---|---|
| un | aller simple | single ticket |
| un | aller-retour | return ticket |
| une | arrivée | arrival |
| le | billet | ticket |
| le | compartiment | compartment |
| la | consigne | luggage locker |
| la | correspondance | connecting train |
| le | départ | departure |
| le | fumeur | smoker |
| la | gare | station |
| un | horaire | timetable |
| le | non-fumeur | non-smoker |
| un | omnibus | local train |
| le | quai | platform |
| le | rapide | express train |
| la | réservation | reservation |
| le | retard | delay |
| la | salle d'attente | waiting-room |
| le | TGV train à grande vitesse | TGV |
| la | voie | track |
| le | voyageur | traveller |
| de | première classe | first class |
| de | seconde classe | second class |
| | arriver* | to arrive |
| | attendre | to wait |
| | changer | to change |
| | partir* | to depart |

### Phrases

| | |
|---|---|
| A quelle heure part le prochain train pour Calais? | When is the next train to Calais? |
| De quel quai? | From which platform? |
| Du quai numéro 3 | From platform 3 |
| A quelle heure est-ce qu'il arrive à Calais? | When does it arrive in Calais? |
| Un aller-retour pour Marseille | One return ticket to Marseilles |
| Deux allers simples pour Calais | Two single tickets to Calais |
| Je voudrais réserver une place | I'd like to reserve a seat |
| Est-ce qu'il faut changer? | Do I have to change? |
| Oui, il faut changer á Lyon | Yes, you have to change at Lyon |
| Non, c'est direct | No, it's a through train |

## En autobus — by bus

| | | |
|---|---|---|
| un | arrêt de bus | bus stop |
| le | carnet | book of tickets |
| le | composteur de billets | machine to date-stamp tickets |
| le | distributeur de tickets | ticket machine |
| la | gare routière | bus station |
| la | ligne | line |
| | composter un billet | to date-stamp a ticket |
| | descendre* du bus | to get out of the bus |
| | monter* dans le bus | to get into the bus |

### Phrases

| | |
|---|---|
| Y a-t-il un arrêt de bus par ici? | Is there a bus stop near here? |
| C'est quelle ligne pour aller à la piscine? | Which bus goes to the swimming pool? |
| Prenez la numéro trois | Take bus (line) no. 3 |
| Pour aller en centre ville, il y a un bus tous les combien? | How often do the buses go to the town centre? |

| | |
|---|---|
| Il y a un bus toutes les vingt minutes | There is a bus every twenty minutes |
| C'est bien le bus pour l'hôtel de ville? | Is this the right bus for the town hall? |

## Par avion — By plane

| | |
|---|---|
| un aéroport | airport |
| un avion | plane |
| le billet | ticket |
| un carrousel | luggage carousel |
| la douane | customs control |
| une hôtesse de l'air | stewardess |
| le passeport | passport |
| le pilote | pilot |
| le vol | flight |
| atterrir | to land |
| décoller | to take off |
| durer | to last |
| rater | to miss |
| voler | to fly |

### Phrases

| | |
|---|---|
| Je voudrais réserver une place | I'd like to book a ticket |
| A quelle heure part le prochain vol pour Londres? | When does the next flight to London leave? |
| Où sont les caddies? | Where are the luggage trolleys? |
| Est-ce qu'il y a un car pour aller à l'aéroport? | Is there a coach to the airport? |

## La traversée de la Manche — The Channel crossing

| | |
|---|---|
| le car-ferry | ferry |
| un hovercraft/ un aéroglisseur | hovercraft |
| la mer | sea |
| le port | port, harbour |
| le tunnel sous la Manche | Channel Tunnel |
| à l'heure | on time |
| agité(e) | rough |
| avec du retard | delayed |
| calme | calm |

### Phrases

| | |
|---|---|
| Comment était la traversée? | What was the crossing like? |
| Elle était très agréable | It was very pleasant |
| Qu'est-ce que tu as fait pendant la traversée? | What did you do during the crossing? |
| J'ai lu un livre | I read a book |
| J'ai dormi | I slept |
| Je me suis promené(e) sur le pont | I went on deck |
| Est-ce que tu as pris le ferry à Douvres? | Did you catch the ferry from Dover? |
| Non, j'ai pris le tunnel à Folkestone | No, I used the tunnel from Folkestone |

# Les excursions — Excursions

## On sort — Going out

| | |
|---|---|
| un acteur | actor |
| une actrice | actress |
| le balcon | balcony |
| le billet | ticket |
| la boîte de nuit | night club |
| la boum | party |
| le centre sportif | sports centre |
| la chaîne de télé | TV channel |
| le cinéma | cinema |
| le club | club |
| le concert | concert |
| la discothèque | disco |
| une excursion | outing |
| une exposition | exhibition |
| la fête | party |
| le film | film |
| la galerie | gallery |
| l' orchestre (m) | stalls |
| la patinoire | ice-rink |
| la pièce de théâtre | play |
| la piscine | swimming pool |
| le pub | pub |
| le restaurant | restaurant |
| la séance | performance |
| les sous-titres (m pl) | subtitles |
| le stade | stadium |
| le terrain de sports | sportsground |
| le théâtre | theatre |
| la version originale (v.o.) | original soundtrack |
| casse-pieds | boring |
| excellent | excellent |
| extra | great |
| intéressant | interesting |
| moche | bad |
| peu intéressant | not interesting |
| sensationel | great |
| commencer | to begin |
| coûter | to cost |
| durer | to last |
| finir | to finish |
| réserver | to book, reserve |

### Phrases

| | |
|---|---|
| On sort ce soir? | Shall we go out tonight? |

| | |
|---|---|
| Oui, je veux bien | Yes, please |
| Non, merci | No, thank you |
| Je regrette, aujourd'hui je ne peux pas | Sorry, I can't make it today |
| J'ai trop de devoirs | I have too much homework |
| Je dois garder mon petit frère | I have to babysit my little brother |
| Je suis déjà pris(e) | I have already got another engagement |
| Je dois d'abord demander à mon correspondant/à ma correspondante | I have to ask my exchange partner first |
| Je ne dois pas sortir aujourd'hui | I am not allowed to go out today |
| Je suis puni(e). Je n'ai pas le droit de sortir | I am grounded |
| Qu'est-ce que tu voudrais faire ce soir? | What would you like to do tonight? |
| Où voudrais-tu aller? | Where would you like to go? |
| Qu'est-ce qu'on peut faire ce soir? | What can we do tonight? |
| Veux-tu aller à la discothèque? | Do you want to go to the disco? |
| On loue une vidéo? | Shall we hire a video? |
| J'aimerais aller au cinéma | I'd like to go to the cinema |
| C'est quel film aujourd'hui? | What film is it today? |
| Il y a un film d'amour | There is a love story |
| Qu'est-ce qu'on donne au théâtre? | What's on at the theatre? |
| Il y a une pièce d'Agatha Christie | There is a play by Agatha Christie |
| As-tu déjà vu 'Apollo 13'? | Have you seen 'Apollo 13'? |
| Est-ce que ça existe déjà en vidéo? | Is it already out on video? |
| A quelle heure est-ce qu'on va se rencontrer? | When shall we meet? |
| A sept heures | At 7 o'clock |
| Où est-ce qu'on va se rencontrer? | Where shall we meet? |
| Chez moi | At my house |
| Devant le cinéma | In front of the cinema |
| A tout à l'heure | See you later |
| A quelle heure commence le film/la pièce? | When does the film/the play begin? |
| A quelle heure finit le film/la pièce? | When does the film/the play finish? |
| C'est combien, un billet? | How much is a ticket? |
| Un billet coûte trente francs | A ticket costs 30 francs |
| Qu'est-ce que tu as fait samedi dernier? | What did you do last Saturday? |
| Le matin je suis allé(e) en ville | I went to town in the morning |
| L'après-midi j'ai fait du sport avec mes amis | In the afternoon I did sport with my friends |
| Le soir, j'ai regardé la télé | In the evening I watched TV |
| Qu'est-ce que tu as fait hier soir? | What did you do yesterday evening? |
| J'ai fait mes devoirs | I did my homework |

## Les jours de fête — Special days

| | | |
|---|---|---|
| la | Nationale | 14th July, Bastille Day |
| le | jour de l'An | New Year's Day |
| la | veille de Noël | Christmas Eve |
| le | jour de Noël | Christmas Day |
| le | jour de Pâques | Easter Day |
| le | jour des Rois | Twelfth Night |
| la | Saint-Sylvestre | New Year's Eve |
| le | Ramadan | Ramadan |
| le | Sabbat | Sabbath |
| la | Pâque juive | Passover |
| le | nouvel an juif | Rosh Hashana |
| un | anniversaire | birthday |
| un | arbre de Noël | Christmas tree |
| le | cadeau | present |
| la | carte | card |
| la | fête | name day |
| le | gâteau | cake |
| le | Père Noël | Father Christmas |
| | acheter | to buy |
| | envoyer | to send |
| | fêter | to celebrate |
| | offrir | to give as a present |

### Phrases

| | |
|---|---|
| J'achète un cadeau à ma sœur | I am buying a present for my sister |
| Je cherche une carte d'anniversaire pour mon cousin/pour ma cousine | I am looking for a birthday card for my cousin |
| Je vais donner du vin à mon grand-père | I am going to give my grandad some wine |
| Mon anniversaire, c'est le trente décembre | My birthday is on the 30th of December |

## Les vacances — Holidays

| | | |
|---|---|---|
| une | agence de voyages | travel agency |
| la | brochure | brochure |
| la | carte routière | road map |
| le | chèque de voyages | traveller's cheque |
| le | dépliant | brochure |
| un | échange | exchange |
| une | excursion | excursion, outing |
| l' | hébergement (m) | accomodation |
| un | office de tourisme | tourist office |
| la | photo | photo |
| le | plan de la ville | map of town |
| le | sac à dos | rucksack |
| le | séjour | stay |
| le | syndicat d'initiative | tourist office |

| | | |
|---|---|---|
| le | touriste | tourist |
| les | vacances (f pl) | holidays |
| la | valise | suitcase |
| la | visite | visit |
| le | voyage | journey |
| | aller* | to go |
| s' | amuser | to enjoy oneself |
| | passer | to spend (time) |
| se | relaxer | to relax |
| se | reposer | to rest |
| | rester* | to stay |
| | voler | to fly |
| | voyager | to travel |

### Phrases

| | |
|---|---|
| Où est-ce que tu vas passer tes vacances? | Where are you going spend your holiday? |
| Je vais passer quinze jours en Espagne | I am going to spend a fortnight in Spain |
| Je vais en France avec ma famille | I am travelling to France with my family |
| Je vais aller à Rome en avion | I am going to fly to Rome |
| Tu vas en vacances avec qui? | Who are you going on holiday with? |
| Tu vas rester combien de temps? | How long are you staying? |
| Comment est-ce que tu voyages en Espagne? | How are you travelling to Spain? |

## Au camping — At the campsite

| | | |
|---|---|---|
| les | allumettes (f pl) | matches |
| le | bloc sanitaire | toilet block |
| la | bouteille de gaz | gas bottle |
| le | camping | camp-site |
| le | camping-car | Dormobile® |
| le | canif | penknife |
| la | caravane | caravan |
| l' | électricité (f) | electricity |
| un | emplacement | pitch |
| le | feu de camp | camp fire |
| le | four à gaz | gas cooker |
| la | lampe | torch |
| le | matelas pneumatique | air bed |
| le | matériel du camping | camping equipment |
| un | ouvre-boîte | tin opener |
| la | réception | reception |
| le | sac de couchage | sleeping bag |
| la | tente | tent |
| | ouvert à l'année | open all year |
| | complet | full |
| a l' | ombre | in the shade |
| | propre | clean |
| | sale | dirty |
| au | soleil | in the sun |
| | camper | to camp |
| | changer | to change |
| | chercher | to look for |
| | faire la cuisine | to cook |
| | monter une tente | to pitch a tent |
| | payer | to pay |

## A l'auberge de jeunesse — In the youth hostel

| | | |
|---|---|---|
| une | auberge de jeunesse | youth hostel |
| la | carte d'adhérent | membership card |
| la | cave | cellar |
| la | couverture | blanket |
| le | dortoir | dormitory |
| la | douche | shower |
| le | drap | sheet |
| la | mère aubergiste | warden (female) |
| la | nuitée | night |
| le | père aubergiste | warden (male) |
| le | réglement | rules of the youth hostel |
| le/la | responsable | party leader, organizer |
| la | salle à manger | dining-room |
| la | salle de séjour | day room |
| le | silence | silence at night, lights out |
| | complet | full |
| | défendu | forbidden |
| à l' | exception de | except |
| | permis | permitted |
| | aider | to help |
| | balayer | to sweep |
| | débarrasser la table | to clear the table |
| | fermer | to shut |
| | louer | to hire |
| | ouvrir | to open |
| | ranger | to tidy up |
| | réserver | to book |

### Phrases

| | |
|---|---|
| Avez-vous encore de la place? | Have you got any beds left? |
| Pour combien de personnes? | For how many persons? |
| Nous sommes quatre, deux filles et deux garçons | There are four of us, two girls and two boys |
| Quels repas prenez-vous? | Which meals would you like? |
| Nous voulons le petit déjeuner et le dîner | We want breakfast and evening meal |
| Avez-vous des draps? | Have you got bed linen? |
| Nous avons besoin de draps pour deux personnes | Yes, we'd like sheets for two people |
| Les dortoirs sont au premier étage | The dormitories are on the first floor |

## A l'hôtel — At the hotel

| | | |
|---|---|---|
| un | ascenseur | lift |
| la | chambre pour deux personnes | double room |
| la | chambre pour une personne | single room |
| la | clé | key |
| en | demi-pension | half board (bed, breakfast and evening meal) |
| avec | douche | with shower |
| un | escalier | staircase |
| la | liste des hôtels | list of hotels |
| le | parking | car park |
| la | pension complète | full board |
| la | plage | beach |
| le | prix | price |
| la | réception | reception |
| le | rez-de-chaussée | ground floor |
| avec | salle de bains | with bathroom |
| le | serveur | waiter |
| la | serveuse | waitress |
| la | sortie de secours | emergency exit |
| le | téléphone | telephone |
| avec | téléviseur | with TV |
| | autre | other |
| | bon marché | good value for money |
| | bruyant | noisy |
| | cher | expensive |
| | compris | included |
| | confortable | comfortable |
| | grand | big |
| | libre | free |
| de | luxe | luxurious |
| | occupé | occupied |
| | petit | small |
| | propre | clean |
| | sale | dirty |
| | seul | alone |
| | avec | with |
| | sans | without |
| | commander | to order |
| | demander | to ask (for) |
| | demander des informations | to ask for information |
| se | plaindre | to complain |
| | réserver | to book |

### Phrases

| | |
|---|---|
| J'ai réservé deux chambres à deux personnes | I reserved two double rooms |
| C'est au nom de MacPherson | It's in the name of MacPherson |
| A quelle heure peut-on dîner? | When is the evening meal served? |
| Est-ce que la TVA est compris? | Is VAT included in the price? |
| Acceptez-vous les cartes VISA? | Do you accept VISA? |
| L'eau dans ma chambre est froide | The water in my room is cold |
| Je voudrais voir le gérant | May I speak to the manager? |
| Est-ce que vous pouvez me donner une autre couverture? | May I have another blanket? |

## A la plage — At the beach

| | | |
|---|---|---|
| le | coup de soleil | sunburn |
| la | crème solaire | suntan lotion |
| le | dériveur | dinghy |
| la | glace | icecream |
| le | maillot | bathing suit |
| la | marée basse | low tide |
| la | marée haute | high tide |
| la | mer | sea |
| le | parasol | parasol |
| la | plage | beach |
| le | port de plaisance | yacht marina |
| le | sable | sand |
| le | voilier | sailing boat |
| | calme | calm |
| | chaud | hot |
| | ensoleillé | sunny |
| se | baigner | to bathe in the sea |
| se | bronzer | to sunbathe |
| | faire de la planche à voile | to windsurf |
| | faire de la voile | to sail |
| | faire du ski nautique | to waterski |
| | faire du skim | to skimboard |

## A la campagne — In the country

| | | |
|---|---|---|
| un | arbre | tree |
| le | champ | field |
| la | ferme | farm |
| la | fleur | flower |
| la | forêt | forest |
| le | gîte | holiday cottage |
| la | montagne | mountain |
| le | paysage | landscape |
| la | prairie | meadow |
| le | sentier | path |
| les | vacances à la ferme (f pl) | farm holiday |
| la | vallée | valley |
| le | village | village |
| | faire une randonnée | to hike |
| se | promener | to go for a walk |

### Phrases

| | |
|---|---|
| Où est-ce que tu vas passer tes vacances? | Where are you spending your holidays? |
| Je vais au bord de la mer | I am going to the seaside |
| Je vais à la montagne | I am going to the mountains |
| Je vais camper | I am going camping |
| Je vais voir mon cousin/ma cousine | I am going to visit my cousin |
| Tu pars en vacances pendant combien de temps? | How long are you going for? |
| Je vais passer quinze jours en vacances | I am on holiday for a fortnight |
| Quel temps fait-il? | What is the weather like? |
| Il fait chaud/du soleil/froid | It is hot/sunny/cold |
| Il pleut tout le temps | It is raining the whole time |
| Qu'est-ce que tu fais à la plage? | What do you do at the beach? |
| Je me bronze | I sunbathe |
| Je nage | I swim |
| Je fais de la planche à voile | I windsurf |
| Qu'est-ce que tu fais le soir? | What do you do in the evenings? |
| Je me promène | I go for walks |
| Je vais au café | I go to the café |
| Qu'est-ce que tu fais à Pâques? | What are you doing at Easter? |
| Je vais en France | I am going to France |
| Je fais un voyage scolaire | I am going on a school trip |
| Qu'est-ce que tu as fait pendant les vacances d'été? | What did you do in the summer holidays? |
| Je suis allé(e) en Ecosse avec mes parents | I went to Scotland with my parents |
| Je suis resté(e) chez moi | I stayed at home |
| Est-ce que tu as visité un musée? | Did you visit a museum? |
| Non, je n'aime pas les musées | No, I don't like museums |

# Les médias — The media

## Les différents médias — Media types

| | | |
|---|---|---|
| le | cinéma | cinema |
| un | illustré | magazine |
| le | journal | newspaper |
| le | magazine | magazine |
| la | presse | press |
| la | radio | radio |
| la | télévision | TV |
| le | théâtre | theatre |

## Les appareils — Equipment

| | | |
|---|---|---|
| une | antenne | aerial |
| une | antenne parabolique | satellite dish |
| le | baladeur | Walkman® |
| le | câble à péage | subscription cable |
| la | cassette vidéo | video cassette |
| la | chaîne stéréo | stereo system |
| le | magnétoscope | VCR |
| la | platine laser | CD player |
| la | télécommande | remote control |
| le | magazine de télé | TV magazine |
| le | téléviseur | TV set |
| la | télévision câblée | cable TV |

## Au cinéma — At the cinema

| | | |
|---|---|---|
| la | comédie | comedy |
| le | dessin animé | cartoon |
| le | film à suspense | thriller |
| le | film d'amour | romantic film |
| le | film d'aventures | adventure film |
| le | film d'épouvante | horror film |
| le | film d'espionnage | spy film |
| le | film de science -fiction | science-fiction film |
| le | film policier | detective film |
| le | western | cowboy film |

### Phrases

| | |
|---|---|
| On va au cinéma ce soir? | Shall we go to the cinema tonight? |
| Qu'est-ce qu'il y a comme film? | What's on? |
| A quelle heure commence le film? | When does the film begin? |
| A quelle heure finit le film? | When does the film end? |
| C'est un film anglais en version originale | It is an English film with the original soundtrack |
| Est-ce que le film est en anglais? | Is the film in English? |
| Non, mais il y a des sous-titres | No, but there are subtitles |

## La télévision, la radio — TV, the radio

| | | |
|---|---|---|
| un | acteur | actor |
| une | actrice | actress |
| le | comédien | comedian/actor |
| la | comédienne | comedienne/actress |
| la | vedette | filmstar |

## Les émissions — Programme types

| | | |
|---|---|---|
| le | documentaire | documentary |
| une | émission de musique | music show |
| le | feuilleton | soap opera/serial |
| les / les | informations (f pl)/ infos (f pl) | news |

| | | |
|---|---|---|
| le | jeu concours | quiz |
| le | mélo | soap |
| la | météo | weather forecast |
| la | publicité | advertisements |
| les | pubs (f pl) | ads |
| le | reportage sportif | sports report |
| le | talk-show | chat show |
| le | journal télévisé | news magazine programme |

| | |
|---|---|
| aimer regarder | to like watching |
| allumer (la radio) | to turn on (the radio) |
| changer de programme | to switch over TV channel |
| écouter | to listen (to) |
| enregistrer | to record |
| éteindre (la radio) | to turn off (the radio) |
| mettre | to play |
| regarder | to watch |

### Phrases

| | |
|---|---|
| Est-ce que tu regardes quelquefois la télé? | Do you sometimes watch TV? |
| Oui, je la regarde tous les jours pendant une heure | Yes, I watch TV every day for an hour |
| Non, je ne regarde pas souvent la télé | No, I don't watch TV very often |
| Quelle est ton émission préférée? | What is your favourite programme? |
| J'aime les films policiers | I like watching detective films |
| Quelles émissions n'aimes-tu pas? | Which programmes don´t you like? |
| Je n'aime pas les films d'amour | I don't like love-films |
| Je trouve les informations casse-pieds | I find the news boring |
| Est-ce que je peux regarder la télé? | May I watch some TV? |
| Est-ce que je peux écouter la radio? | May I listen to the radio? |
| Est-ce que tu pourrais augmenter le son? | Could you please turn the volume up? |
| Est-ce que tu peux baisser le son? | Could you please turn the volume down? |

## La lecture — Reading

| | | |
|---|---|---|
| la | bande dessinée | comic strip |
| un | illustré | magazine |
| le | livre | book |
| le | roman | novel |
| le | roman d'aventure | adventure novel |
| le | roman policier | detective novel |

### Phrases

| | |
|---|---|
| Tu aimes lire? | Do you like reading? |
| Oui, je lis beaucoup | Yes, I like reading a lot |
| Quel genre de livres est-ce que tu lis? | What sort of books do you read? |
| J'aime lire des romans | I like reading novels |
| Je lis des romans policiers | I like reading detective novels |

# Irregular Verb Table

| **Infinitif**<br>**Infinitive** | **Présent**<br>**Present** | **Imparfait**<br>**Imperfect** | **Passé Composé**<br>**Perfect** | **Futur**<br>**Future** |
|---|---|---|---|---|
| aller | je vais | j'allais | je suis allé(e) | j'irai |
| *to go* | tu vas | tu allais | tu es allé(e) | tu iras |
| | il/elle va | il/elle allait | il est allé | il/elle ira |
| | nous allons | nous allions | elle est allée | nous irons |
| | vous allez | vous alliez | nous sommes allé(e)s | vous irez |
| | ils/elles vont | ils/elles allaient | vous êtes allé(e)(s) | ils iront |
| | | | ils sont allés | |
| | | | elles sont allées | |
| apprendre | j'apprends | j'apprenais | j'ai appris | j'apprendrai |
| *to learn* | tu apprends | tu apprenais | tu as appris | tu apprendras |
| | il/elle apprend | il/elle apprenait | il/elle a appris | il/elle apprendra |
| | nous apprenons | nous apprenions | nous avons appris | nous apprendrons |
| | vous apprenez | vous appreniez | vous avez appris | vous apprendrez |
| | ils/elles apprennent | ils/elles apprenaient | ils/elles ont appris | ils/elles apprendront |
| s'asseoir | je m'assieds | je m'asseyais | je me suis assis(e) | je m'assiérai |
| *to sit down* | tu t'assieds | tu t'asseyais | tu t'es assis(e) | tu t'assiéras |
| | il/elle s'assied | il/elle s'asseyait | il s'est assis | il/elle s'assiéra |
| | nous nous asseyons | nous nous asseyions | elle s'est assise | nous nous assiérons |
| | vous vous asseyez | vous vous asseyiez | nous nous sommes assis(es) | vous vous assiérez |
| | ils/elles s'asseyent | ils/elles s'asseyaient | vous vous êtes assis(e)(es) | ils/elles s'assiéront |
| | | | ils se sont assis | |
| | | | elles se sont assises | |
| avoir | j'ai | j'avais | j'ai eu | j'aurai |
| *to have* | tu as | tu avais | tu as eu | tu auras |
| | il /elle a | il/elle avait | il/elle a eu | il/elle aura |
| | nous avons | nous avions | nous avons eu | nous aurons |
| | vous avez | vous aviez | vous avez eu | vous aurez |
| | ils /elles ont | ils/elles avaient | ils/elles ont eu | ils/elles auront |
| battre | je bats | je battais | j'ai battu | je battrai |
| *to beat* | tu bats | tu battais | tu as battu | tu battras |
| | il/elle bat | il/elle battait | il/elle a battu | il/elle battra |
| | nous battons | nous battions | nous avons battu | nous battrons |
| | vous battez | vous battiez | vous avez battu | vous battrez |
| | ils/elles battent | ils/elles battaient | ils/elles ont battu | ils/elles battront |

| Infinitif<br>Infinitive | Présent<br>Present | Imparfait<br>Imperfect | Passé Composé<br>Perfect | Futur<br>Future |
|---|---|---|---|---|
| boire | je bois | je buvais | j'ai bu | je boirai |
| *to drink* | tu bois | tu buvais | tu as bu | tu boiras |
| | il/elle boit | il/elle buvait | il/elle a bu | il/elle boira |
| | nous buvons | nous buvions | nous avons bu | nous boirons |
| | vous buvez | vous buviez | vous avez bu | vous boirez |
| | ils/elles boivent | ils/elles buvaient | ils/elles ont bu | ils/elles boiront |
| comprendre | je comprends | je comprenais | j'ai compris | je comprendrai |
| *to understand* | tu comprends | tu comprenais | tu as compris | tu comprendras |
| | il/elle comprend | il/elle comprenait | il/elle a compris | il/elle comprendra |
| | nous comprenons | nous comprenions | nous avons compris | nous comprendrons |
| | vous comprenez | vous compreniez | vous avez compris | vous comprendrez |
| | ils/elles comprennent | ils/elles comprenaient | ils/elles ont compris | ils/elles comprendront |
| conduire | je conduis | je conduisais | j'ai conduit | je conduirai |
| *to drive* | tu conduis | tu conduisais | tu as conduit | tu conduiras |
| | il/elle conduit | il/elle conduisait | il/elle a conduit | il/elle conduira |
| | nous conduisons | nous conduisions | nous avons conduit | nous conduirons |
| | vous conduisez | vous conduisiez | vous avez conduit | vous conduirez |
| | ils/elles conduisent | ils/elles conduisaient | ils/elles ont conduit | ils/elles conduiront |
| connaître | je connais | je connaissais | j'ai connu | je connaîtrai |
| *to know* | tu connais | tu connaissais | tu as connu | tu connaîtras |
| *(a person, place, book,* | il/elle connaît | il/elle connaissait | il/elle a connu | il/elle connaîtra |
| *film)* | nous connaissons | nous connaissions | nous avons connu | nous connaîtrons |
| | vous connaissez | vous connaissiez | vous avez connu | vous connaîtrez |
| | ils/elles connaissent | ils/elles connaissaient | ils/elles ont connu | ils/elles connaîtront |
| construire | je construis | je construisais | j'ai construit | je construirai |
| *to build* | tu construis | tu construisais | tu as construit | tu construiras |
| | il/elle construit | il construisait | il/elle a construit | il/elle construira |
| | nous construisons | nous construisions | nous avons construit | nous construirons |
| | vous construisez | vous construisiez | vous avez construit | vous construirez |
| | ils/elles construisent | ils/elles construisaient | ils/elles ont construit | ils/elles construiront |
| contenir | je contiens | je contenais | j'ai contenu | je contiendrai |
| *to contain,* | tu contiens | tu contenais | tu as contenu | tu contiendras |
| *to hold back* | il/elle contient | il/elle contenait | il/elle a contenu | il/elle contiendra |
| | nous contenons | nous contenions | nous avons contenu | nous contiendrons |
| | vous contenez | vous conteniez | vous avez contenu | vous contiendrez |
| | ils/elles contiennent | ils/elles contenaient | ils/elles ont contenu | ils/elles contiendront |

| Infinitif<br>Infinitive | Présent<br>Present | Imparfait<br>Imperfect | Passé Composé<br>Perfect | Futur<br>Future |
|---|---|---|---|---|
| coudre | je couds | je cousais | j'ai cousu | je coudrai |
| *to sew* | tu couds | tu cousais | tu as cousu | tu coudras |
| | il/elle coud | il/elle cousait | il/elle a cousu | il/elle coudra |
| | nous cousons | nous cousions | nous avons cousu | nous coudrons |
| | vous cousez | vous cousiez | vous avez cousu | vous coudrez |
| | ils/elles cousent | ils/elles cousaient | ils/elles ont cousu | ils/elles coudront |
| courir | je cours | je courais | j'ai couru | je courrai |
| *to run* | tu cours | tu courais | tu as couru | tu courras |
| | il/elle court | il/elle courait | il/elle a couru | il/elle courra |
| | nous courons | nous courions | nous avons couru | nous courrons |
| | vous courez | vous couriez | vous avez couru | vous courrez |
| | ils/elles courent | ils/elles couraient | ils/elles ont couru | ils/elles courront |
| couvrir | je couvre | je couvrais | j'ai couvert | je couvrirai |
| *to cover* | tu couvres | tu couvrais | tu as couvert | tu couvriras |
| | il/elle couvre | il/elle couvrait | il/elle a couvert | il/elle couvrira |
| | nous couvrons | nous couvrions | nous avons couvert | nous couvrirons |
| | vous couvrez | vous couvriez | vous avez couvert | vous couvrirez |
| | ils/elles couvrent | ils/elles couvraient | ils/elles ont couvert | ils/elles couvriront |
| craindre | je crains | je craignais | j'ai craint | je craindrai |
| *to fear,* | tu crains | tu craignais | tu as craint | tu craindras |
| *to be afraid* | il/elle craint | il/elle craignait | il/elle a craint | il/elle craindra |
| | nous craignons | nous craignions | nous avons craint | nous craindrons |
| | vous craignez | vous craigniez | vous avez craint | vous craindrez |
| | ils/elles craignent | ils/elles craignaient | ils/elles ont craint | ils/elles craindront |
| croire | je crois | je croyais | j'ai cru | je croirai |
| *to believe,* | tu crois | tu croyais | tu as cru | tu croiras |
| *to think* | il/elle croit | il/elle croyait | il/elle a cru | il/elle croira |
| | nous croyons | nous croyions | nous avons cru | nous croirons |
| | vous croyez | vous croyiez | vous avez cru | vous croirez |
| | ils/elles croient | ils/elles croyaient | ils/elles ont cru | ils/elles croiront |
| découvrir | je découvre | je découvrais | j'ai découvert | je découvrirai |
| *to discover* | tu découvres | tu découvrais | tu as découvert | tu découvriras |
| | il/elle découvre | il/elle découvrait | il/elle a découvert | il/elle découvrira |
| | nous découvrons | nous découvrions | nous avons découvert | nous découvrirons |
| | vous découvrez | vous découvriez | vous avez découvert | vous découvrirez |
| | ils/elles découvrent | ils/elles découvraient | ils/elles ont découvert | ils/elles découvriront |

| Infinitif<br>Infinitive | Présent<br>Present | Imparfait<br>Imperfect | Passé Composé<br>Perfect | Futur<br>Future |
|---|---|---|---|---|
| descendre | je descends | je descendais | je suis descendu(e) | je descendrai |
| *to go down* | tu descends | tu descendais | tu es descendu(e) | tu descendras |
| | il/elle descend | il/elle descendait | il est descendu | il/elle descendra |
| | nous descendons | nous descendions | elle est descendue | nous descendrons |
| | vous descendez | vous descendiez | nous sommes descendu(e)s | vous descendrez |
| | ils/elles descendent | ils/elles descendaient | vous êtes descendu(e)(s) | ils/elles descendront |
| | | | ils sont descendus | |
| | | | elles sont descendues | |
| détruire | je détruis | je détruisais | j'ai détruit | je détruirai |
| *to destroy* | tu détruis | tu détruisais | tu as détruit | tu détruiras |
| | il/elle détruit | il/elle détruisait | il/elle a détruit | il/elle détruira |
| | nous détruisons | nous détruisions | nous avons détruit | nous détruirons |
| | vous détruisez | vous détruisiez | vous avez détruit | vous détruirez |
| | ils/elles détruisent | ils/elles détruisaient | ils/elles ont détruit | ils/elles détruiront |
| devenir | je deviens | je devenais | je suis devenu(e) | je deviendrai |
| *to become* | tu deviens | tu devenais | tu es devenu(e) | tu deviendras |
| | il/elle devient | il/elle devenait | il est devenu | il/elle deviendra |
| | nous devenons | nous devenions | elle est devenue | nous deviendrons |
| | vous devenez | vous deveniez | nous sommes devenu(e)s | vous deviendrez |
| | ils/elles deviennent | ils/elles devenaient | vous êtes devenu(e)(s) | ils/elles deviendront |
| | | | ils sont devenus | |
| | | | elles sont devenues | |
| devoir | je dois | je devais | j'ai dû | je devrai |
| *to have to* | tu dois | tu devais | tu as dû | tu devras |
| | il/elle doit | il/elle devait | il/elle a dû | il/elle devra |
| | nous devons | nous devions | nous avons dû | nous devrons |
| | vous devez | vous deviez | vous avez dû | vous devrez |
| | ils/elles doivent | ils/elles devaient | ils/elles ont dû | ils/elles devront |
| dire | je dis | je disais | j'ai dit | je dirai |
| *to say,* | tu dis | tu disais | tu as dit | tu diras |
| *to tell* | il/elle dit | il/elle disait | il/elle a dit | il/elle dira |
| | nous disons | nous disions | nous avons dit | nous dirons |
| | vous dites | vous disiez | vous avez dit | vous direz |
| | ils/elles disent | ils/elles disaient | ils/elles ont dit | ils/elles diront |
| disparaître | je disparais | je disparaissais | j'ai disparu | je disparaîtrai |
| *to disappear* | tu disparais | tu disparaissais | tu as disparu | tu disparaîtras |
| | il/elle disparaît | il/elle disparaissait | il/elle a disparu | il/elle disparaîtra |
| | nous disparaissons | nous disparaissions | nous avons disparu | nous disparaîtrons |
| | vous disparaissez | vous disparaissiez | vous avez disparu | vous disparaîtrez |
| | ils/elles disparaissent | ils/elles disparaissaient | ils/elles ont disparu | ils/elles disparaîtront |

| **Infinitif**<br>**Infinitive** | **Présent**<br>**Present** | **Imparfait**<br>**Imperfect** | **Passé Composé**<br>**Perfect** | **Futur**<br>**Future** |
|---|---|---|---|---|
| dormir | je dors | je dormais | j'ai dormi | je dormirai |
| *to sleep* | tu dors | tu dormais | tu as dormi | tu dormiras |
| | il/elle dort | il/elle dormait | il/elle a dormi | il/elle dormira |
| | nous dormons | nous dormions | nous avons dormi | nous dormirons |
| | vous dormez | vous dormiez | vous avez dormi | vous dormirez |
| | ils/elles dorment | ils/elles dormaient | ils/elles ont dormi | ils/elles dormiront |
| écrire | j'écris | j'écrivais | j'ai écrit | j'écrirai |
| *to write* | tu écris | tu écrivais | tu as écrit | tu écriras |
| | il/elle écrit | il/elle écrivait | il/elle a écrit | il/elle écrira |
| | nous écrivons | nous écrivions | nous avons écrit | nous écrirons |
| | vous écrivez | vous écriviez | vous avez écrit | vous écrirez |
| | ils/elles écrivent | ils/elles écrivaient | ils/elles ont écrit | ils/elles écriront |
| s'endormir | je m'endors | je m'endormais | je me suis endormi(e) | je m'endormirai |
| *to go to sleep,* | tu t'endors | tu t'endormais | tu t'es endormi(e) | tu t'endormiras |
| *fall asleep* | il/elle s'endort | il/elle s'endormait | il s'est endormi | il/elle s'endormira |
| | nous nous endormons | nous nous endormions | elle s'est endormie | nous nous endormirons |
| | vous vous endormez | vous vous endormiez | nous nous sommes endormi(e)s | vous vous endormirez |
| | ils/elles s'endorment | ils/elles s'endormaient | vous vous êtes endormi(e)(s) | ils/elles s'endormiront |
| | | | ils se sont endormis | |
| | | | elles se sont endormies | |
| entendre | j'entends | j'entendais | j'ai entendu | j'entendrai |
| *to hear* | tu entends | tu entendais | tu as entendu | tu entendras |
| | il/elle entend | il/elle entendait | il/elle a entendu | il/elle entendra |
| | nous entendons | nous entendions | nous avons entendu | nous entendrons |
| | vous entendez | vous entendiez | vous avez entendu | vous entendrez |
| | ils/elles entendent | ils/elles entendaient | ils/elles ont entendu | ils/elles entendront |
| entretenir | j'entretiens | j'entretenais | j'ai entretenu | j'entretiendrai |
| *to maintain* | tu entretiens | tu entretenais | tu as entretenu | tu entretiendras |
| | il /elle entretient | il/elle entretenait | il/elle a entretenu | il /elle entretiendra |
| | nous entretenons | nous entretenions | nous avons entretenu | nous entretiendrons |
| | vous entretenez | vous entreteniez | vous avez entretenu | vous entretiendrez |
| | ils/elles entretiennent | ils/elles entretenaient | ils/elles ont entretenu | ils/elles entretiendront |
| envoyer | j'envoie | j'envoyais | j'ai envoyé | j'enverrai |
| *to send* | tu envoies | tu envoyais | tu as envoyé | tu enverras |
| | il/elle envoie | il/elle envoyait | il/elle a envoyé | il/elle enverra |
| | nous envoyons | nous envoyions | nous avons envoyé | nous enverrons |
| | vous envoyez | vous envoyiez | vous avez envoyé | vous enverrez |
| | ils/elles envoient | ils/elles envoyaient | ils/elles ont envoyé | ils/elles enverront |

| **Infinitif**<br>**Infinitive** | **Présent**<br>**Present** | **Imparfait**<br>**Imperfect** | **Passé Composé**<br>**Perfect** | **Futur**<br>**Future** |
|---|---|---|---|---|
| éteindre | j'éteins | j'éteignais | j'ai éteint | j'éteindrai |
| *to extinguish,* | tu éteins | tu éteignais | tu as éteint | tu éteindras |
| *to switch off* | il/elle éteint | il/elle éteignait | il/elle a éteint | il/elle éteindra |
| | nous éteignons | nous éteignions | nous avons éteint | nous éteindrons |
| | vous éteignez | vous éteigniez | vous avez éteint | vous éteindrez |
| | ils/elles éteignent | ils/elles éteignaient | ils/elles ont éteint | ils/elles éteindront |
| être | je suis | j'étais | j'ai été | je serai |
| *to be* | tu es | tu étais | tu as été | tu seras |
| | il/elle est | il/elle était | il/elle a été | il/elle sera |
| | nous sommes | nous étions | nous avons été | nous serons |
| | vous êtes | vous étiez | vous avez été | vous serez |
| | ils/elles sont | ils/elles étaient | ils/elles ont été | ils/elles seront |
| faire | je fais | je faisais | j'ai fait | je ferai |
| *to do,* | tu fais | tu faisais | tu as fait | tu feras |
| *to make* | il/elle fait | il/elle faisait | il/elle a fait | il/elle fera |
| | nous faisons | nous faisions | nous avons fait | nous ferons |
| | vous faites | vous faisiez | vous avez fait | vous ferez |
| | ils/elles font | ils/elles faisaient | ils/elles ont fait | ils/elles feront |
| falloir | il faut | il fallait | il a fallu | il faudra |
| *to have to* | | | | |
| lire | je lis | je lisais | j'ai lu | je lirai |
| *to read* | tu lis | tu lisais | tu as lu | tu liras |
| | il/elle lit | il/elle lisait | il/elle a lu | il/elle lira |
| | nous lisons | nous lisions | nous avons lu | nous lirons |
| | vous lisez | vous lisiez | vous avez lu | vous lirez |
| | ils/elles lisent | ils/elles lisaient | ils/elles ont lu | ils/elles liront |
| mettre | je mets | je mettais | j'ai mis | je mettrai |
| *to put* | tu mets | tu mettais | tu as mis | tu mettras |
| | il/elle met | il/elle mettait | il/elle a mis | il/elle mettra |
| | nous mettons | nous mettions | nous avons mis | nous mettrons |
| | vous mettez | vous mettiez | vous avez mis | vous mettrez |
| | ils/elles mettent | ils/elles mettaient | ils/elles ont mis | ils/elles mettront |
| mourir | je meurs | je mourais | je suis mort(e) | je mourrai |
| *to die* | tu meurs | tu mourais | tu es mort(e) | tu mourras |
| | il/elle meurt | il/elle mourait | il est mort | il/elle mourra |
| | nous mourons | nous mourions | elle est morte | nous mourrons |
| | vous mourez | vous mouriez | nous sommes mort(e)s | vous mourrez |
| | ils/elles meurent | ils/elles mouraient | vous êtes mort(e)(s) | ils/elles mourront |
| | | | ils sont morts | |
| | | | elles sont mortes | |

| **Infinitif**<br>**Infinitive** | **Présent**<br>**Present** | **Imparfait**<br>**Imperfect** | **Passé Composé**<br>**Perfect** | **Futur**<br>**Future** |
|---|---|---|---|---|
| naître | je nais | je naissais | je suis né(e) | je naîtrai |
| *to be born* | tu nais | tu naissais | tu es né(e) | tu naîtras |
| | il/elle naît | il/elle naissait | il est né | il/elle naîtra |
| | nous naissons | nous naissions | elle est née | nous naîtrons |
| | vous naissez | vous naissiez | nous sommes né(e)s | vous naîtrez |
| | ils/elles naissent | ils/elles naissaient | vous êtes né(e)(s) | ils/elles naîtront |
| | | | ils sont nés | |
| | | | elles sont nées | |
| obtenir | j'obtiens | j'obtenais | j'ai obtenu | j'obtiendrai |
| *to obtain* | tu obtiens | tu obtenais | tu as obtenu | tu obtiendras |
| | il/elle obtient | il/elle obtenait | il/elle a obtenu | il/elle obtiendra |
| | nous obtenons | nous obtenions | nous avons obtenu | nous obtiendrons |
| | vous obtenez | vous obteniez | vous avez obtenu | vous obtiendrez |
| | ils/elles obtiennent | ils/elles obtenaient | ils/elles ont obtenu | ils/elles obtiendront |
| offrir | j'offre | j'offrais | j'ai offert | j'offrirai |
| *to offer* | tu offres | tu offrais | tu as offert | tu offriras |
| | il/elle offre | il/elle offrait | il/elle a offert | il/elle offrira |
| | nous offrons | nous offrions | nous avons offert | nous offrirons |
| | vous offrez | vous offriez | vous avez offert | vous offrirez |
| | ils/elles offrent | ils/elles offraient | ils/elles ont offert | ils/elles offriront |
| ouvrir | j'ouvre | j'ouvrais | j'ai ouvert | j'ouvrirai |
| *to open* | tu ouvres | tu ouvrais | tu as ouvert | tu ouvriras |
| | il/elle ouvre | il/elle ouvrait | il/elle a ouvert | il/elle ouvrira |
| | nous ouvrons | nous ouvrions | nous avons ouvert | nous ouvrirons |
| | vous ouvrez | vous ouvriez | vous avez ouvert | vous ouvrirez |
| | ils/elles ouvrent | ils/elles ouvraient | ils/elles ont ouvert | ils/elles ouvriront |
| paraître | je parais | je paraissais | j'ai paru | je paraîtrai |
| *to appear,* | tu parais | tu paraissais | tu as paru | tu paraîtras |
| *to seem* | il/elle paraît | il/elle paraissait | il/elle a paru | il/elle paraîtra |
| | nous paraissons | nous paraissions | nous avons paru | nous paraîtrons |
| | vous paraissez | vous paraissiez | vous avez paru | vous paraîtrez |
| | ils/elles paraissent | ils/elles paraissaient | ils/elles ont paru | ils/elles paraîtront |
| partir | je pars | je partais | je suis parti(e) | je partirai |
| *to leave,* | tu pars | tu partais | tu es parti(e) | tu partiras |
| *to go away* | il/elle part | il/elle partait | il est parti | il/elle partira |
| | nous partons | nous partions | elle est partie | nous partirons |
| | vous partez | vous partiez | nous sommes parti(e)s | vous partirez |
| | ils/elles partent | ils/elles partaient | vous êtes parti(e)(s) | ils/elles partiront |
| | | | ils sont partis | |
| | | | elles sont parties | |

| **Infinitif**<br>**Infinitive** | **Présent**<br>**Present** | **Imparfait**<br>**Imperfect** | **Passé Composé**<br>**Perfect** | **Futur**<br>**Future** |
|---|---|---|---|---|
| pouvoir | je peux (puis-je?) | je pouvais | j'ai pu | je pourrai |
| *to be able to* | tu peux | tu pouvais | tu as pu | tu pourras |
| | il/elle peut | il/elle pouvait | il/elle a pu | il/elle pourra |
| | nous pouvons | nous pouvions | nous avons pu | nous pourrons |
| | vous pouvez | vous pouviez | vous avez pu | vous pourrez |
| | ils/elles peuvent | ils/elles pouvaient | ils/elles ont pu | ils/elles pourront |
| prendre | je prends | je prenais | j'ai pris | je prendrai |
| *to take* | tu prends | tu prenais | tu as pris | tu prendras |
| | il/elle prend | il/elle prenait | il/elle a pris | il/elle prendra |
| | nous prenons | nous prenions | nous avons pris | nous prendrons |
| | vous prenez | vous preniez | vous avez pris | vous prendrez |
| | ils/elles prennent | ils/elles prenaient | ils/elles ont pris | ils/elles prendront |
| prévenir | je préviens | je prévenais | j'ai prévenu | je préviendrai |
| *to warn, to inform* | tu préviens | tu prévenais | tu as prévenu | tu préviendras |
| | il/elle prévient | il/elle prévenait | il/elle a prévenu | il/elle préviendra |
| | nous prévenons | nous prévenions | nous avons prévenu | nous préviendrons |
| | vous prévenez | vous préveniez | vous avez prévenu | vous préviendrez |
| | ils/elles préviennent | ils/elles prévenaient | ils/elles ont prévenu | ils/elles préviendront |
| recevoir | je reçois | je recevais | j'ai reçu | je recevrai |
| *to receive* | tu reçois | tu recevais | tu as reçu | tu recevras |
| | il/elle reçoit | il/elle recevait | il/elle a reçu | il/elle recevra |
| | nous recevons | nous recevions | nous avons reçu | nous recevrons |
| | vous recevez | vous receviez | vous avez reçu | vous recevrez |
| | ils/elles reçoivent | ils/elles recevaient | ils/elles ont reçu | ils/elles recevront |
| reconnaître | je reconnais | je reconnaissais | j'ai reconnu | je reconnaîtrai |
| *to recognize* | tu reconnais | tu reconnaissais | tu as reconnu | tu reconnaîtras |
| | il/elle reconnaît | il/elle reconnaissait | il/elle a reconnu | il/elle reconnaîtra |
| | nous reconnaissons | nous reconnaissions | nous avons reconnu | nous reconnaîtrons |
| | vous reconnaissez | vous reconnaissiez | vous avez reconnu | vous reconnaîtrez |
| | ils/elles reconnaissent | ils/elles reconnaissaient | ils/elles ont reconnu | ils/elles reconnaîtront |
| repartir | je repars | je repartais | je suis reparti(e) | je repartirai |
| *to leave again* | tu repars | tu repartais | tu es reparti(e) | tu repartiras |
| | il/elle repart | il/elle repartait | il est reparti | il/elle repartira |
| | nous repartons | nous repartions | elle est repartie | nous repartirons |
| | vous repartez | vous repartiez | nous sommes reparti(e)s | vous repartirez |
| | ils/elles repartent | ils/elles repartaient | vous êtes reparti(e)(s) | ils/elles repartiront |
| | | | ils sont repartis | |
| | | | elles sont reparties | |

| Infinitif<br>Infinitive | Présent<br>Present | Imparfait<br>Imperfect | Passé Composé<br>Perfect | Futur<br>Future |
|---|---|---|---|---|
| reprendre | je reprends | je reprenais | j'ai repris | je reprendrai |
| *to take/get back,* | tu reprends | tu reprenais | tu as repris | tu reprendras |
| *to resume* | il/elle reprend | il/elle reprenait | il/elle a repris | il/elle reprendra |
| | nous reprenons | nous reprenions | nous avons repris | nous reprendrons |
| | vous reprenez | vous repreniez | vous avez repris | vous reprendrez |
| | ils/elles reprennent | ils/elles reprenaient | ils/elles ont repris | ils/elles reprendront |
| retenir | je retiens | je retenais | j'ai retenu | je retiendrai |
| *to hold back,* | tu retiens | tu retenais | tu as retenu | tu retiendras |
| *to keep* | il/elle retient | il/elle retenait | il/elle a retenu | il/elle retiendra |
| | nous retenons | nous retenions | nous avons retenu | noue retiendrons |
| | vous retenez | vous reteniez | vous avez retenu | vous retiendrez |
| | ils/elles retiennent | ils/elles retenaient | ils/elles ont retenu | ils/elles retiendront |
| revenir | je reviens | je revenais | je suis revenu(e) | je reviendrai |
| *to come back,* | tu reviens | tu revenais | tu es revenu(e) | tu reviendras |
| *to return* | il/elle revient | il/elle revenait | il est revenu | il/elle reviendra |
| | nous revenons | nous revenions | elle est revenue | nous reviendrons |
| | vous revenez | voue reveniez | nous sommes revenu(e)s | vous reviendrez |
| | ils/elles reviennent | ils/elles revenaient | vous êtes revenu(e)(s) | ils/elles reviendront |
| | | | ils sont revenus | |
| | | | elles sont revenues | |
| rire | je ris | je riais | j'ai ri | je rirai |
| *to laugh* | tu ris | tu riais | tu as ri | tu riras |
| | il/elle rit | il/elle riait | il/elle a ri | il/elle rira |
| | nous rions | nous riions | nous avons ri | nous rirons |
| | vous riez | vous riiez | vous avez ri | vous rirez |
| | ils/elles rient | ils/elles riaient | ils/elles ont ri | ils/elles riront |
| savoir | je sais | je savais | j'ai su | je saurai |
| *to know* | tu sais | tu savais | tu as su | tu sauras |
| *(a fact, or how to do* | il/elle sait | il/elle savait | il/elle a su | il/elle saura |
| *something)* | nous savons | nous savions | nous avons su | nous saurons |
| | vous savez | vous saviez | vous avez su | vous saurez |
| | ils/elles savent | ils/elles savaient | ils/elles ont su | ils/elles sauront |
| sentir | je sens | je sentais | j'ai senti | je sentirai |
| *to smell,* | tu sens | tu sentais | tu as senti | tu sentiras |
| *to feel,* | il/elle sent | il/elle sentait | il/elle a senti | il/elle sentira |
| *to sense* | nous sentons | nous sentions | nous avons senti | nous sentirons |
| | vous sentez | vous sentiez | vous avez senti | vous sentirez |
| | ils/elles sentent | ils/elles sentaient | ils/elles ont senti | ils/elles sentiront |

| **Infinitif**<br>**Infinitive** | **Présent**<br>**Present** | **Imparfait**<br>**Imperfect** | **Passé Composé**<br>**Perfect** | **Futur**<br>**Future** |
|---|---|---|---|---|
| se sentir<br>*to feel (ill, well, etc.)* | je me sens<br>tu te sens<br>il/elle se sent<br>nous nous sentons<br>vous vous sentez<br>ils/elles se sentent | je me sentais<br>tu te sentais<br>il/elle se sentait<br>nous nous sentions<br>vous vous sentiez<br>ils/elles se sentaient | je me suis senti(e)<br>tu t'es senti(e)<br>il s'est senti<br>elle s'est sentie<br>nous nous sommes senti(e)s<br>vous vous êtes senti(e)(s)<br>ils se sont sentis<br>elles se sont senties | je me sentirai<br>tu te sentiras<br>il/elle se sentira<br>nous nous sentirons<br>vous vous sentirez<br>ils/elles se sentiront |
| servir<br>*to serve* | je sers<br>tu sers<br>il/elle sert<br>nous servons<br>vous servez<br>ils/elles servent | je servais<br>tu servais<br>il/elle servait<br>nous servions<br>vous serviez<br>ils/elles servaient | j'ai servi<br>tu as servi<br>il/elle a servi<br>nous avons servi<br>vous avez servi<br>ils/elles ont servi | je servirai<br>tu serviras<br>il/elle servira<br>nous servirons<br>vous servirez<br>ils/elles serviront |
| se servir (de)<br>*to use* | je me sers<br>tu te sers<br>il/elle se sert<br>nous nous servons<br>vous vous servez<br>ils/elles se servent | je me servais<br>tu te servais<br>il/elle se servait<br>nous nous servions<br>vous vous serviez<br>ils/elles se servaient | je me suis servi(e)<br>tu t'es servi(e)<br>il s'est servi<br>elle s'est servie<br>nous nous sommes servi(e)s<br>vous vous êtes servi(e)(s)<br>ils se sont servis<br>elles se sont servies | je me servirai<br>tu te serviras<br>il/elle se servira<br>nous nous servirons<br>vous vous servirez<br>ils/elles se serviront |
| sortir<br>*to go out* | je sors<br>tu sors<br>il/elle sort<br>nous sortons<br>vous sortez<br>ils/elles sortent | je sortais<br>tu sortais<br>il/elle sortait<br>nous sortions<br>vous sortiez<br>ils/elles sortaient | je suis sorti(e)<br>tu es sorti(e)<br>il est sorti<br>elle est sortie<br>nous sommes sorti(e)s<br>vous êtes sorti(e)(s)<br>ils sont sortis<br>elles sont sorties | je sortirai<br>tu sortiras<br>il/elle sortira<br>nous sortirons<br>vous sortirez<br>ils/elles sortiront |
| souffrir<br>*to suffer* | je souffre<br>tu souffres<br>il/elle souffre<br>nous souffrons<br>vous souffrez<br>ils /elles souffrent | je souffrais<br>tu souffrais<br>il/elle souffrait<br>nous souffrions<br>vous souffriez<br>ils /elles souffraient | j'ai souffert<br>tu as souffert<br>il/elle a souffert<br>nous avons souffert<br>vous avez souffert<br>ils/elles ont souffert | je souffrirai<br>tu souffriras<br>il/elle souffrira<br>nous souffrirons<br>vous souffrirez<br>ils/elles souffriront |

| Infinitif<br>Infinitive | Présent<br>Present | Imparfait<br>Imperfect | Passé Composé<br>Perfect | Futur<br>Future |
|---|---|---|---|---|
| sourire | je souris | je souriais | j'ai souri | je sourirai |
| *to smile* | tu souris | tu souriais | tu as souri | tu souriras |
| | il/elle sourit | il/elle souriait | il/elle a souri | il/elle sourira |
| | nous sourions | nous souriions | nous avons souri | nous sourirons |
| | vous souriez | vous souriiez | vous avez souri | vous sourirez |
| | ils/elles sourient | ils/elles souriaient | ils/elles ont souri | ils/elles souriront |
| suivre | je suis | je suivais | j'ai suivi | je suivrai |
| *to follow* | tu suis | tu suivais | tu as suivi | tu suivras |
| | il/elle suit | il/elle suivait | il/elle a suivi | il/elle suivra |
| | nous suivons | nous suivions | nous avons suivi | nous suivrons |
| | vous suivez | vous suiviez | vous avez suivi | vous suivrez |
| | ils/elles suivent | ils/elles suivaient | ils/elles ont suivi | ils/elles suivront |
| surprendre | je surprends | je surprenais | j'ai surpris | je surprendrai |
| *to surprise* | tu surprends | tu surprenais | tu as surpris | tu surprendras |
| | il/elle surprend | il/elle surprenait | il/elle a surpris | il/elle surprendra |
| | nous surprenons | nous surprenions | nous avons surpris | nous surprendrons |
| | vous surprenez | vous surpreniez | vous avez surpris | vous surprendrez |
| | ils/elles surprennent | ils/elles surprenaient | ils/elles ont surpris | ils/elles surprendront |
| tenir | je tiens | je tenais | j'ai tenu | je tiendrai |
| *to hold* | tu tiens | tu tenais | tu as tenu | tu tiendras |
| | il/elle tient | il/elle tenait | il/elle a tenu | il/elle tiendra |
| | nous tenons | nous tenions | nous avons tenu | nous tiendrons |
| | vous tenez | vous teniez | vous avez tenu | vous tiendrez |
| | ils/elles tiennent | ils/elles tenaient | ils/elles ont tenu | ils/elles tiendront |
| se tenir | je me tiens | je me tenais | je me suis tenu(e) | je me tiendrai |
| *to stand* | tu te tiens | tu te tenais | tu t'es tenu(e) | tu te tiendras |
| | il/elle se tient | il/elle se tenait | il s'est tenu | il/elle se tiendra |
| | nous nous tenons | nous nous tenions | elle s'est tenue | nous nous tiendrons |
| | vous vous tenez | vous vous teniez | nous nous sommes tenu(e)s | vous vous tiendrez |
| | ils/elles se tiennent | ils/elles se tenaient | vous vous êtes tenu(e)(s) | ils/elles se tiendront |
| | | | ils se sont tenus | |
| | | | elles se sont tenues | |
| venir | je viens | je venais | je suis venu(e) | je viendrai |
| *to come* | tu viens | tu venais | tu es venu(e) | tu viendras |
| | il/elle vient | il/elle venait | il est venu | il/elle viendra |
| | nous venons | nous venions | elle est venue | nous viendrons |
| | vous venez | vous veniez | nous sommes venu(e)s | vous viendrez |
| | ils/elles viennent | ils/elles venaient | vous êtes venu(e)(s) | ils/elles viendront |
| | | | ils sont venus | |
| | | | elles sont venues | |

| Infinitif<br>Infinitive | Présent<br>Present | Imparfait<br>Imperfect | Passé Composé<br>Perfect | Futur<br>Future |
|---|---|---|---|---|
| vivre | je vis | je vivais | j'ai vécu | je vivrai |
| *to live* | tu vis | tu vivais | tu as vécu | tu vivras |
| *to be alive* | il/elle vit | il/elle vivait | il/elle a vécu | il/elle vivra |
| | nous vivons | nous vivions | nous avons vécu | nous vivrons |
| | vous vivez | vous viviez | vous avez vécu | vous vivrez |
| | ils/elles vivent | ils/elles vivaient | ils/elles ont vécu | ils/elles vivront |
| voir | je vois | je voyais | j'ai vu | je verrai |
| *to see* | tu vois | tu voyais | tu as vu | tu verras |
| | il/elle voit | il/elle voyait | il/elle a vu | il/elle verra |
| | nous voyons | nous voyions | nous avons vu | nous verrons |
| | vous voyez | vous voyiez | vous avez vu | vous verrez |
| | ils/elles voient | ils/elles voyaient | ils/elles ont | ils/elles verront |
| vouloir | je veux | je voulais | j'ai voulu | je voudrai |
| *to wish,* | tu veux | tu voulais | tu as voulu | tu voudras |
| *to want* | il/elle veut | il/elle voulait | il/elle a voulu | il/elle voudra |
| | nous voulons | nous voulions | nous avons voulu | nous voudrons |
| | vous voulez | vous vouliez | vous avez voulu | vous voudrez |
| | ils/elles veulent | ils/elles voulaient | ils/elles ont voulu | ils/elles voudront |

# Mini-dictionary

In this section you can find both an French–English dictionary and a English–French dictionary.

Before each French word in the French–English dictionary you are given, where appropriate, the **gender** followed by the English translation.

| l' | argent (m) | money |
|---|---|---|

After each English word in the English–French dictionary you are given, where appropriate, the **gender** of the French word and its **plural ending** in brackets. For example:

| money | l' | argent (m) |
|---|---|---|


- French–English 142
- English–French 173

# French–English

# *Mini-Dictionary*

## Key

| | |
|---|---|
| (e) | feminine form |
| (s) | plural form |
| (m) | masculine |
| (f) | feminine |
| (m pl) | masculine plural |
| (f pl) | feminine plural |
| (sing) | singular |
| * | verb takes *être* in the perfect tense |

| | | | |
|---|---|---|---|
| | à | | to, at, in |
| | à côté de | | next to, beside |
| un | abri | | shed |
| un | abricot | | apricot |
| d' | accord | | agreed |
| | acheter | to | buy |
| un | acteur | | actor |
| une | actrice | | actress |
| un/une | adolescent(e) | | adolescent |
| une | adresse | | address |
| un | adulte | | adult |
| un | aéroport | | airport |
| l' | âge (m) | | age |
| une | agence de voyages | | travel agency |
| un | agent de police | | police officer |
| | agité(e) | | rough |
| l' | agneau (m) | | lamb |
| | aider | to | help |
| l' | ail (m) | | garlic |
| | aimable | | likeable |
| | aimer | | to like |
| | aimer regarder | to | like watching |
| une | allée | | avenue |
| l' | allemand (m) | | German |
| | aller* en ville | to | go into town |
| un | aller simple | | single ticket |
| | aller* | to | go |
| un | aller-retour | | return ticket |
| | allumer (la radio) | to | turn on (the radio) |
| les | allumettes (f pl) | | matches |
| un | ami | | friend (male) |
| une | amie | | friend (female) |
| | amusant | | fun/funny |
| s' | amuser | to | enjoy oneself |

| | | | |
|---|---|---|---|
| un | ananas | | pineapple |
| l' | anglais (m) | | English |
| un | anniversaire | | birthday |
| une | antenne | | aerial |
| une | antenne parabolique | | satellite dish |
| un | appareil-photo | | camera |
| un | appartement | | flat |
| s' | appeler | to | be called |
| | apprendre | to | learn |
| | apprendre par cœur | to | learn by heart |
| | après | | after |
| | après les feux | | after the lights |
| l' | après-midi (m) | | afternoon |
| un | arbre | | tree |
| un | arbre de Noël | | Christmas tree |
| un | arbuste | | bush |
| l' | argent (m) | | money |
| une | armoire | | wardrobe |
| un | arrêt de bus | | bus stop |
| une | arrivée | | arrival |
| | arriver* | to | arrive |
| | arroser | to | water |
| les | arts ménagers (m) | | home economics |
| un | ascenseur | | lift |
| un | aspirateur | | vacuum cleaner |
| une | assemblée | | assembly |
| une | assiette | | plate |
| l' | athlétisme (m) | | athletics |
| | attendre | to | wait (for) |
| | atterrir | to | land |
| | au coin de la rue | | on the corner of the street |
| | au nord de | | north of |
| | au sud de | | south of |
| une | auberge de jeunesse | | youth hostel |
| une | auto | | car |
| | autre | | other |
| | avant | | before |
| | avec | | with |
| | avec du retard | | delayed |
| par | avion | | by air mail/by plane |
| un | avion | | plane |
| la | baguette | | stick of French bread |
| se | baigner | to | bathe in the sea |
| la | baignoire | | bath tub |

| | | | |
|---|---|---|---|
| le | baladeur | | Walkman® |
| le | balai | | broom |
| | Balance | | Libra |
| | balayer | to | sweep |
| le | balcon | | balcony |
| la | banane | | banana |
| le | banc | | bench |
| la | bande dessinée | | comic strip |
| la | banlieue | | suburbs |
| la | banque | | bank |
| le | bar | | bar |
| la | base de données | | database |
| les | baskets (m pl) | | trainers |
| la | batterie | | drum kit |
| le | beau-père | | stepfather, father-in-law |
| | beaucoup | a | lot |
| le | bébé | | baby |
| | Bélier | | Aries |
| la | belle-mère | | stepmother, mother-in-law |
| en | béton | of | concrete |
| la | bibliothèque | | library/bookcase |
| la | bicyclette | | bicycle |
| le | bidet | | bidet |
| la | bière/de la bière | | beer/some beer |
| le | bifteck | | steak |
| le | billet | | banknote/ticket |
| la | biologie | | biology |
| le | biscuit | | biscuit |
| | blanc | | white |
| | bleu | | blue |
| | bleu marine | | navy blue |
| le | bloc sanitaire | | toilet block |
| le | blouson | | blouson jacket |
| le | bœuf | | beef |
| le | bois | | wood |
| la | boîte aux lettres | | letter box |
| la | boîte de nuit | | night club |
| | bon marché | | cheap, good value for money |
| | bonjour | | good morning, good day, good afternoon |
| | bonne nuit | | good night |
| | bonsoir | | good evening |
| la | botte | | boot |
| la | bouche | | mouth |
| la | boucherie | | butcher's shop |

| | | | |
|---|---|---|---|
| le | bouchon | | plug |
| la | boulangerie | | baker's/bread shop |
| la | boum | | party |
| le | bouquet de fleurs | | bunch of flowers |
| la | bouteille de gaz | | gas bottle |
| la | boutique | | shop |
| le | bras | | arm |
| | briller | to | shine |
| en | brique | | of brick |
| la | brochure | | brochure |
| se | bronzer | to | sunbathe |
| la | brosse à dents | | toothbrush |
| | brosser | to | brush |
| se | brosser les dents | to | brush one's teeth |
| le | brouillard | | fog |
| | brun | | brown |
| | bruyant | | noisy, loud |
| le | bug | | bug |
| le | bulletin scolaire | | school report |
| le | bungalow | | bungalow |
| le | bureau | | desk/study |
| le | bus | | bus |
| la | cabine téléphonique | | phone box |
| le | cabinet | | surgery |
| le | câble à péage | | subscription cable |
| le | cadeau | | present |
| le | café | | café |
| le | café/du café | | coffee (black)/ some coffee |
| le | café crème | | white coffee |
| le | café express | | espresso coffee |
| le | cahier | | exercise book |
| la | caisse | | cash register/till |
| | calculer | to | calculate |
| le | caleçon (sing) | | leggings |
| | calme | | calm, quiet |
| au | calme | | calmly |
| le | caméscope | | camrecorder |
| le | camion | | lorry |
| la | camionnette | | van |
| la | campagne | | country (side) |
| | camper | to | camp |
| le | camping | | campsite/camping |
| le | camping-car | | Dormobile® |
| le | canapé | | sofa |

| | | | |
|---|---|---|---|
| le | canard | | duck |
| le | canari | | canary |
| | Cancer | | Cancer |
| le | canif | | penknife |
| | Capricorne | | Capricorn |
| le | car | | coach |
| le | car-ferry | | ferry |
| la | caravane | | caravan |
| le | carnet | | book of tickets |
| la | carotte | | carrot |
| le | carrefour | | crossroads |
| le | carrousel | | luggage carousel |
| la | carte | | card |
| la | carte d'adhérent | | membership card |
| la | carte d'identité | | identity card |
| la | carte postale | | postcard |
| la | carte routière | | road map |
| la | casquette | | cap |
| | casse-pieds | | boring |
| la | casserole | | saucepan |
| la | cassette | | cassette |
| la | cassette vidéo | | video cassette |
| le | cassis | | blackcurrant |
| le | catalogue | | disk manager |
| la | cathédrale | | cathedral |
| la | cave | | cellar |
| le | CD | | CD |
| le | CD ROM | | CD ROM |
| le | CDI | | resource centre |
| | CEDEX | | PO box |
| la | ceinture | | belt |
| le | centime | | centime |
| le | centre commercial | | shopping centre |
| au | centre de | in the | middle of |
| le | centre sportif | | sports centre |
| le | centre-ville | | town centre |
| la | cerise | | cherry |
| le | CES | | comprehensive school (11–15) |
| la | chaîne de télé | | TV channel |
| la | chaîne stéréo | | stereo (system) |
| la | chaise | | chair |
| la | chambre (à coucher) | | bedroom |
| la | chambre d'amis | | guest room |
| la | chambre pour deux personnes | | double room |

| | | | |
|---|---|---|---|
| la | chambre pour une personne | | single room |
| le | champ | | field |
| le | champignon | | mushroom |
| le | change | | currency exchange |
| | changer | to | change |
| se | changer | to | get changed |
| | changer de l'argent | to | change money |
| | changer de programme | to | switch over TV channel |
| la | chanson | | song |
| | chanter | to | sing |
| le | chanteur favori | | favourite singer (male) |
| la | chanteuse favorite | | favourite singer (female) |
| le | chapeau | | hat |
| la | charcuterie | | delicatessen/processed meats |
| | charger | to | load |
| le | chariot | | shopping trolley |
| le | chat | | cat |
| | chaud | | hot |
| le | chauffage central | | central heating |
| le | chauffeur | | driver |
| la | chaussette | | sock |
| la | chaussure | | shoe |
| la | cheminée | | chimney/open fireplace |
| la | chemise | | shirt |
| le | chemisier | | blouse |
| le | chèque | | cheque |
| le | chèque de voyage | | traveller's cheque |
| | cher | | expensive |
| | chercher | to | look for |
| le | cheval | | horse |
| la | cheville | | ankle |
| | chez | | at the house of |
| le | chien | | dog |
| la | chimie | | chemistry |
| les | chips (m pl) | | crisps |
| le | chocolat | | chocolate |
| le | chocolat chaud | | hot chocolate |
| le | chocolat froid | | cold chocolate |
| | choisir | to | choose/select |
| au | chômage | | unemployed |
| la | chorale | | choir |
| le | chou | | cabbage |
| le | chou-chou | | scrunchie |
| le | chou-fleur | | cauliflower |

| | | | |
|---|---|---|---|
| les | choux de Bruxelles (m pl) | | sprouts |
| le | cidre/du cidre | | cider/some cider |
| le | cinéma | | cinema |
| le | citron | | lemon |
| le | citron pressé | | freshly squeezed lemon juice |
| la | clarinette | | clarinet |
| le | clavier | | keyboard |
| la | clé | | key |
| le/la | client(e) | | customer |
| le | club | | club |
| le | club des jeunes | | youth club |
| le | cobaye/cochon d'Inde | | guinea pig |
| le | coca | | cola |
| le | code postal | | postcode |
| le | coiffeur | | hairdresser (male) |
| la | coiffeuse | | hairdresser (female) |
| le | coin (de la rue) | | corner |
| le | colis | | parcel |
| le | collant (sing) | | tights |
| la | collection | | collection |
| | collectionner | to | collect |
| le | collège | | comprehensive school (11–15) |
| la | colline | | hill |
| | combien (de)...? | | how many...? |
| la | comédie | | comedy |
| le | comédien | | comedian/actor |
| la | comédienne | | comedienne/actress |
| | commander | to | order (food, etc.) |
| | commencer | to | begin, start |
| | comment est...? | | what is...like? |
| | comment? | | how? |
| le/la | commerçant(e) | | trader/shopkeeper |
| le | compartiment | | compartment |
| | complet | | full |
| | composter un billet | to | date-stamp a ticket |
| le | composteur de billets | | machine to date-stamp tickets |
| le | comprimé | | tablet |
| | compris | | included |
| | compter | to | count |
| le | concert | | concert |
| le/la | concierge | | caretaker |
| le | concombre | | cucumber |
| | conduire | to | drive |
| | confortable | | comfortable |

| | | | |
|---|---|---|---|
| le | congé de mi-trimestre | | half-term holidays |
| le | congélateur | | freezer |
| la | consigne | | luggage locker |
| | construire | to | build |
| | copier | to | copy |
| la | correspondance | | connecting train |
| le | correspondant | | penfriend/exchange partner (male) |
| la | correspondante | | penfriend/exchange partner (female) |
| | corriger | to | correct |
| en | coton | | made of cotton |
| le | coton hydrophile | | cotton wool |
| se | coucher | to | go bed |
| | coudre | to | sew |
| la | couette | | duvet |
| le | couloir | | corridor |
| le | coup de soleil | | sunburn |
| la | cour | | playground |
| le | courrier | | mail |
| le | cours | | lesson |
| le | court de tennis | | tennis court |
| le | cousin | | cousin (male) |
| la | cousine | | cousin (female) |
| | coûter | to | cost |
| la | couverture | | blanket |
| la | craie | | chalk |
| le | crayon | | pencil |
| le | crayon de couleur | | coloured pencil |
| la | crème | | cream |
| la | crème solaire | | suntan lotion |
| la | crémerie | | cheese shop |
| la | crêpe | | pancake |
| le | cricket | | cricket |
| le | croque-monsieur | | toasted ham and cheese sandwich |
| les | crudités (m) | | fresh raw vegetables |
| en | cuir | | made of leather |
| la | cuisine | | kitchen |
| la | cuisinière | | cooker |
| le | cyclisme | | cycling |
| la | dame | | lady |
| | dans | | in |
| | danser | to | dance |
| | de | | from, of |
| | débarrasser la table | to | clear the table |
| | décoller | to | take off (aircraft) |

| | | | |
|---|---|---|---|
| | défendu | | forbidden |
| le | déjeuner | | lunch |
| | délicat | | dainty, delicate |
| à | demain | | see you tomorrow |
| | demander | to | ask (for) |
| | demander des informations | to | ask for information |
| | déménager | to | move house |
| le | demi-frère | | half-brother |
| en | demi-pension | | half board (bed, breakfast and evening meal) |
| la | demi-sœur | | half-sister |
| la | dent | | tooth |
| le | dentifrice | | toothpaste |
| le | dentiste | | dentist |
| le | départ | | departure |
| | dépenser (pour) | to | spend (on) |
| le | dépliant | | brochure |
| le | dériveur | | dinghy |
| | derrière | | behind |
| | derrière l'église | | behind the church |
| | descendre* du bus | to | get off the bus |
| se | déshabiller | to | get undressed |
| le | dessert | | dessert |
| le | dessin | | art |
| le | dessin animé | | cartoon |
| | dessiner | to | draw |
| | deux points (m) | | colon |
| | devant | | in front of |
| les | devoirs (m pl) | | homework |
| la | diarrhée | | diarrhoea |
| | difficile | | difficult |
| la | dinde | | turkey |
| le | dîner | | evening meal |
| le | directeur | | headmaster |
| la | directrice | | headmistress |
| la | discothèque | | disco |
| se | disputer | to | argue |
| le | disque dur | | hard disk |
| la | disquette | | disk |
| le | distributeur de billets | | cashpoint |
| le | distributeur de tickets | | ticket machine |
| | divorcé(e) | | divorced |
| à | dix kilomètres | | 10 km away |
| le | documentaire | | documentary |
| le | doigt | | finger |

| | | | |
|---|---|---|---|
| | donner à manger | to | feed |
| | dormir | to | sleep |
| le | dortoir | | dormitory |
| le | dos | | back |
| la | douane | | customs control |
| la | douche | | shower |
| avec | douche | | with shower |
| la | douleur | | pain |
| le | drap | | sheet |
| à | droite | | right |
| à | droite de | on the | right of |
| | durer | to | last |
| l' | eau (f) | | water |
| l' | eau minérale (f)/de l'eau minérale (f) | | mineral water/some mineral water |
| un | échange | | exchange |
| une | écharpe | | scarf |
| une | école maternelle | | nursery school |
| une | école primaire | | primary school |
| | économe | | careful with money |
| | écouter | to | listen to |
| un | écran | | screen |
| | écrire | to | write |
| | éditer | to | edit |
| | effacer | to | delete |
| une | église | | church |
| un | électricien | | electrician |
| l' | électricité (f) | | electricity |
| un | élève | | pupil (male) |
| une | élève | | pupil (female) |
| une | émission de musique | | music show |
| un | emplacement | | pitch |
| un | emploi du temps | | timetable (school) |
| | employé | | employed |
| un | employé de bureau | | office worker (male) |
| une | employée de bureau | | office worker (female) |
| | en | | by, in, with |
| | en face de | | opposite |
| | en face de la mairie | | opposite the town hall |
| | enchanté(e) | | pleased to meet you |
| un | enfant | | child |
| | ennuyeux | | boring |
| | enregistrer | to | record on cassette |
| un | enseignement | | teaching |
| | ensoleillé | | sunny |

| | | | |
|---|---|---|---|
| s' | entendre bien/mal avec | to | get on well/badly with |
| s' | entraîner | to | train |
| | entre | | between |
| une | entrée | | entrance |
| | envoyer | to | send |
| une | épicerie | | grocer's |
| les | épinards (m pl) | | spinach |
| une | éponge | | sponge |
| une | équipe | | team |
| l' | équitation (f) | | riding |
| une | erreur | | mistake |
| un | escalator | | escalator |
| un | escalier | | staircase |
| une | escalope de dinde | | turkey escalope |
| l' | espagnol (m) | | Spanish |
| | essayer | to | try |
| | essuyer la vaisselle | to | dry up |
| à l' | est | in the | east |
| à l' | est de | | east of |
| un | estomac | | stomach |
| un | étage | | floor, storey |
| une | étagère | | shelf |
| un | étang | | pool |
| | éteindre (la radio) | to | turn off (the radio) |
| | être collé(e) | to | have a detention |
| | être présent(e) | to | be present |
| | être reçu(e) | to | pass (an exam) |
| un | évier | | sink |
| | excellent | | excellent |
| à l' | exception de | | except |
| une | excursion | | excursion, outing |
| | excusez-moi | | excuse me, sorry |
| un | exemple | | example |
| | expliquer | to | explain |
| s' | expliquer avec | to | have an argument with |
| une | exposition | | exhibition |
| | extra | | great |
| | facile | | easy |
| le | facteur | | postman |
| la | factrice | | postwoman |
| | faire | to | make, to do |
| | faire chaud | to | be hot (weather) |
| | faire de l'équitation | to | ride |
| | faire de la musique | to | make music |

| | | | |
|---|---|---|---|
| | faire de la planche à voile | to | windsurf |
| | faire de la voile | to | sail |
| | faire des commissions | to | shop |
| | faire des courses | to | go shopping |
| | faire des devoirs | to | do homework |
| | faire des économies | to | save (money) |
| | faire des photos | to | take photos |
| | faire du bricolage | to | do DIY |
| | faire du brouillard | to | be foggy |
| | faire du cyclisme | to | cycle |
| | faire du lèche-vitrines | to | go window shopping |
| | faire du patin à roulettes | to | roller-skate |
| | faire du ski | to | ski |
| | faire du ski nautique | to | waterski |
| | faire du skim | to | skimboard |
| | faire du sport | to | do sport |
| | faire du vent | to | be windy |
| | faire froid | to | be cold (weather) |
| | faire la cuisine | to | cook |
| | faire la vaisselle | to | wash up |
| | faire une expérience | to | do an experiment |
| | faire une randonnée | to | hike |
| la | famille | | family |
| la | faute | | mistake |
| le | fauteuil | | armchair |
| | faxer | to | fax |
| la | femme | | wife, woman |
| la | femme de ménage | | cleaner |
| la | fenêtre | | window |
| la | ferme | | farm |
| | fermé | | closed |
| | fermer | to | close, shut |
| la | fête | | name day/party |
| | fêter | to | celebrate |
| le | feu de camp | | camp fire |
| le | feuilleton | | serial/soap opera |
| le | feutre | | felt-tip |
| les | feux (m pl) | | traffic lights |
| | fiancé(e) | | engaged |
| le/la | fiancé(e) | | fiancé(e) |
| la | fièvre | | high temperature |
| la | fille | | girl, daughter |
| pour | filles | | for girls |
| le | film | | film |

| | | | |
|---|---|---|---|
| le | film à suspense | | thriller |
| le | film d'amour | | romantic film |
| le | film d'aventures | | adventure film |
| le | film d'épouvante | | horror film |
| le | film d'espionnage | | spy film |
| le | film de science-fiction | | science-fiction film |
| le | film policier | | detective film |
| le | fils | | son |
| | finir | to | end, finish |
| la | fleur | | flower |
| la | flûte | | flute |
| la | flûte à bec | | recorder |
| le/la | fonctionnaire | | public service worker |
| le | foot/football | | football |
| la | forêt | | forest |
| | formater | to | format |
| le | four | | oven |
| le | four à gaz | | gas cooker |
| le | four à micro-ondes | | microwave oven |
| le | foyer de la jeunesse | | youth centre |
| la | fraise | | strawberry |
| la | framboise | | raspberry |
| le | franc | | franc |
| le | français | | French |
| le | frère | | brother |
| le | frigo | | fridge |
| les | frites (f pl) | | chips |
| | froid | | cold |
| le | fromage | | cheese |
| le | fruit | | fruit |
| le | fumeur | | smoker |
| | gagner | to | win |
| la | galerie | | gallery |
| le | gant | | glove |
| le | gant de toilette | | flannel |
| le | garçon | | boy |
| pour | garçons | | for boys |
| la | gare | | station |
| la | gare routière | | bus station |
| la | gare SNCF | | railway station |
| le | gâteau | | cake |
| à | gauche | | left |
| à | gauche de | on the | left of |
| le | gaz | | gas |

| | | | |
|---|---|---|---|
| le | gazon | | lawn |
| | geler | to | freeze |
| | Gémeaux | | Gemini |
| | généreux | | generous |
| le | genou | | knee |
| | gentil | | affectionate |
| la | géographie | | geography |
| le/la | gérant(e) | | manager |
| la | gerbille | | gerbil |
| le | gîte | | holiday cottage |
| la | glace | | ice-cream |
| la | gomme | | rubber |
| la | gorge | | throat |
| | grand | | big, tall |
| le | grand magasin | | department store |
| la | grand-mère | | grandmother |
| les | grand-parents (pl) | | grandparents |
| le | grand-père | | grandfather |
| la | grande surface | | hypermarket |
| les | grandes vacances (f pl) | | summer holidays |
| le | grenier | | loft |
| la | grippe | | flu |
| | gris | | grey |
| | gris clair | | light grey |
| | gris foncé | | dark grey |
| le | groupe | | group |
| le | groupe favori | | favourite group |
| le | guichet | | counter |
| les | guillemets | | speech marks |
| la | guitare | | guitar |
| le | gymnase | | gymnasium |
| la | gymnastique | | gymnastics |
| s' | habiller | to | get dressed |
| | habiter | to | live |
| un | hamster | | hamster |
| le | haricot | | bean |
| le | haricot vert | | green bean |
| l' | hébergement (m) | | accommodation |
| à l' | heure | | on time |
| les | heures d'ouverture (f pl) | | opening times |
| l' | histoire (f) | | history |
| l' | histoire/géo | | humanities |
| | historique | | historic |
| une | HLM | | council flat |

| | | | |
|---|---|---|---|
| un | homme | | man |
| un | hôpital | | hospital |
| un | horaire | | timetable |
| les | hors d' oeuvre (m) | | starters |
| un | hôtel | | hotel |
| un | hôtel de ville | | town hall |
| une | hôtesse de l'air | | stewardess |
| la | housse | | duvet cover |
| un | hovercraft | | hovercraft |
| une | île | | island |
| un | illustré | | magazine |
| une | image | | picture |
| un | immeuble | | block of flats |
| une | impasse | | cul-de-sac |
| un | imperméable | | waterproof coat |
| | important | | important |
| une | imprimante | | printer |
| un | infirmier | | nurse (male) |
| une | infirmière | | nurse (female) |
| les | informations (les infos) (f pl) | | news |
| l' | informatique (f) | | IT |
| un | ingénieur | | engineer |
| une | insolation | | sunstroke |
| un | instituteur | | primary school teacher (male) |
| une | institutrice | | primary school teacher (female) |
| l' | instruction civique (f) | | citizenship/PSE |
| un | instrument | | instrument |
| | intéressant | | interesting |
| | inutile | | useless |
| | isolé | | out of the way |
| l' | italien (m) | | Italian |
| la | jambe | | leg |
| le | jambon | | ham |
| le | jardin potager | | vegetable garden |
| | jaune | | yellow |
| le | jean (sing) | | pair of jeans |
| le | jeu | | game |
| le | jeu concours | | quiz |
| le | jeu de société | | board game |
| le | jeu électronique | | computer game |
| la | jeunesse | | youth, young people |
| le | jogging | | tracksuit |
| la | jonquille | | daffodil |
| | jouer aux cartes | to | play cards |

| | | | |
|---|---|---|---|
| | jouer aux échecs | to | play chess |
| le | jour | | day |
| le | jour de l'An | | New Year's Day |
| le | jour de Noël | | Christmas Day |
| le | jour de Pâques | | Easter Day |
| le | jour des Rois | | Twelfth Night |
| le | journal | | newspaper |
| le | journal télévisé | | news magazine programme |
| la | journée | | day |
| la | jupe | | skirt |
| le | jus de fruit/du jus de fruit | | fruit juice/some fruit juice |
| à | l'heure | | hourly |
| le | laboratoire | | laboratory |
| le | lac | | lake |
| en | laine | | made of wool |
| le | lait/du lait | | milk/some milk |
| la | laitue | | lettuce |
| la | lampe | | lamp, torch |
| le | lapin | | rabbit |
| le | latin | | Latin |
| le | lavabo | | basin, sink |
| le | lave-linge | | washing-machine |
| le | lave-vaisselle | | dish washer |
| se | laver | to | wash |
| la | leçon | | lesson |
| le | lecteur de disquettes | | disk drive |
| la | lecture | | reading |
| le | légume | | vegetable |
| | lentement | | slowly |
| la | lettre | | letter |
| se | lever | to | get up |
| | libre | | free |
| le | libre-service | | self-service |
| le | lieu de naissance | | place of birth |
| la | ligne | | line |
| la | limonade/de la limonade | | lemonade/some lemonade |
| | Lion | | Leo |
| | lire | to | read |
| la | liste des hôtels | | list of hotels |
| le | lit | | bed |
| le | livre | | book |
| le | livre illustré | | picture book |
| la | livre sterling | | pound sterling |
| | loin de | | far from |

| | | | |
|---|---|---|---|
| | louer | to | hire |
| de | luxe | | luxurious |
| le | lycée | | sixth form college/tertiary college (15–18) |
| le | maçon | | bricklayer, builder |
| | Madame | | Mrs, Ms |
| | Mademoiselle | | Miss |
| le | magasin | | shop |
| le | magasin d'alimentation générale | | general food shop |
| le | magasin de vêtements | | clothes shop |
| le | magazine | | magazine |
| le | magazine de télé | | TV magazine |
| le | magnétophone | | cassette recorder |
| le | magnétoscope | | VCR |
| le | maillot | | bathing suit |
| la | main | | hand |
| la | mairie | | town hall |
| la | maison | | house |
| la | maison jumelée | | semi-detached house |
| la | majuscule | | written with a capital letter |
| le | mal de mer | | seasickness |
| la | maladie | | illness |
| la | maman | | mummy |
| la | mami | | grandma |
| | manger | to | eat |
| le | manteau | | coat |
| le | manuel | | textbook |
| les | marchandises (f pl) | | goods |
| le | marché | | market |
| la | mare | | pond |
| la | marée basse | | low tide |
| la | marée haute | | high tide |
| le | mari | | husband |
| | marié(e) | | married |
| la | marmelade | | jam |
| | marron | | chestnut brown |
| le | match | | match |
| le | matelas pneumatique | | air bed |
| le | matériel du camping | | camping equipment |
| les | maths (f pl) | | maths |
| le | matin | | morning |
| le | mécanicien | | mechanic |
| la | mécanicienne | | mechanic (female) |
| | méchant | | vicious |
| le | médecin | | doctor |

| | | | |
|---|---|---|---|
| le | médicament | | medicine |
| le | mélo | | soap (opera) |
| le | melon | | melon |
| le | membre | | member |
| le | ménage | | housework |
| le | menu | | menu |
| la | mer | | sea |
| | merci | | thank you |
| la | mère | | mother |
| la | mère aubergiste | | warden (female) |
| la | météo | | weather forecast |
| le | métro | | underground |
| | mettre | to | play |
| | mettre la table | to | lay the table |
| la | minuscule | | written with a lower-case (small) letter |
| le | miroir | | mirror |
| | mixte | | mixed |
| | moche | | horrible, ugly |
| le | modellisme | | making models |
| | moderne | | modern |
| le | mois | | month |
| par | mois | | per month |
| le | moniteur | | monitor |
| | Monsieur | | Mr, Sir, gentleman |
| la | montagne | | mountain |
| | monter une tente | to | pitch a tent |
| | monter* dans le bus | to | get into the bus |
| la | moquette | | fitted carpet |
| | mort(e) | | dead |
| la | moto | | motorbike |
| les | mots croisés (m pl) | | crosswords |
| le | moyen de transport | | means of transport |
| le | mur | | wall |
| le | musée | | museum |
| la | musique classique | | classical music |
| la | musique folklorique | | folk music |
| la | musique pop | | pop music |
| | nager | to | swim |
| la | nappe | | tablecloth |
| la | natation | | swimming |
| la | neige | | snow |
| | neiger | to | snow |
| | nettoyer | to | clean |
| le | nez | | nose |

| | | | |
|---|---|---|---|
| | noir | | black |
| le | nom/nom de famille | | name/surname |
| | non | | no |
| le | non-fumeur | | non-smoker |
| au | nord | in the | north |
| la | note | | mark, grade |
| le | nouvel an juif | | Rosh Hashana |
| le | nuage | | cloud |
| la | nuitée | | night (time) |
| le | numéro de téléphone | | telephone number |
| | occupé | | occupied |
| un | œil (pl: les yeux) | | eye |
| un | œuf | | egg |
| un | office de tourisme | | tourist information office |
| | offrir | to | give as a present |
| un | oignon | | onion |
| un | oiseau | | bird |
| à l' | ombre | in the | shade |
| une | omelette aux champignons | | mushroom omelette |
| un | omnibus | | local train |
| | on | | one, we, 'you', 'they' |
| un | oncle | | uncle |
| un | orage | | thunderstorm |
| une | orange | | orange |
| un | orangina | | Orangina® |
| un | orchestre | | orchestra |
| l' | orchestre (m) | | stalls |
| un | ordinateur | | computer |
| une | ordonnance | | prescription |
| une | oreille | | ear |
| un | oreiller | | pillow |
| | où? | | where? |
| | oublier | to | forget |
| à l' | ouest | in the | west |
| à l' | ouest de | | west of |
| | oui | | yes |
| | ouvert | | open |
| un | ouvre-boîte | | tin opener |
| un | ouvrier | | worker (male, unskilled) |
| une | ouvrière | | worker (female, unskilled) |
| | ouvrir | to | open |
| le | pain | | bread, French loaf |
| le | pamplemousse | | grapefruit |
| le | panier | | shopping basket |

| | | | |
|---|---|---|---|
| le | pansement | | bandage, dressing |
| le | pantalon (sing) | | trousers |
| le | papa | | daddy |
| le | papi | | grandpa |
| le | papier | | paper |
| la | Pâque juive | | Passover |
| le | paquet | | package |
| le | paragraphe | | paragraph |
| le | parasol | | parasol |
| | pardon | | pardon |
| le | parent | | parent |
| le/la | parent(e) | | relative of any kind |
| la | parenthèse | | bracket |
| le | parking | | car park |
| | parler | to | talk |
| | partager | to | share |
| la | partie | | match |
| | partir* | to | depart |
| | pas du tout | | not at all |
| le | passeport | | passport |
| | passer | to | spend (time) |
| | passer l'aspirateur | to | hoover |
| | passer le bac | to | take A Level or GNVQ |
| la | pastèque | | water melon |
| la | pastille | | cough sweet |
| le | pâté de campagne | | country pâté |
| les | pâtes (f pl) | | pasta |
| | patiner | to | ice-skate |
| la | patinoire | | ice-rink |
| la | pâtisserie | | cake shop |
| | pauvre | | poor |
| le | pavillon | | detached house |
| | payer | to | pay (for) |
| le | pays | | country |
| le | paysage | | landscape |
| la | pêche | | peach |
| | pêcher | to | fish |
| se | peigner | to | comb one's hair |
| | peindre | to | paint |
| la | pendule | | clock |
| la | pension complète | | full board |
| | perdre | to | lose |
| le | père | | father |
| le | père aubergiste | | warden (male) |

| | | | |
|---|---|---|---|
| le | Père Noël | | Father Christmas |
| | permis | | permitted |
| la | perruche | | budgie |
| | petit | | small |
| le | petit déjeuner | | breakfast |
| les | petits pois (m pl) | | peas |
| le | petits-fils | | grandson |
| la | petite-fille | | granddaughter |
| un | peu | a | little |
| | peu intéressant | | not interesting |
| | peut-être | | perhaps |
| | peut-on...? | | can you...? |
| la | pharmacie | | chemist's |
| la | photo | | photo |
| la | photo familiale | | family photo |
| la | phrase | | sentence |
| la | physique | | physics |
| le | piano | | piano |
| la | pièce | | coin |
| la | pièce d'identité | | ID |
| la | pièce de théâtre | | play |
| le | pied | | foot |
| le | pilote | | pilot |
| la | piqûre | | injection/insect bite |
| la | piscine | | swimming pool |
| le | placard | | cupboard |
| la | place | | square, place |
| le | plafond | | ceiling |
| la | plage | | beach |
| se | plaindre | to | complain |
| le | plan de la ville | | map of town |
| le | plancher | | floor |
| le | plat chaud | | cooked dish |
| la | plate-bande | | flower bed |
| la | platine laser | | CD player |
| | pleuvoir | to | rain |
| le | plombage | | filling |
| la | pluie | | rain |
| la | poêle | | frying pan |
| le | point | | full stop |
| le | point d'exclamation | | exclamation mark |
| le | point d'interrogation | | question mark |
| le | point virgule | | semicolon |
| la | poire | | pear |

| | | | |
|---|---|---|---|
| le | poisson | | fish |
| le | poisson rouge | | goldfish |
| la | poissonnerie | | fish shop |
| | Poissons | | Pisces |
| | pollué | | polluted |
| en | polycoton | | made of polyester/cotton |
| la | pomme | | apple |
| la | pomme de terre | | potato |
| le | pommier | | apple tree |
| le | poney | | pony |
| le | pont | | bridge |
| le | porc | | pork |
| le | port | | port, harbour |
| le | port de plaisance | | yacht marina |
| la | porte | | door |
| | porter | to | wear |
| la | poste | | post office |
| | poster | to | post |
| le | poster | | poster |
| la | poterie | | pottery |
| la | poubelle | | rubbish bin |
| le | poulet | | chicken |
| le | poulet rôti | | roast chicken |
| | pour | | for, in order to |
| | pourquoi? | | why? |
| | poussez | | push |
| la | prairie | | meadow |
| de | première classe | | first class |
| | prendre | to | take |
| | prendre le petit déjeuner | to | have breakfast |
| | prendre un bain | to | take a bath |
| | prendre une douche | to | shower |
| le | prénom | | first name, Christian name |
| | près de | | near |
| la | presse | | press |
| le | prix | | price |
| | probablement | | probably |
| le | problème | | problem |
| le/la | prof (professeur) | | teacher (secondary) |
| | promener | to | take (a dog) for a walk |
| se | promener (à la campagne) | to | go for a walk (in the country) |
| en | promotion | | on special offer |
| | propre | | clean |
| le | proviseur | | head of a lycée |

| | | | |
|---|---|---|---|
| la | prune | | plum |
| le | pub | | pub |
| la | publicité | | advertisements |
| les | pubs (f pl) | | ads |
| la | puce | | micro-chip |
| | puis-je...? | | may I...? can I...? |
| le | pull | | pullover |
| | punir | to | punish |
| le | pyjama (sing) | | pyjamas |
| | qu'est-ce que...? | | what...? |
| | qui est-ce qui...? | | who...? |
| le | quai | | platform |
| | quand? | | when? |
| le | quartier | | district, part of a town |
| | quel, quels? (m) | | which? |
| à | quelle heure...? | | at what time...? |
| | quelle, quelles? (f) | | which? |
| la | question | | question |
| | qui? | | who? |
| la | quincaillerie | | ironmonger's shop |
| | quitter la maison | to | leave the house |
| le | radiateur | | radiator |
| la | radio | | radio |
| le | raisin | | grape |
| le | Ramadan | | Ramadan |
| | ranger | to | tidy up |
| le | rapide | | express train |
| | rapidement | | fast, quickly |
| se | raser | to | shave |
| le | rat | | rat |
| | rater | to | miss |
| le | rayon | | department |
| la | réception | | reception |
| la | réceptionniste | | receptionist |
| la | récréation | | break |
| | redoubler une année | to | repeat a year |
| le | réfectoire | | canteen |
| | regarder | to | watch |
| | regarder la télé | to | watch TV |
| la | région | | region, area |
| la | règle | | rule/ruler |
| le | réglement | | rules (e.g. of the youth hostel) |
| se | relaxer | to | relax |
| la | religion | | religious studies |

| | | | |
|---|---|---|---|
| | rencontrer des amis | to | meet friends |
| le | rendez-vous | | appointment |
| | rénover | to | renovate |
| la | rentrée | | start of school year |
| | rentrer* (à la maison) | to | come back (home) |
| | répéter | to | repeat, to practise |
| | répondre (à) | to | answer |
| la | réponse | | answer |
| le | reportage sportif | | sports report |
| se | reposer | to | rest |
| la | réservation | | reservation |
| | réserver | to | book, to reserve |
| le/la | responsable | | party leader, organizer |
| le | restaurant | | restaurant |
| | restaurer | to | restore |
| | rester* | to | stay |
| le | retard | | delay |
| en | retard | | late |
| le | rétro-projecteur | | overhead projector |
| le | réveil | | alarm clock |
| se | réveiller | to | wake up |
| au | revoir | | goodbye |
| le | rez-de-chaussée | | ground floor |
| le | rhume | | cold |
| | riche | | rich |
| le | rideau | | curtain |
| la | rivière | | river |
| le | riz | | rice |
| la | robe | | dress |
| le | robinet | | tap |
| le | roman | | novel |
| le | roman d'aventure | | adventure novel |
| le | roman policier | | detective novel |
| le | rond-point | | roundabout |
| | rose | | pink |
| la | rose | | rose |
| le | rôti | | roast |
| | rouge | | red |
| la | route | | road (main) |
| la | route départementale | | B road |
| le | routier | | lorry driver |
| la | rue | | street |
| le | ruisseau | | brook |
| | s'il te plaît/s'il vous plaît | | please |

| | | | |
|---|---|---|---|
| le | Sabbat | | Sabbath |
| le | sable | | sand |
| le | sac à dos | | rucksack |
| le | sac banane | | bumbag |
| le | sac de couchage | | sleeping bag |
| | Sagittaire | | Sagittarius |
| la | Saint-Sylvestre | | New Year's Eve |
| la | salade | | salad |
| la | salade de tomates | | tomato salad |
| | sale | | dirty |
| la | salle à manger | | dining-room |
| la | salle d'attente | | waiting-room |
| avec | salle de bain | | with bathroom |
| la | salle de bains | | bathroom |
| la | salle de classe | | classroom |
| la | salle de gym | | gym |
| la | salle de séjour | | day room/living-room |
| la | salle des professeurs | | staffroom |
| la | salle polyvalente | | multipurpose room |
| le | salon | | living-room |
| | salut! | | hi! |
| la | sandale | | sandal |
| le | sandwich au fromage | | cheese sandwich |
| le | sandwich au jambon | | ham sandwich |
| le | sang | | blood |
| | sans | | without |
| le | sapin | | fir tree |
| la | sardine | | sardine |
| la | saucisse | | sausage |
| le | saucisson | | salami-type sausage |
| | sauvegarder | to | save |
| le | savon | | soap |
| les | sciences (f pl) | | science |
| | Scorpion | | Scorpio |
| la | séance | | performance |
| de | seconde classe | | second class |
| la | secrétaire | | secretary |
| le | séjour | | living-room |
| le | séjour | | stay |
| par | semaine | | per week |
| le | sens unique | | one-way street |
| | sensationel | | great |
| le | sentier | | path |
| le | serpent | | snake |

| | | | |
|---|---|---|---|
| la | serre | | greenhouse |
| le | serveur | | waiter |
| la | serveuse | | waitress |
| la | serviette | | towel |
| la | serviette de bain | | bath towel |
| la | serviette hygiénique | | sanitary towel |
| | seul | | alone |
| le | short (sing) | | shorts |
| la | signature | | signature |
| le | signe du zodiaque | | star sign |
| | signer | to | sign |
| le | silence | | silence at night, lights out |
| le | sirop | | cough mixture |
| | situé | | situated |
| le | slip | | pants |
| la | société | | club |
| la | sœur | | sister |
| en | soie | | made of silk |
| | soigné | | tidy |
| le | soir | | evening |
| la | soirée | | evening (time) |
| au | soleil | in the | sun |
| le | soleil | | sun |
| | sonner (à la porte) | to | ring (door bell) |
| la | sortie de secours | | emergency exit |
| | sortir* | to | go out |
| la | souris | | mouse |
| | sous | | under |
| les | sous-titres (m pl) | | subtitles |
| le | soutien-gorge | | bra |
| le | sparadrap | | sticking plaster |
| le | sport | | sport |
| les | sports aquatiques (m pl) | | watersports |
| les | sports d'hiver (m pl) | | winter sports |
| le | stade | | stadium |
| la | station service | | filling station |
| le | steak | | steak |
| le | steak grillé | | grilled steak |
| le | stylo | | ink pen |
| le | stylo (à bille) | | biro |
| au | sud | in the | south |
| | sur | | on |
| le | survêtement | | tracksuit |
| le | syndicat d'initiative | | tourist information office |

| | | | |
|---|---|---|---|
| le | T-shirt | | T-shirt |
| le | tabac | | tobacconist's shop |
| la | table | | desk/table |
| la | table basse | | coffee table |
| la | table de chevet | | bedside table |
| le | tableau | | picture/board |
| le | talk show | | chat show |
| la | tante | | aunt |
| le | tapis | | rug |
| | tapisser | to | hang wallpaper |
| la | tarte aux pommes | | apple tart |
| la | tasse | | cup |
| | Taureau | | Taurus |
| le | taux de change | | exchange rate |
| la | technologie | | technology |
| la | télé (télévision) | | TV |
| la | télécommande | | remote control |
| | télécopier | to | fax |
| le | téléphone | | telephone |
| le | téléviseur | | TV set |
| avec | téléviseur | | with TV |
| la | télévision câblée | | cable TV |
| à | temps | in | time |
| le | temps libre | | free time, leisure time |
| à | temps partiel | | part-time |
| le | tennis | | tennis |
| la | tente | | tent |
| le | terrain de sports | | sportsground |
| la | terrasse | | patio |
| la | tête | | head |
| le | TGV | | TGV |
| le | thé/du thé | | tea/some tea |
| le | thé au citron | | tea with lemon |
| le | thé au lait | | tea with milk |
| le | théâtre | | theatre |
| le | timbre | | stamp |
| la | tirelire | | piggy bank/money-box |
| | tirez | | pull |
| les | toilettes (f pl) | | toilets |
| le | toit | | roof |
| la | tomate | | tomato |
| | tondre le gazon | to | mow the lawn |
| la | tortue | | tortoise |
| | tôt | | early |

| | | | |
|---|---|---|---|
| | toucher un chèque | to | cash a cheque |
| le | touriste | | tourist |
| | tourner | to | turn |
| à | tout à l'heure | | see you later |
| | tout droit | | straight on |
| | tout près | | very near |
| le | train | | train |
| le | train à grande vitesse | | TGV |
| le | trait d'union | | hyphen |
| le | traitement de texte | | word processing |
| le | tramway | | tram |
| les | transports publics (m pl) | | public transport |
| le | travail | | work |
| | travailler | to | work |
| les | travellers (m pl) | | traveller's cheques |
| la | traversée de la Manche | | Channel crossing |
| | traverser | to | cross |
| | tricoter | to | knit |
| le | trimestre | | term |
| le | trombone | | trombone |
| la | trompette | | trumpet |
| la | trousse | | pencil case |
| | trouver | to | find |
| la | truite | | trout |
| le | tube | | hit song/tube |
| le | tunnel sous la Manche | | Channel Tunnel |
| un | uniforme | | uniform |
| une | usine | | factory |
| | utile | | useful |
| les | vacances (f pl) | | (school) holidays |
| les | vacances à la ferme (f pl) | | farm holiday |
| les | vacances de Noël (f pl) | | Christmas holidays |
| les | vacances de Pâques (f pl) | | Easter holidays |
| la | valise | | suitcase |
| la | vallée | | valley |
| le | vase | | vase |
| le | veau | | veal |
| la | vedette | | film-star |
| la | veille de Noël | | Christmas Eve |
| le | vélo | | bicycle |
| le | vélomoteur | | moped |
| le | vendeur | | sales shop assistant (male) |
| la | vendeuse | | sales shop assistant (female) |
| à | vendre | | for sale |

| | | | |
|---|---|---|---|
| | vendre | to | sell |
| le | vent | | wind |
| le | ventre | | abdomen |
| le | verre | | glass |
| | vers | | towards (place), at about (time) |
| | Verseau | | Aquarius |
| la | version originale (v.o.) | | original soundtrack |
| | vert | | green |
| le | vestiaire | | changing room |
| le | veston | | jacket |
| | veuf/veuve | | widowed |
| la | viande | | meat |
| | Vierge | | Virgo |
| | vieux | | old |
| le | village | | village |
| la | ville | | town |
| la | ville industrielle | | industrial town |
| le | vin/du vin | | wine/some wine |
| le | vin blanc | | white wine |
| le | vin rouge | | red wine |
| le | violon | | violin |
| le | violoncelle | | cello |
| la | virgule | | comma |
| la | visite | | visit |
| | visiter | to | visit (a monument) |
| | visiter un château | to | visit a stately home |
| la | vitrine | | shop window |
| la | voie | | track |
| le | voilier | | sailing boat |
| | voir | to | see |
| | voir des amis | to | meet friends |
| la | voiture | | car |
| le | vol | | flight |
| la | volaille | | poultry |
| | voler | to | fly |
| le | volet | | shutter |
| le | voyage | | journey |
| | voyager | to | travel |
| le | voyageur | | traveller |
| le | WC | | toilet |
| le | weekend | | weekend |
| le | western | | cowboy film |
| | y a-t-il...? | | Is there...?/Are there...? |
| le | yaourt | | yoghurt |

| | | |
|---|---|---|
| la | zone industrielle | industrial estate |
| la | zone piétonne | pedestrian precinct |

# English–French

# *Mini-Dictionary*

## Key

| | |
|---|---|
| (e) | feminine form |
| (s) | plural form |
| (m) | masculine |
| (f) | feminine |
| (m pl) | masculine plural |
| (f pl) | feminine plural |
| (sing) | singular |
| * | verb takes *être* in the perfect tense |

| | | | |
|---|---|---|---|
| | abdomen | le | ventre |
| | accommodation | l' | hébergement (m) |
| | actor | un | acteur |
| | actress | une | actrice |
| | address | une | adresse |
| | adolescent | un/une | adolescent(e) |
| | ads | les | pubs (f pl) |
| | adult | un | adulte |
| | adventure film | le | film d'aventures |
| | adventure novel | le | roman d'aventure |
| | advertisements | la | publicité |
| | aerial | une | antenne |
| | affectionate | | gentil |
| | after | | après |
| | after the lights | | après les feux |
| | afternoon | l' | après-midi (m) |
| | age | l' | âge (m) |
| | agreed | d' | accord |
| | air bed | le | matelas pneumatique |
| | airport | un | aéroport |
| | alarm clock | le | réveil |
| | alone | | seul |
| | ankle | la | cheville |
| | answer | la | réponse |
| to | answer | | répondre (à) |
| | apple | la | pomme |
| | apple tart | la | tarte aux pommes |
| | apple tree | le | pommier |
| | appointment | le | rendez-vous |
| | apricot | un | abricot |
| | Aquarius | | Verseau |
| | Are there...? | | Y a-t-il...? |
| to | argue | se | disputer |
| | Aries | | Bélier |
| | arm | le | bras |

| | | | |
|---|---|---|---|
| | armchair | le | fauteuil |
| | arrival | une | arrivée |
| to | arrive | | arriver* |
| | art | le | dessin |
| to | ask (for) | | demander |
| to | ask for information | | demander des informations |
| | assembly | une | assemblée |
| | at the house of | | chez |
| | at what time...? | à | quelle heure...? |
| | athletics | l' | athlétisme (m) |
| | aunt | la | tante |
| | avenue | une | allée |
| | (10 km) away | à | (10 kilomètres) |
| | B road | la | route départementale |
| | baby | le | bébé |
| | back | le | dos |
| | bad | | moche |
| | baker's shop | la | boulangerie |
| | balcony | le | balcon |
| | banana | la | banane |
| | bandage, dressing | le | pansement |
| | bank | la | banque |
| | bank note | le | billet |
| | bar | le | bar |
| | basin | le | lavabo |
| | bath towel | la | serviette de bain |
| | bath tub | la | baignoire |
| to | bathe in the sea | se | baigner |
| | bathing suit | le | maillot |
| | bathroom | la | salle de bains |
| to | be called | s' | appeler |
| to | be cold (weather) | | faire froid |
| to | be foggy | | faire du brouillard |
| to | be hot (weather) | | faire chaud |
| to | be present | | être présent(e) |
| to | be windy | | faire du vent |
| | beach | la | plage |
| | bean | le | haricot |
| | bed | le | lit |
| | bedside table | la | table de chevet |
| | bedroom | la | chambre (à coucher) |
| | beef | le | bœuf |
| | beer | la | bière |
| some | beer | de la | bière |

| | | | |
|---|---|---|---|
| | before | | avant |
| to | begin, start | | commencer |
| | behind | | derrière |
| | behind the church | | derrière l'église |
| | belt | la | ceinture |
| | bench | le | banc |
| | beside | | à côté de |
| | between | | entre |
| | bicycle | la | bicyclette |
| | bicycle | le | vélo |
| | bidet | le | bidet |
| | big, tall | | grand |
| | biology | la | biologie |
| | bird | un | oiseau |
| | biro | le | stylo (à bille) |
| | birthday | un | anniversaire |
| | biscuit | le | biscuit |
| | black | | noir |
| | blackcurrant | le | cassis |
| | blanket | la | couverture |
| | block of flats | un | immeuble |
| | blood | le | sang |
| | blouse | le | chemisier |
| | blouson jacket | le | blouson |
| | blue | | bleu |
| | board | le | tableau |
| | board game | le | jeu de société |
| | book | le | livre |
| to | book | | réserver |
| | book of tickets | le | carnet |
| | bookcase | la | bibliothèque |
| | boot | la | botte |
| | boring | | casse-pieds, ennuyeux |
| | boy | le | garçon |
| | bra | le | soutien-gorge |
| | bracket | la | parenthèse |
| | bread shop | la | boulangerie |
| | bread, French loaf | le | pain |
| | break | la | récréation |
| | breakfast | le | petit déjeuner |
| | bricklayer, builder | le | maçon |
| | bridge | le | pont |
| | brochure | la | brochure/le dépliant |
| | brook | le | ruisseau |

| | | | |
|---|---|---|---|
| | broom | le | balai |
| | brother | le | frère |
| | brown | | brun |
| to | brush | | brosser |
| to | brush one's teeth | se | brosser les dents |
| | budgie | la | perruche |
| | bug | le | bug |
| to | build | | construire |
| | bumbag | le | sac banane |
| | bunch of flowers | le | bouquet de fleurs |
| | bungalow | le | bungalow |
| | bus | le | bus |
| | bus station | la | gare routière |
| | bus stop | un | arrêt de bus |
| | bush | un | arbuste |
| | butcher's shop | la | boucherie |
| to | buy | | acheter |
| | by air mail/by plane | par | avion |
| | by, in, with | | en |
| | cabbage | le | chou |
| | cable TV | la | télévision câblée |
| | café | le | café |
| | cake | le | gâteau |
| | cake shop | la | pâtisserie |
| to | calculate | | calculer |
| | calm | | calme |
| | calmly | au | calme |
| | camera | un | appareil-photo |
| to | camp | | camper |
| | campfire | le | feu de camp |
| | campsite/camping | le | camping |
| | camping equipment | le | matériel du camping |
| | camrecorder | le | caméscope |
| | can you...? | | peut-on...? |
| | canary | le | canari |
| | Cancer | | Cancer |
| | canteen | le | réfectoire |
| | cap | la | casquette |
| | Capricorn | | Capricorne |
| | car | une | auto/la voiture |
| | car park | le | parking |
| | caravan | la | caravane |
| | card | la | carte |
| | careful with money | | économe |

| | | | |
|---|---|---|---|
| | caretaker | le/la | concierge |
| | carrot | la | carotte |
| | cartoon | le | dessin animé |
| to | cash a cheque | | toucher un chèque |
| | cash register, till | la | caisse |
| | cashpoint | le | distributeur de billets |
| | cassette | la | cassette |
| | cassette recorder | le | magnétophone |
| | cat | le | chat |
| | cathedral | la | cathédrale |
| | cauliflower | le | chou-fleur |
| | CD | le | CD |
| | CD player | la | platine laser |
| | CD ROM | le | CD ROM |
| | ceiling | le | plafond |
| to | celebrate | | fêter |
| | cellar | la | cave |
| | cello | le | violoncelle |
| | centime | le | centime |
| | central heating | le | chauffage central |
| | chair | la | chaise |
| | chalk | la | craie |
| to | change | | changer |
| to | change money | | changer de l'argent |
| | changing room | le | vestiaire |
| | Channel crossing | la | traversée de la Manche |
| | Channel Tunnel | le | tunnel sous la Manche |
| | chat show | le | talk show |
| | cheap, good value for money | | bon marché |
| | cheese | le | fromage |
| | cheese sandwich | le | sandwich au fromage |
| | cheese shop | la | crémerie |
| | chemist's | la | pharmacie |
| | chemistry | la | chimie |
| | cheque | le | chèque |
| | cherry | la | cerise |
| | chestnut brown | | marron |
| | chicken | le | poulet |
| | child | un | enfant |
| | chimney | la | cheminée |
| | chips | les | frites (f pl) |
| | chocolate | le | chocolat |
| | choir | la | chorale |
| to | choose | | choisir |

| | | | |
|---|---|---|---|
| | Christmas Day | le | jour de Noël |
| | Christmas Eve | la | veille de Noël |
| | Christmas holidays | les | vacances de Noël (f pl) |
| | Christmas tree | un | arbre de Noël |
| | church | une | église |
| | cider | le | cidre |
| (some) | cider | du | cidre |
| | cinema | le | cinéma |
| | citizenship/PSE | l' | instruction civique (f) |
| | clarinet | la | clarinette |
| | classical music | la | musique classique |
| | classroom | la | salle de classe |
| | clean | | propre |
| to | clean | | nettoyer |
| | cleaner | la | femme de ménage |
| to | clear the table | | débarrasser la table |
| | clock | la | pendule |
| to | close | | fermer |
| | closed | | fermé |
| | clothes shop | le | magasin de vêtements |
| | cloud | le | nuage |
| | club | la | société/le club |
| | coach | le | car |
| | coat | le | manteau |
| | coffee (black) | le | café |
| | (some) coffee | du | café |
| | coffee table | la | table basse |
| | coin | la | pièce |
| | cola | le | coca |
| | cold | | froid |
| | cold | le | rhume |
| | cold chocolate | le | chocolat froid |
| to | collect | | collectionner |
| | collection | la | collection |
| | colon | | deux points (m) |
| | coloured pencil | le | crayon de couleur |
| to | comb one's hair | se | peigner |
| to | come back (home) | | rentrer* (à la maison) |
| | comedian/actor | le | comédien |
| | comedienne/actress | la | comédienne |
| | comedy | la | comédie |
| | comfortable | | confortable |
| | comic strip | la | bande dessinée |
| | comma | la | virgule |

| | | | |
|---|---|---|---|
| | compartment | le | compartiment |
| to | complain | se | plaindre |
| | comprehensive school (11–15) | le | collège/le CES |
| | computer | un | ordinateur |
| | computer game | le | jeu électronique |
| | concert | le | concert |
| | connecting train | la | correspondance |
| to | cook | | faire la cuisine |
| | cooked dish | le | plat chaud |
| | cooker | la | cuisinière |
| to | copy | | copier |
| | corner | le | coin (de la rue) |
| to | correct | | corriger |
| | corridor | le | couloir |
| to | cost | | coûter |
| | cotton wool | le | coton hydrophile |
| | cough mixture | le | sirop |
| | cough sweet | la | pastille |
| | council flat | une | HLM |
| to | count | | compter |
| | counter | le | guichet |
| | country | le | pays |
| | country (side) | la | campagne |
| | country pâté | le | pâté de campagne |
| | cousin (female) | la | cousine |
| | cousin (male) | le | cousin |
| | cowboy film | le | western |
| | cream | la | crème |
| | cricket | le | cricket |
| | crisps | les | chips (m pl) |
| to | cross | | traverser |
| | crossroads | le | carrefour |
| | crosswords | les | mots croisés (m pl) |
| | cucumber | le | concombre |
| | cul-de-sac | une | impasse |
| | cup | la | tasse |
| | cupboard | le | placard |
| | currency exchange | le | change |
| | curtain | le | rideau |
| | customer | le/la | client(e) |
| | customs control | la | douane |
| to | cycle | | faire du cyclisme |
| | cycling | le | cyclisme |
| | daddy | le | papa |

| | | | |
|---|---|---|---|
| | daffodil | la | jonquille |
| | dainty, delicate | | délicat |
| to | dance | | danser |
| | dark grey | | gris foncé |
| | database | la | base de données |
| to | date-stamp a ticket | | composter un billet |
| | day | le | jour |
| | day(time) | la | journée |
| | day room | la | salle de séjour |
| | dead | | mort(e) |
| | delay | le | retard |
| | delayed | | avec du retard |
| to | delete | | effacer |
| | delicatessen | la | charcuterie |
| | dentist | le | dentiste |
| to | depart | | partir* |
| | department | le | rayon |
| | department store | le | grand magasin |
| | departure | le | départ |
| | desk | la | bureau/la table |
| | dessert | le | dessert |
| | detached house | le | pavillon |
| | detective film | le | film policier |
| | detective novel | le | roman policier |
| | diarrhoea | la | diarrhée |
| | difficult | | difficile |
| | dinghy | le | dériveur |
| | dining-room | la | salle à manger |
| | dirty | | sale |
| | disco | la | discothèque |
| | dishwasher | le | lave-vaisselle |
| | disk | la | disquette |
| | disk drive | le | lecteur de disquettes |
| | disk manager | le | catalogue |
| | district, part of a town | le | quartier |
| | divorced | | divorcé(e) |
| to | do an experiment | | faire une expérience |
| to | do DIY | | faire du bricolage |
| to | do homework | | faire des devoirs |
| to | do sport | | faire du sport |
| | doctor | le | médecin |
| | documentary | le | documentaire |
| | dog | le | chien |
| | door | la | porte |

| | | | |
|---|---|---|---|
| | dormitory | le | dortoir |
| | Dormobile® | le | camping-car |
| | double room | la | chambre pour deux personnes |
| to | draw | | dessiner |
| | dress | la | robe |
| to | drive | | conduire |
| | driver | le | chauffeur |
| | drum kit | la | batterie |
| to | dry up | | essuyer la vaisselle |
| | duck | le | canard |
| | duvet | la | couette |
| | duvet cover | la | housse |
| | ear | une | oreille |
| | early | | tôt |
| in the | east | à l' | est |
| | east of | | à l'est de |
| | Easter Day | le | jour de Pâques |
| | Easter holiday | les | vacances de Pâques (f pl) |
| | easy | | facile |
| to | eat | | manger |
| to | edit | | éditer |
| | egg | un | oeuf |
| | electrician | un | électricien |
| | electricity | l' | électricité (f) |
| | emergency exit | la | sortie de secours |
| | employed | | employé |
| to | end, finish | | finir |
| | engaged | | fiancé(e) |
| | engineer | un | ingénieur |
| | English | l' | anglais (m) |
| to | enjoy oneself | s' | amuser |
| | entrance | une | entrée |
| | escalator | un | escalator |
| | evening | le | soir |
| | evening (time) | la | soirée |
| | evening meal | le | dîner |
| | example | un | exemple |
| | excellent | | excellent |
| | except | à l' | exception de |
| | exchange | un | échange |
| | exchange rate | le | taux de change |
| | exclamation mark | le | point d'exclamation |
| | excursion, outing | une | excursion |
| | excuse me, sorry | | excusez-moi |

| | | | |
|---|---|---|---|
| | exercise book | le | cahier |
| | exhibition | une | exposition |
| | expensive | | cher |
| to | explain | | expliquer |
| | express train | le | rapide |
| | espresso coffee | le | café express |
| | eye | un | œil (pl: les yeux) |
| | factory | une | usine |
| | family | la | famille |
| | family photo | la | photo familiale |
| | far from | | loin de |
| | farm | la | ferme |
| | farm holiday | les | vacances à la ferme (f pl) |
| | fast, quickly | | rapidement |
| | father | le | père |
| | Father Christmas | le | Père Noël |
| | favourite group | le | groupe favori |
| | favourite singer (male) | le | chanteur favori |
| | favourite singer (female) | la | chanteuse favorite |
| to | fax | | faxer/télécopier |
| to | feed | | donner à manger |
| | felt-tip | le | feutre |
| | ferry | le | car-ferry |
| | fiancé(e) | le/la | fiancé(e) |
| | field | le | champ |
| | filling | le | plombage |
| | filling station | la | station service |
| | film | le | film |
| | film-star | la | vedette |
| to | find | | trouver |
| | finger | le | doigt |
| to | finish | | finir |
| | fir tree | le | sapin |
| | first class | de | première classe |
| | first name, Christian name | le | prénom |
| | fish | le | poisson |
| to | fish | | pêcher |
| | fish shop | la | poissonnerie |
| | fitted carpet | la | moquette |
| | flannel | le | gant de toilette |
| | flat | un | appartement |
| | flight | le | vol |
| | floor | le | plancher |
| | floor, storey | un | étage |

| | | | |
|---|---|---|---|
| | flower | la | fleur |
| | flower bed | la | plate-bande |
| | flu | la | grippe |
| | flute | la | flûte |
| to | fly | | voler |
| | fog | le | brouillard |
| | folk music | la | musique folklorique |
| | foot | le | pied |
| | football | le | foot/football |
| | for boys | pour | garçons |
| | for girls | pour | filles |
| | for sale | à | vendre |
| | for, in order to | | pour |
| | forbidden | | défendu |
| | forest | la | forêt |
| to | forget | | oublier |
| to | format | | formater |
| | franc | le | franc |
| | free | | libre |
| | free time, leisure time | le | temps libre |
| to | freeze | | geler |
| | freezer | le | congélateur |
| | French | le | français |
| | fresh raw vegetables | les | crudités (m) |
| | freshly squeezed lemon juice | le | citron pressé |
| | fridge | le | frigo |
| | friend (male) | un | ami |
| | friend (female) | une | amie |
| | from, of | de | |
| | fruit | le | fruit |
| | fruit juice | le | jus de fruit |
| (some) | fruit juice | du | jus de fruit |
| | frying pan | la | poêle |
| | full | | complet |
| | full board | la | pension complète |
| | full stop | le | point |
| | fun, funny | | amusant |
| | gallery | la | galerie |
| | game | le | jeu |
| | garlic | l' | ail (m) |
| | gas | le | gaz |
| | gas bottle | la | bouteille de gaz |
| | gas cooker | le | four à gaz |
| | Gemini | | Gémeaux |

| | | | |
|---|---|---|---|
| | general food shop | le | magasin d'alimentation générale |
| | generous | | généreux |
| | geography | la | géographie |
| | gerbil | la | gerbille |
| | German | l' | allemand (m) |
| to | get changed | se | changer |
| to | get dressed | s' | habiller |
| to | get in the bus | | monter* dans le bus |
| to | get off the bus | | descendre* du bus |
| to | get on well/badly with | s' | entendre bien/mal avec |
| to | get undressed | se | déshabiller |
| to | get up | se | lever |
| | girl, daughter | la | fille |
| to | give as a present | | offrir |
| | glass | le | verre |
| | glove | le | gant |
| to | go | | aller* |
| to | go to bed | se | coucher |
| to | go for a walk | se | promener |
| to | go for a walk (in the country) | se | promener (à la campagne) |
| to | go into town | | aller* en ville |
| to | go out | | sortir* |
| to | go shopping | | faire des courses |
| to | go window shopping | | faire du lèche-vitrines |
| | goldfish | le | poisson rouge |
| | goodbye | au | revoir |
| | good evening | | bonsoir |
| | good morning, good day, good afternoon | | bonjour |
| | good night | | bonne nuit |
| | good value for money | | bon marché |
| | goods | les | marchandises (f pl) |
| | granddaughter | la | petite-fille |
| | grandfather | le | grand-père |
| | grandma | la | mami |
| | grandmother | la | grand-mère |
| | grandpa | le | papi |
| | grandparents | les | grand-parents (pl) |
| | grandson | le | petit-fils |
| | grape | le | raisin |
| | grapefruit | le | pamplemousse |
| | great | | extra, sensationel |
| | green | | vert |
| | green bean | le | haricot vert |
| | greenhouse | la | serre |

| | | | |
|---|---|---|---|
| | grey | | gris |
| | grilled steak | le | steak grillé |
| | grocer's | une | épicerie |
| | ground floor | le | rez-de-chaussée |
| | group | le | groupe |
| | guest room | la | chambre d'amis |
| | guinea pig | le | cobaye/cochon d'Inde |
| | guitar | la | guitare |
| | gym | la | salle de gym |
| | gymnasium | le | gymnase |
| | gymnastics | la | gymnastique |
| | hairdresser (male) | le | coiffeur |
| | hairdresser (female) | la | coiffeuse |
| | half board (bed, breakfast and evening meal) | en | demi-pension |
| | half-brother | le | demi-frère |
| | half-sister | la | demi-soeur |
| | half-term holidays | le | congé de mi-trimestre |
| | ham | le | jambon |
| | ham sandwich | le | sandwich au jambon |
| | hamster | un | hamster |
| | hand | la | main |
| to | hang wallpaper | | tapisser |
| | hard disk | le | disque dur |
| | hat | le | chapeau |
| to | have a detention | | être collé(e) |
| to | have an argument with | s' | expliquer avec |
| to | have breakfast | | prendre le petit déjeuner |
| | head | la | tête |
| | head of a lycée | le | proviseur |
| | headmaster | le | directeur |
| | headmistress | la | directrice |
| to | help | | aider |
| | hi! | | salut! |
| | high temperature | la | fièvre |
| | high tide | la | marée haute |
| to | hike | | faire une randonnée |
| | hill | la | colline |
| to | hire | | louer |
| | historic | | historique |
| | history | l' | histoire (f) |
| | hit song | le | tube |
| | holiday cottage | le | gîte |
| | holidays | les | vacances (f pl) |
| | home economics | les | arts ménagers (m) |

| | | | |
|---|---|---|---|
| | homework | les | devoirs (m pl) |
| to | hoover | | passer l'aspirateur |
| | horror film | le | film d'épouvante |
| | horse | le | cheval |
| | hospital | un | hôpital |
| | hot | | chaud |
| | hot chocolate | le | chocolat chaud |
| | hotel | un | hôtel |
| | hourly | à | l'heure |
| | house | la | maison |
| | housework | le | ménage |
| | hovercraft | un | hovercraft |
| | how many...? | | combien (de)...? |
| | how? | | comment? |
| | humanities | l' | histoire/géo |
| | husband | le | mari |
| | hypermarket | la | grande surface |
| | hyphen | le | trait d'union |
| | ice-cream | la | glace |
| | ice-rink | la | patinoire |
| to | ice-skate | | patiner |
| | ID | la | pièce d'identité |
| | identity card | la | carte d'identité |
| | illness | la | maladie |
| | important | | important |
| | in | | dans |
| in | front of | | devant |
| | included | | compris |
| | industrial estate | la | zone industrielle |
| | industrial town | la | ville industrielle |
| | injection | la | piqûre |
| | ink pen | le | stylo |
| | insect bite | la | piqûre |
| | instrument | un | instrument |
| | interesting | | intéressant |
| | ironmonger's shop | la | quincaillerie |
| | Is there...? | | Y a-t-il...? |
| | island | une | île |
| | IT | l' | informatique (f) |
| | Italian | l' | italien (m) |
| | jacket | le | veston |
| | jam | la | marmelade |
| | journey | le | voyage |
| | key | la | clé |

| | | | |
|---|---|---|---|
| | keyboard | le | clavier |
| | kitchen | la | cuisine |
| | knee | le | genou |
| to | knit | | tricoter |
| | laboratory | le | laboratoire |
| | lady | la | dame |
| | lake | le | lac |
| | lamb | l' | agneau (m) |
| | lamp | la | lampe |
| to | land | | atterrir |
| | landscape | le | paysage |
| | large, tall | | grand |
| to | last | | durer |
| | late | en | retard |
| | Latin | le | latin |
| | lawn | le | gazon |
| to | lay the table | | mettre la table |
| to | learn | | apprendre |
| to | learn by heart | | apprendre par coeur |
| to | leave the house | | quitter la maison |
| | left | à | gauche |
| on the | left of | à | gauche de |
| | leg | la | jambe |
| | leggings | le | caleçon (sing) |
| | lemon | le | citron |
| | lemonade | la | limonade |
| (some) | lemonade | de la | limonade |
| | Leo | | Lion |
| | lesson | le | cours |
| | lesson | la | leçon |
| | letter | la | lettre |
| | letter box | la | boîte aux lettres |
| | lettuce | la | laitue |
| | Libra | | Balance |
| | library | la | bibliothèque |
| | lift | un | ascenseur |
| | light grey | | gris clair |
| to | like | | aimer |
| to | like watching | | aimer regarder |
| | likeable | | aimable |
| | line | la | ligne |
| | list of hotels | la | liste des hôtels |
| to | listen to | | écouter |
| a | little | un | peu |

| | | | |
|---|---|---|---|
| to | live | | habiter |
| | living-room | la | salle de séjour/le salon/le séjour |
| to | load | | charger |
| | local train | un | omnibus |
| | loft | le | grenier |
| to | look for | | chercher |
| | lorry | le | camion |
| | lorry driver | le | routier |
| to | lose | | perdre |
| a | lot | | beaucoup |
| | low tide | la | marée basse |
| | luggage carousel | le | carrousel |
| | luggage locker | la | consigne |
| | lunch | le | déjeuner |
| | luxurious | de | luxe |
| | machine to date-stamp tickets | le | composteur de billets |
| | made of cotton | en | coton |
| | made of leather | en | cuir |
| | made of polyester/cotton | en | polycoton |
| | made of silk | en | soie |
| | made of wool | en | laine |
| | magazine | un | illustré/magazine |
| | mail | le | courrier |
| to | make music | | faire de la musique |
| | making models | le | modellisme |
| | man | un | homme |
| | manager | le/la | gérant(e) |
| | map of town | le | plan de la ville |
| | mark, grade | la | note |
| | market | le | marché |
| | married | | marié(e) |
| | match | le | match/la partie |
| | matches | les | allumettes (f pl) |
| | maths | les | maths (f pl) |
| | may I...? can I...? | | puis-je...? |
| | meadow | la | prairie |
| | means of transport | le | moyen de transport |
| | meat | la | viande |
| | mechanic (male) | le | mécanicien |
| | mechanic (female) | la | mécanicienne |
| | medicine | le | médicament |
| to | meet friends | | voir des amis, rencontrer des amis |
| | melon | le | melon |
| | member | le | membre |

| | | | |
|---|---|---|---|
| | membership card | la | carte d'adhérent |
| | menu | le | menu |
| | microchip | la | puce |
| | microwave oven | le | four à micro-ondes |
| in the | middle of | au | centre de |
| | milk | le | lait |
| | (some) milk | du | lait |
| | mineral water | l' | eau minérale (f) |
| (some) | mineral water | de l' | eau minérale (f) |
| | mirror | le | miroir |
| | Miss | | Mademoiselle |
| to | miss | | rater |
| | mistake | une | erreur/la faute |
| | mixed | | mixte |
| | modern | | moderne |
| | money | l' | argent (m) |
| | monitor | le | moniteur |
| | month | le | mois |
| | moped | le | vélomoteur |
| | morning | le | matin |
| | mother | la | mère |
| | motorbike | la | moto |
| | mountain | la | montagne |
| | mouse | la | souris |
| | mouth | la | bouche |
| to | move house | | déménager |
| to | mow the lawn | | tondre le gazon |
| | Mr, Sir, gentleman | | Monsieur |
| | Mrs, Ms | | Madame |
| | multipurpose room | la | salle polyvalente |
| | mummy | la | maman |
| | museum | le | musée |
| | mushroom | le | champignon |
| | mushroom omelette | une | omelette aux champignons |
| | music show | une | émission de musique |
| (sur) | name | le | nom/nom de famille |
| | name day | la | fête |
| | navy blue | | bleu marine |
| | near | | près de |
| | New Year's Day | le | jour de l'An |
| | New Year's Eve | la | Saint-Sylvestre |
| | news | les | informations/les infos (f pl) |
| | news magazine programme | le | journal télévisé |
| | newspaper | le | journal |

| | | | |
|---|---|---|---|
| | next to, beside | | à côté de |
| | night (time) | la | nuitée |
| | night (= evening) | le | soir |
| | night club | la | boîte de nuit |
| | no | | non |
| | noisy, loud | | bruyant |
| | non-smoker | le | non-fumeur |
| in the | north | au | nord |
| | north of | | au nord de |
| | nose | le | nez |
| | not at all | | pas du tout |
| | not interesting | | peu intéressant |
| | note | le | billet |
| | novel | le | roman |
| | nurse (male) | un | infirmier |
| | nurse (female) | une | infirmière |
| | nursery school | une | école maternelle |
| | occupied | | occupé |
| | of brick | en | brique |
| | of concrete | en | béton |
| | office worker (male) | un | employé de bureau |
| | office worker (female) | une | employée de bureau |
| | old | | vieux |
| | on | | sur |
| | on special offer | en | promotion |
| | on the corner of the street | | au coin de la rue |
| | on time | à l' | heure |
| | one-way street | le | sens unique |
| | onion | un | oignon |
| | open | | ouvert |
| to | open | | ouvrir |
| | open fireplace | la | cheminée |
| | opening times | les | heures d'ouverture (f pl) |
| | opposite | | en face de |
| | opposite the town hall | | en face de la mairie |
| | orange | une | orange |
| | Orangina® | un | orangina |
| | orchestra | un | orchestre |
| to | order (food, etc.) | | commander |
| | original soundtrack | la | version originale (v.o.) |
| | other | | autre |
| | out of the way | | isolé |
| | outing | une | excursion |
| | oven | le | four |

| | | | |
|---|---|---|---|
| | overhead projector | le | rétro-projecteur |
| | package | le | paquet |
| | pain | la | douleur |
| to | paint | | peindre |
| | pair of jeans | le | jean (sing) |
| | pancake | la | crêpe |
| | pants | le | slip |
| | paper | le | papier |
| | paragraph | le | paragraphe |
| | parasol | le | parasol |
| | parcel | le | colis |
| | pardon | | pardon |
| | parent | le | parent |
| | part of town, quarter, area | le | quartier |
| | part-time | à | temps partiel |
| | party | la | boum/la fête |
| | party leader, organizer | le/la | responsable |
| to | pass (an exam) | | être reçu(e) |
| | Passover | la | Pâque juive |
| | passport | le | passeport |
| | pasta | les | pâtes (f pl) |
| | path | le | sentier |
| | patio | la | terrasse |
| to | pay (for) | | payer |
| | peas | les | petits pois (m pl) |
| | peach | la | pêche |
| | pear | la | poire |
| | pedestrian precinct | la | zone piétonne |
| | penfriend (male) | le | correspondant |
| | penfriend (female) | la | correspondante |
| | pencil | le | crayon |
| | pencil case | la | trousse |
| | penknife | le | canif |
| | per month | par | mois |
| | per week | par | semaine |
| | performance | la | séance |
| | perhaps | | peut-être |
| | permitted | | permis |
| | phone box | la | cabine téléphonique |
| | photo | la | photo |
| | physics | la | physique |
| | piano | le | piano |
| | picture | une | image/le tableau |
| | picture book | le | livre illustré |

| | | | |
|---|---|---|---|
| | piggy bank | la | tirelire |
| | pillow | un | oreiller |
| | pilot | le | pilote |
| | pineapple | un | ananas |
| | pink | | rose |
| | Pisces | | Poissons |
| | pitch | un | emplacement |
| to | pitch a tent | | monter une tente |
| | place of birth | le | lieu de naissance |
| | plane | un | avion |
| | plate | une | assiette |
| | platform | le | quai |
| | play | la | pièce de théâtre |
| to | play | | mettre |
| to | play cards | | jouer aux cartes |
| to | play chess | | jouer aux échecs |
| | playground | la | cour |
| | playground shelter | le | préau |
| | please | | s'il te plaît/s'il vous plaît |
| | pleased to meet you | | enchanté(e) |
| | plug | le | bouchon |
| | plum | la | prune |
| | PO box | | CEDEX |
| | police officer | un | agent de police |
| | polluted | | pollué |
| | pond | la | mare |
| | pony | le | poney |
| | pool | un | étang |
| | poor | | pauvre |
| | pop music | la | musique pop |
| | pork | le | porc |
| | port, harbour | le | port |
| to | post | | poster |
| | postcard | la | carte postale |
| | postcode | le | code postal |
| | poster | le | poster |
| | postman | le | facteur |
| | post office | la | poste |
| | postwoman | la | factrice |
| | potato | la | pomme de terre |
| | pottery | la | poterie |
| | poultry | la | volaille |
| | pound sterling | la | livre sterling |
| to | practise | | répéter |

| | | | |
|---|---|---|---|
| | prescription | une | ordonnance |
| | present | le | cadeau |
| | press | la | presse |
| | price | le | prix |
| | primary school | une | école primaire |
| | primary school teacher (male) | un | instituteur |
| | primary school teacher (female) | une | institutrice |
| | printer | une | imprimante |
| | probably | | probablement |
| | problem | le | problème |
| | processed meats | la | charcuterie |
| | pub | le | pub |
| | public service worker | le/la | fonctionnaire |
| | public transport | les | transports publics (m pl) |
| | pull | | tirez |
| | pullover | le | pull |
| | punctually | à l' | heure |
| to | punish | | punir |
| | pupil (male) | un | élève |
| | pupil (female) | une | élève |
| | push | | poussez |
| | pyjamas | le | pyjama (sing) |
| | question | la | question |
| | question mark | le | point d'interrogation |
| | quiet | | calme |
| | quiz | le | jeu concours |
| | rabbit | le | lapin |
| | radiator | le | radiateur |
| | radio | la | radio |
| | railway station | la | gare SNCF |
| | rain | la | pluie |
| to | rain | | pleuvoir |
| | Ramadan | le | Ramadan |
| | raspberry | la | framboise |
| | rat | le | rat |
| to | read | | lire |
| | reading | la | lecture |
| | reception | la | réception |
| | receptionist | la | réceptionniste |
| to | record on cassette | | enregistrer |
| | recorder | la | flûte à bec |
| | red | | rouge |
| | red wine | le | vin rouge |
| | region, area | la | région |

| | | | |
|---|---|---|---|
| | relative of any kind | le/la | parent(e) |
| to | relax | se | relaxer |
| | religious studies | la | religion |
| | remote control | la | télécommande |
| to | renovate | | rénover |
| to | repeat | | répéter |
| to | repeat a year | | redoubler une année |
| | reservation | la | réservation |
| to | reserve | | réserver |
| | resource centre | le | CDI |
| to | rest | se | reposer |
| | restaurant | le | restaurant |
| to | restore | | restaurer |
| | return ticket | un | aller-retour |
| | rice | le | riz |
| | rich | | riche |
| to | ride | | faire de l'équitation |
| | riding | l' | équitation (f) |
| | right | à | droite |
| on the | right of | à | droite de |
| to | ring (door bell) | | sonner (à la porte) |
| | river | la | rivière |
| | road (main) | la | route |
| | road map | la | carte routière |
| | roast | le | rôti |
| | roast chicken | le | poulet rôti |
| to | roller-skate | | faire du patin à roulettes |
| | romantic film | le | film d'amour |
| | roof | le | toit |
| | rose | la | rose |
| | Rosh Hashana | le | nouvel an juif |
| | rough | | agité(e) |
| | roundabout | le | rond-point |
| | rubber | la | gomme |
| | rubbish bin | la | poubelle |
| | rucksack | le | sac à dos |
| | rug | le | tapis |
| | rule/ruler | la | règle |
| | rules of the youth hostel | le | réglement |
| | Sabbath | le | Sabbat |
| | Sagittarius | | Sagittaire |
| to | sail | | faire de la voile |
| | sailing boat | le | voilier |
| | salad | la | salade |

| | | | |
|---|---|---|---|
| | salami-type sausage | le | saucisson |
| | sales assistant (male) | le | vendeur |
| | sales assistant (female) | la | vendeuse |
| | sand | le | sable |
| | sandal | la | sandale |
| | sanitary towel | la | serviette hygiénique |
| | sardine | la | sardine |
| | satellite dish | une | antenne parabolique |
| | saucepan | la | casserole |
| | sausage | la | saucisse |
| to | save | | sauvegarder |
| to | save (money) | | faire des économies |
| | scarf | une | écharpe |
| | school holidays | les | vacances (f pl) |
| | school report | le | bulletin scolaire |
| | science | les | sciences (f pl) |
| | science-fiction film | le | film de science-fiction |
| | Scorpio | | Scorpion |
| | screen | un | écran |
| | scrunchie | le | chou-chou |
| | sea | la | mer |
| | seasickness | le | mal de mer |
| | second class | de | seconde classe |
| | secretary | la | secrétaire |
| to | see | | voir |
| | see you later | à | tout à l'heure |
| | see you tomorrow | à | demain |
| to | select | | choisir |
| | self-service | le | libre-service |
| to | sell | | vendre |
| | semicolon | le | point virgule |
| | semi-detached house | la | maison jumelée |
| to | send | | envoyer |
| | sentence | la | phrase |
| | serial | le | feuilleton |
| to | sew | | coudre |
| in the | shade | à l' | ombre |
| to | share | | partager |
| to | shave | se | raser |
| | shed | un | abri |
| | sheet | le | drap |
| | shelf | une | étagère |
| to | shine | | briller |
| | shirt | la | chemise |

| | | | |
|---|---|---|---|
| | shoe | la | chaussure |
| | shop | la | boutique/le magasin |
| to | shop | | faire des commissions/faire des courses |
| | shop assistant (male) | le | vendeur |
| | shop assistant (female) | la | vendeuse |
| | shop window | la | vitrine |
| | shopkeeper | le/la | commerçant(e) |
| | shopping basket | le | panier |
| | shopping centre | le | centre commercial |
| | shopping trolley | le | chariot |
| | shorts | le | short (sing) |
| | shower | la | douche |
| to | shower | | prendre une douche |
| to | shut | | fermer |
| | shutter | le | volet |
| to | sign | | signer |
| | signature | la | signature |
| | silence at night, lights out | le | silence |
| to | sing | | chanter |
| | single room | la | chambre pour une personne |
| | single ticket | un | aller simple |
| | sink | le | lavabo/un évier |
| | sister | la | soeur |
| | situated | | situé |
| | sixth form college/tertiary college (15–18) | le | lycée |
| to | ski | | faire du ski |
| to | skimboard | | faire du skim |
| | skirt | la | jupe |
| to | sleep | | dormir |
| | sleeping bag | le | sac de couchage |
| | slowly | | lentement |
| | small | | petit |
| | smoker | le | fumeur |
| | snake | le | serpent |
| | snow | la | neige |
| to | snow | | neiger |
| | soap | le | savon |
| | soap opera | le | feuilleton/le mélo |
| | sock | la | chaussette |
| | sofa | le | canapé |
| | son | le | fils |
| | song | la | chanson |
| in the | south | au | sud |
| | south of | | au sud de |

| | | | |
|---|---|---|---|
| | Spanish | l' | espagnol (m) |
| | speech marks | les | guillemets |
| to | spend (on) | | dépenser (pour) |
| to | spend (time) | | passer |
| | spinach | les | épinards (m pl) |
| | sponge | une | éponge |
| | sport | le | sport |
| | sports centre | le | centre sportif |
| | sports report | le | reportage sportif |
| | sportsground | le | terrain de sports |
| | sprouts | les | choux de Bruxelles (m pl) |
| | spy film | le | film d'espionnage |
| | square, place | la | place |
| | stadium | le | stade |
| | staffroom | la | salle des professeurs |
| | staircase | un | escalier |
| | stalls | l' | orchestre (m) |
| | stamp | le | timbre |
| | star sign | le | signe du zodiaque |
| | start of school year | la | rentrée |
| | starter | les | hors d'œuvre (m) |
| | station | la | gare |
| | stay | le | séjour |
| to | stay | | rester* |
| | steak | le | bifteck/le steak |
| | stepfather, father-in-law | le | beau-père |
| | stepmother, mother-in-law | la | belle-mère |
| | stereo (system) | la | chaîne stéréo |
| | stewardess | une | hôtesse de l'air |
| | stick of French bread | la | baguette |
| | sticking plaster | le | sparadrap |
| | stomach | un | estomac |
| | straight on | | tout droit |
| | strawberry | la | fraise |
| | street | la | rue |
| | study | le | bureau |
| | subscription cable | le | câble à péage |
| | subtitles | les | sous-titres (m pl) |
| | suburbs | la | banlieue |
| | suitcase | la | valise |
| | summer holidays | les | grandes vacances (f pl) |
| in the | sun | au | soleil |
| | sun | le | soleil |
| | sunburn | le | coup de soleil |

| | | | |
|---|---|---|---|
| | sunstroke | une | insolation |
| | suntan lotion | la | crème solaire |
| to | sunbathe | se | bronzer |
| | sunburn | le | coup de soleil |
| | sunny | | ensoleillé |
| | surgery | le | cabinet |
| | surname | le | nom de famille |
| to | sweep | | balayer |
| to | swim | | nager |
| | swimming | la | natation |
| | swimming pool | la | piscine |
| to | switch over TV channel | | changer de programme |
| | T-shirt | le | T-shirt |
| | table | la | table |
| | tablecloth | la | nappe |
| | tablet | le | comprimé |
| to | take | | prendre |
| to | take (a dog) for a walk | | promener |
| to | take a bath | | prendre un bain |
| to | take A Level or GNVQ | | passer le bac |
| to | take off (aircraft) | | décoller |
| to | take photos | | faire des photos |
| to | talk | | parler |
| | tap | le | robinet |
| | Taurus | | Taureau |
| | tea | le | thé |
| | (some) tea | du | thé |
| | tea with lemon | le | thé au citron |
| | tea with milk | le | thé au lait |
| | teacher (male, primary) | un | instituteur |
| | teacher (female, primary) | une | institutrice |
| | teacher (secondary) | le/la | prof |
| | teacher (secondary) | le | professeur |
| | teaching | un | enseignement |
| | team | une | équipe |
| | technology | la | technologie |
| | telephone | le | téléphone |
| | telephone number | le | numéro de téléphone |
| | tennis | le | tennis |
| | tennis court | le | court de tennis |
| | tent | la | tente |
| | term | le | trimestre |
| | textbook | le | manuel |
| | TGV | le | TGV/le train à grande vitesse |

| | | | |
|---|---|---|---|
| | thank you | | merci |
| | theatre | le | théâtre |
| | thriller | le | film à suspense |
| | throat | la | gorge |
| | thunderstorm | un | orage |
| | ticket | le | billet |
| | ticket machine | le | distributeur de tickets |
| | tidy | | soigné |
| to | tidy up | | ranger |
| | tights | le | collant (sing) |
| in | time | à | temps |
| | timetable | un | horaire |
| | timetable (school) | un | emploi du temps |
| | tin opener | un | ouvre-boîte |
| | to, at, in | à | |
| | toasted ham and cheese sandwich | le | croque-monsieur |
| | tobacconist's shop | le | tabac |
| | toilet | le | WC |
| | toilet block | le | bloc sanitaire |
| | toilets | les | toilettes (f pl) |
| | tomato | la | tomate |
| | tomato salad | la | salade de tomates |
| | tooth | la | dent |
| | toothbrush | la | brosse à dents |
| | toothpaste | le | dentifrice |
| | torch | la | lampe |
| | tortoise | la | tortue |
| | tourist | le | touriste |
| | tourist information office | un | office de tourisme/le syndicat d'initiative |
| | towards(place), at about (time) | | vers |
| | towel | la | serviette |
| | town | la | ville |
| | town centre | le | centre-ville |
| | town hall | un | hôtel de ville |
| | town hall | la | mairie |
| | track | la | voie |
| | tracksuit | le | jogging/le survêtement |
| | trader | le/la | commerçant(e) |
| | traffic lights | les | feux (m pl) |
| to | train | s' | entraîner |
| | train | le | train |
| | trainers | les | baskets (m pl) |
| | tram | le | tramway |
| to | travel | | voyager |

| | | | |
|---|---|---|---|
| | travel agency | une | agence de voyages |
| | traveller | le | voyageur |
| | traveller's cheque | le | chèque de voyages |
| | traveller's cheques | les | travellers (m pl) |
| | tree | un | arbre |
| | trombone | le | trombone |
| | trousers | le | pantalon (sing) |
| | trout | la | truite |
| | trumpet | la | trompette |
| to | try | | essayer |
| | tube | le | tube |
| | turkey | la | dinde |
| | turkey escalope | une | escalope de dinde |
| to | turn | | tourner |
| to | turn off (the radio) | | éteindre (la radio) |
| to | turn on (the radio) | | allumer (la radio) |
| | TV | la | télé/la télévision |
| | TV channel | la | chaîne de télé |
| | TV magazine | le | magazine de télé |
| | TV set | le | téléviseur |
| | Twelfth Night | le | jour des Rois |
| | uncle | un | oncle |
| | under | | sous |
| | underground | le | métro |
| | unemployed | au | chômage |
| | uniform | un | uniforme |
| | useful | | utile |
| | useless | | inutile |
| | vacuum cleaner | un | aspirateur |
| | valley | la | vallée |
| | van | la | camionnette |
| | vase | le | vase |
| | VCR | le | magnétoscope |
| | veal | le | veau |
| | vegetable | le | légume |
| | vegetable garden | le | jardin potager |
| | very near | | tout près |
| | vicious | | méchant |
| | video cassette | la | cassette vidéo |
| | video recorder | le | magnétoscope |
| | village | le | village |
| | violin | le | violon |
| | Virgo | | Vierge |
| | visit | la | visite |

| | | | |
|---|---|---|---|
| to | visit (a monument) | | visiter |
| to | visit a stately home | | visiter un château |
| to | wait (for) | | attendre |
| | waiter | le | serveur |
| | waiting-room | la | salle d'attente |
| | waitress | la | serveuse |
| to | wake up | se | réveiller |
| | Walkman® | le | baladeur |
| | wall | le | mur |
| | warden (male) | le | père aubergiste |
| | warden (female) | la | mère aubergiste |
| | wardrobe | une | armoire |
| to | wash | se | laver |
| to | wash up | | faire la vaisselle |
| | washing-machine | le | lave-linge |
| to | watch | | regarder |
| to | watch TV | | regarder la télé |
| to | water | | arroser |
| | water | l' | eau (f) |
| | water melon | la | pastèque |
| | waterproof coat | un | imperméable |
| to | waterski | | faire du ski nautique |
| | watersports | les | sports aquatiques (m pl) |
| to | wear | | porter |
| | weather forecast | la | météo |
| | weekend | le | weekend |
| in the | west | à l' | ouest |
| | west of | à l' | ouest de |
| | what is...like? | | comment est...? |
| | what? | | qu'est-ce que...? |
| | when? | | quand? |
| | where? | | où? |
| | which? | | quel, quels? (m) |
| | which? | | quelle, quelles? (f) |
| | white | | blanc |
| | white coffee | le | café crème |
| | white wine | le | vin blanc |
| | who? | | qui? |
| | why? | | pourquoi? |
| | widowed | | veuf/veuve |
| | wife | la | femme |
| to | win | | gagner |
| | wind | le | vent |
| | window | la | fenêtre |

| | | | |
|---|---|---|---|
| to | windsurf | | faire de la planche à voile |
| | wine | le | vin |
| (some) | wine | du | vin |
| | winter sports | les | sports d'hiver (m pl) |
| | with | | avec |
| | with bathroom | | avec salle de bains |
| | with shower | | avec douche |
| | with TV | | avec téléviseur |
| | without | | sans |
| | woman | la | femme |
| | wood | le | bois |
| | word processing | le | traitement de texte |
| to | work | | travailler |
| | work | le | travail |
| | worker (male, unskilled) | un | ouvrier |
| | worker (female, unskilled) | une | ouvrière |
| to | write | | écrire |
| | written with a capital letter | la | majuscule |
| | written with a lower-case (small) letter | la | minuscule |
| | yacht marina | le | port de plaisance |
| | yellow | | jaune |
| | yes | | oui |
| | yoghurt | le | yaourt |
| | youth centre | le | foyer de la jeunesse |
| | youth club | le | club des jeunes |
| | youth hostel | une | auberge de jeunesse |
| | youth, young people | la | jeunesse |